The Minstrel-Boy to the war is gone,
In the ranks of death you'll find him;
His father's sword he has girded on,
and his wild harp slung behind him.

THOMAS MOORE

The Blackbird

ROSS WILSON

The Minstrel Boy

FRANCIS LEDWIDGE,
AND THE LITERATURE OF HIS TIME

including six previously unpublished poems

HUBERT DUNN

BOOKLINK

for Henriqueta,
Eugenia, Sebastian
and Josephine

Francis Ledwidge
ROSS WILSON

Published by Booklink, Ireland
Publisher: Dr Claude Costecalde

© Text, 2006, Hubert Dunn
© Paintings, the private collection of Mr and Mrs Hubert Dunn

Design by Dunbar Design, Ireland

Printed in Ireland by Universities Press

ISBN 0-9554097-0-5

Contents

The River Boyne near Slane

PAUL WALLS

ONE

THE FOUNTAINS
OF HIS JOY

John Synge, I, and Augusta Gregory, thought
All that we did, all that we said or sang
Must come from contact with the soil, from that
Contact everything Antaeus-like grew strong

The Municipal Gallery revisited, WB Yeats

IT WAS IN SLANE, COUNTY MEATH that the poet Francis Ledwidge grew up and grew strong. Nature in all her ways was the chief inspiration of his poetry. His joy was living in nature, walking in nature, rejoicing in nature. His fulfilment was in writing of the seasons, the grass, the trees, the leaves, the meadows, the flowers, the rivers, the birds, the cattle, the sheep. No part of the country, in which he lived and moved, failed to inspire him. His absorption in the sights and sounds of the country around Slane was total. It consumed him. It broke out in his earliest poetry and sustained him through years of war.

He wrote of himself: 'I have always been very quiet and bashful and a great mystery in my own place. I avoided the evening play of neighbouring children to find

A View from Slane

CATHERINE FLANAGAN

some secret place in a wood by the Boyne and there imagine fairy dances and hunts, fires and feasts. I saw curious shapes in shadows and clouds and loved to watch the change of the leaves and flowers. I heard voices in the rain and the wind and strange whisperings in the waters. I loved all wandering people and things and several times tried to become part of a gypsy caravan. I read of Troy and Nineveh and the Nomads of the Sahara. I wrote wander songs for cuckoos and winter songs for the robin. I hated gardens where gaudy flowers were trained in rows but loved the wild things of change and circumstance.'

Francis Ledwidge's earliest poems were informed by the inspirations detailed in this passage. The County Meath, in particular the country surrounding Slane and the Boyne Valley, had, and still has, a beauty essential to itself. It is green. It is lush. It is open. It is fertile and it is well wooded. It is a miracle of lovely colours dependent on the sun, rain, or storm that maybe about. It has lengthy views of peacefulness, particularly from places close to Francis Ledwidge's early life. He lived two miles from the Hill of Slane. The view from it extends generously south over the central plain of Ireland. He often walked up to it. It was easily accessible by bicycle to the Hill of Tara, Ireland's Holy Hill. Its legends were a source of some of his most powerful writing.

The Hill of Slane

PAUL WALLS

The Hill of Tara has been desolate for fourteen hundred years; for the two thousand years before that it was the capital of the High Kings of Ireland. On Easter Saturday 433, St Patrick lit a fire on the Hill of Slane in honour of the Pascal feast. This incensed King Laoghaire. It was a serious breach of correct behaviour for anyone to light a fire ahead of the King. The King drove his chariots to Slane. He met St Patrick. St Patrick did not succeed in converting King Laoghaire. He died a pagan in 458.

King Diarmaid was the last High King of Ireland to rule at Tara. He was the last of one hundred and thirty-six Pagan and six Christian Kings to rule from there. His successor removed from Tara. Tara and the Hill of Slane are significant landmarks in County Meath. The panoramas from the Hill of Tara north to the mountains of Mourne and south to the Wicklow mountains and the Plains of the Pale are more magnificent than those from the Hill of Slane. Francis Ledwidge knew them both well.

The River Boyne flowed through the heart of Francis Ledwidge. 'The Boyne and its tributaries spreading like a fan, permeate the whole area and the Boyne River basin is almost coincident with the County. The principal towns lie on the river and most of the biological and archaeological interest of Meath, as well as most of its scenic beauty, are associated with the course of the Boyne. No river in Ireland offers a combination of scenic beauty and historical interest to compare with the Boyne.' *The Way that I Went*, by Robert Praeger.

The beauty of County Meath is not the rugged beauty of the West coast of Ireland. It is not the savage beauty of County Donegal. It is not the magnificent beauty of County Sligo dominated by Benbulben. Francis Ledwidge could never have written of anything in County Meath as WB Yeats wrote of Benbulben:

> Swear by those horsemen, by those women
> Complexion and form prove superhuman,
> That pale, long-visaged company
> That air in immortality
> Completeness of their passions won;
> Now they ride the wintry dawn
> Where Ben Bulben sets the scene.
> Here's the gist of what they mean.
>
> *Under Benbulben*, WB Yeats

It is not the lonely beauty of County Mayo. Francis Ledwidge could never have written of County Meath as Louis MacNiece wrote of County Mayo:

> But in Mayo the tumbledown walls went leapfrog over the moors
> The sugar and salt in the pubs were damp in the castors
> And the water was brown as beer upon the shores
>
> Of desolate loughs, and stumps of hoary bog oak
> Stuck up here and there
> And as the twilight filtered on the heather
> Water-music filled the air.
>
> *In Mayo*, Louis MacNiece

It is not the mystical beauty of Connemara and the Twelve Pins. It is not the rocky beauty of County Clare or the semi-tropical beauty of parts of County Kerry.

It is the beauty of grass, of rivers, of trees, of meadows, of flowers, of birds which was the vital source of Francis Ledwidge's joy and of his best poetry. Nature and all things natural were the principal subject matter of his earliest poems.

SPRING

The dews drip roses on the meadows
Where the meek daisies dot the sward.
And AEolus whispers through the shadows,
'Behold the handmaid of the Lord!'
The golden news the skylark waketh
And 'thwart the heavens his flight is curled;
Attend ye as the first note breaketh
And chrism droppeth on the world.

DESIRE IN SPRING

I love the cradle songs that mothers sing
In lonely places when the twilight drops,
The slow endearing melodies that bring
Sleep to the weeping lids; and, when she stops,
I love the roadside birds upon the tops
Of dusty hedges in a world of spring.

And when the sunny rain drips from the edge
Of midday wind, and meadows lean one way,
And a long whisper passes thro' the sedge,
Beside the ruffled water let me stay,
While these old airs upon my memory play,
And silent changes colour up the hedge.

These are two of Ledwidge's earlier poems. They were written before he joined the army in 1914. They appeared in the First Edition of his poetry to be published under the title *Songs Of The Fields*. The introduction to this edition was written by Lord Dunsany and dated June 1914. Lord Dunsany's introduction ended 'I hope that not too many will be attracted to this book on account of the author being a peasant, lest he come to be praised by the how-interesting! school; for know that neither in any class, nor in any country, nor in any age, shall you predict the footfall of Pegasus, who touches the earth where he pleaseth and is bridled by whom he will.'

We will see in due course the friendship and support which Lord Dunsany, himself a distinguished writer and playwright, as well as a great aristocrat, sportsman and traveller, gave to Francis Ledwidge; and how much Francis Ledwidge looked to him for encouragement in his life as a poet.

However, it is not only that nature's ways were a chief source of Francis Ledwidge's inspiration as a poet. It soon became apparent in his poetry that he saw nature as a living person; that he related to nature as to a human personality.

AUGUST

She'll come at dusky first of day,
White over yellow harvest's song.
Upon her dewy rainbow way
She shall be beautiful and strong.
The lidless eye of noon shall spray
Tan on her ankles in the hay,
Shall kiss her brown the whole day long.

I'll know her in the windrows, tall
Above the crickets of the hay.
I'll know her when her odd eyes fall,
One May-blue, one November-grey.
I'll watch her from the red barn wall
Take down her rusty scythe, and call,
And I will follow her away.

This poem appears after halfway in *Songs Of The Fields*. It is clear that Francis Ledwidge's style had matured significantly by the time at which it was written. It is one of his most acclaimed poems. It was selected for the *Oxford Book of Irish Verse* 1958. In addition to including so many of Francis Ledwidge's loves in the country around Slane it might have been written to and about a friend alive and living near him.

JUNE

Broom out the floor now, lay the fender by,
And plant this bee-sucked bough of woodbine there,
And let the window down. The butterfly
Floats in upon the sunbeam, and the fair
Tanned face of June, the nomad gipsy, laughs
Above her widespread wares, the while she tells
The farmers' fortunes in the fields, and quaffs
The water from the spider-peopled wells.

The hedges are all drowned in green grass seas,
And bobbing poppies flare like Elmo's light,
While siren-like the pollen-stainéd bees
Drone in the clover depths. And up the height
The cuckoo's voice is hoarse and broke with joy.
And on the lowland crops the crows make raid,
Nor fear the clappers of the farmer's boy,
Who sleeps, like drunken Noah, in the shade.

And loop this red rose in that hazel ring
That snares your little ear, for June is short
And we must joy in it and dance and sing,
And from her bounty draw her rosy worth.
Ay! soon the swallows will be flying south,
The wind wheel north to gather in the snow,
Even the roses split on youth's red mouth
Will soon blow down the road all roses go.

June appears slightly earlier in *Songs Of The Fields* than August; no doubt because it was written in June 1914 rather than August 1914. The descriptions of the 'bee-sucked bough', 'the butterfly', 'the fair tanned face of June', 'the hedges', 'the poppies', 'the cuckoo's voice', 'the crows' and 'the red rose', are so detailed that it would seem this poem must have been inspired in June in County Meath. Again it is written as if to and about a nomad gipsy living in and about Slane. It is not clear whether there were or are travellers in County Meath in 1914; no doubt a few. *June* appears in the Penguin Book of Irish Verse – Second Edition 1981.

THE HILLS

The hills are crying from the fields to me,
And calling me with music from a choir
Of waters in their woods where I can see
The bloom unfolded on the whins like fire.
And, as the evening moon climbs ever higher
And blots away the shadows from the slope,
They cry to me like things devoid of hope.

Pigeons are home. Day droops. The fields are cold.
Now a slow wind comes labouring up the sky
With a small cloud long steeped in sunset gold,
Like Jason with the precious fleece anigh
The harbour of Iolcos. Day's bright eye
Is filmed with the twilight, and the rill
Shines like a scimitar upon the hill.

And moonbeams drooping thro' the coloured wood
Are full of little people wingéd white.
I'll wander thro' the moon-pale solitude
That calls across the intervening night
With river voices at their utmost height,
Sweet as rain-water in the blackbird's flute
That strikes the world in admiration mute.

The Hills was also included in *Songs Of The Fields*. It is indicative of the universal influence which nature had on Francis Ledwidge. The hills around Slane were alive and speaking to him. The River voices were the music of the Boyne, a significantly broad and strong river flowing past Slane.

We will see in due course how the inspiration of nature as a living force survived the ravages of war in Francis Ledwidge's later poetry as he withstood the shocks of the Gallipoli campaign, the desolation of the Balkan battle and the horrors of the Western front. In the meantime, mention of the blackbird's flute in this poem can take us to look at a central source of his poetry, birds and in particular the blackbird.

BEHIND THE CLOSED EYE

I walk the old frequented ways
That wind around the tangled braes,
I live again the sunny days
Ere I the city knew.

And scenes of old again are born,
The woodbine lassoing the thorn,
And drooping Ruth-like in the corn
The poppies weep the dew...

Above me smokes the little town,
With its whitewashed walls and roofs of brown
And its octagon spire toned smoothly down
As the holy minds within.

And wondrous impudently sweet,
Half of him passion, half conceit,
The blackbird calls adown the street
Like the piper of Hamelin.

I hear him, and I feel the lure
Drawing me back to the homely moor,
I'll go and close the mountains' door
On the city's strife and din.

This poem is placed second in *Songs Of The Fields*. It was written when Francis Ledwidge was not yet sixteen. He was working in a grocer's shop in Dublin. It is indicative of his love of country and home rather than the city. He was so unenthusiastic about Dublin that after writing *Behind The Closed Eye* he got out of bed and walked the thirty miles home from Dublin to Slane. The road from Dublin to Slane is one of the straightest in Ireland. It was constructed with particular concentration on its straightness at the request of the Prince of Wales, later King George IV, who was emotionally interested in the Marchioness Conyingham, then resident at Slane Castle. He was keen to travel from Dublin to Slane with the maximum expedition after arriving in Ireland.

Behind The Closed Eye was one of Francis Ledwidge's earliest poems. It exhibits the lack of sophistication which we have already noticed in the first verse 'ways', 'braes', 'and days'. But it also introduces one of his most exciting loves, the blackbird which features significantly in his poetry.

These early poems of Francis Ledwidge, with birds, and particularly the blackbird at their heart shadow in their language his lament for the Irish poets executed after the Easter Rising of 1916. The Easter Rising of 1916 affected him very deeply. The executions of Patrick Pearse, Thomas McDonagh and Joseph Plunkett struck him to the heart. It will be necessary to return to these momentous events in due course; in particular their effect upon Francis Ledwidge, then in 1916 serving in the British Army. *The Blackbirds* was written by him in July 1916. He was in barracks in England having survived the Gallipoli campaign, having served in Serbia and having spent a time of recovery in a hospital in Egypt. It is going ahead in the chronology to look at *The Blackbirds* at this early stage. But it is fascinating to note the dramatic change and the maturity in Francis Ledwidge's writing in the two years from the early Blackbird poems written in 1914 and *The Blackbirds* written in July 1916.

THE BLACKBIRDS

I heard the Poor Old Woman say:
'At break of day the fowler came,
And took my blackbirds from their songs
Who loved me well thro' shame and blame.

No more from lovely distances
Their songs shall bless me mile by mile,
Nor to white Ashbourne call me down
To wear my crown another while.

With bended flowers the angels mark
For the skylark the place they lie,
From there its little family
Shall dip their wings first in the sky.

And when the first surprise of flight
Sweet songs excite, from the far dawn
Shall there come blackbirds loud with love,
Sweet echoes of the singers gone.

But in the lonely hush of eve
Weeping I grieve the silent bills.'
I heard the Poor Old Woman say
In Derry of the little hills.

Francis Ledwidge did some of his Army training in the City of Londonderry. No doubt he was familiar with the hauntingly beautiful country which surrounds it towards Claudy and the foothills of the Sperrin mountains. The lonely hush of eve is exactly County Londonderry. Derry of the little hills is exactly what it is. We will return to this poem in its proper context of Francis Ledwidge's reaction to the executions of the poets after the Easter Rising. It is so lovely that it is no hardship to look at it twice.

Another way of understanding Francis Ledwidge's passion for the ways of nature was his extreme disinclination to become a city dweller. There never was any chance that he would become what is somewhat inelegantly referred to as a metropolitan bum. He wrote, 'I could not bear brick horizons.'

In March 1914, Francis Ledwidge visited Manchester and stayed a few days. He cared for it even less than Dublin. He took the images of blackbirds with him. Visions of cherry time and the Boyne sustained him.

IN MANCHESTER

There is a noise of feet that move in sin
Under the side-faced moon here where I stray,
Want by me like a Nemesis. The din
Of noon is in my ears, but far away
My thoughts are, where Peace shuts the blackbirds' wings
And it is cherry time by all the springs.

And this same moon floats like a trail of fire
Down the long Boyne, and darts white arrows thro'
The mill wood; her white skirt is on the weir,
She walks thro' crystal mazes of the dew,
And rests awhile upon the dewy slope'
While I will hope again the old, old hope.

With wandering we are worn my muse and I,
And, if I sing, my song knows nought of mirth.
I often think my soul is an old lie
In sackcloth, it repents so much of birth.
But I will build it yet a cloister home
Near the peace of lakes when I have ceased to roam.

The family cottage at Janeville was on the road from Slane to Drogheda. It had three bedrooms, a large kitchen, a living room and half an acre of garden. The family had been allotted the cottage in 1886 by the Rural District Council. The family then were Mr and Mrs Ledwidge, Patrick, Mary, Thomas, Kitty, Michael and Anne. By 1903, when Francis Ledwidge, aged 16, had shaken the dust of Dublin off his feet to return to Slane only his mother and a younger brother Joe were still living in the family home. His father had died in March 1892; by 1903 Patrick had died of

The Ledwidge Home
SIMON McKINSTRY

tuberculosis. Mary, Thomas, Kitty and Michael had moved on from Slane.

The intervening years from 1892, when Francis Ledwidge's father had died, to the time immediately concerning us, 1903, had been stringent for Mrs Ledwidge and her children. In 1892 the youngest child Joseph was three months old. The only state assistance was outdoor relief of a shilling per week per child. Mrs Ledwidge did casual work for neighbouring farmers at the rate of two and six per day. This involved haymaking, potato picking, and turnip thinning in summer. In winter, when agricultural work was not available she washed and mended clothes. In later years Francis Ledwidge wrote, 'There were four brothers of us and three sisters. I am the second youngest. For these my mother laboured night and day, as none of them were strong enough to provide for their own wants. She never complained and even when my eldest brother Patrick advanced in strength she persisted in his regular attendance at school until he qualified at book-keeping and left home for Dublin.'

On one occasion the bailiff and two policemen came to evict the family for arrears of rent. The local doctor certified that Patrick, who had returned home from Dublin, was not fit to be moved. He died of tuberculosis. There was no money to pay for his coffin. The parish paid.

The Ledwidge children who had left home tried to help their mother while two younger brothers remained at home in Slane. None of them were in skilled employment. Their wages were humble. They had little to send home. When Francis

Ledwidge and his brother Joe returned from school they joined their mother in the
fields to help with her work in the months of daylight.

Francis Ledwidge left school at thirteen, in the spring of 1901. He worked as a
farmer's boy for seven shillings a week plus meals. Farm labouring was a depressed
occupation in terms of wages and hours of work. He was tall and strong for his years.
He could make up rhymes. He wrote them on gates and boulders. He was well liked
by other labourers and was never out of work. He had a short period as a trainee
houseboy at Slane Castle, seat of the Marquis Conyngham. The Marchioness
Coyngham detailed the day's menus to the cook who committed them to a slate.
Francis Ledwidge, aged fourteen, amused himself by substituting pigs' feet, cabbage
and spuds for her Ladyship's directions on the cook's slate. The cook was displeased.

Slane Castle

CATHERINE FLANAGAN

The Centre of Slane
SIMON McKINSTRY

Francis Ledwidge was sacked and returned to farm work where he was happier. Aged fifteen, Francis Ledwidge became a grocer's apprentice in Drogheda. He worked until the shop closed at 11pm or 12 midnight. As an apprentice he had to work for four years for food and lodgings without pay. He was allowed home from Saturday afternoon to Sunday evening.

His mother then arranged for him to take his elder brother Michael's place at Dalys, Rathfarnam. Michael was moving on to better things.

After Dalys, he worked for three years as garden boy to the Taylor-Carlyle's who lived near Newgrange for a wage of £21 a year plus keep. In 1906 the Taylor-Carlyle's returned to Dublin. Francis Ledwidge was nineteen. He returned to casual farm labour. In 1907, he obtained employment as a road worker; roadwork was desirable if somewhat arduous labour. It was desirable as the wage was 17s 6p per week. It was hard work. Starting time was 8am to 6pm in summer, dusk in winter. It involved bicycling from home to the appointed place.

The years as garden boy at Newgrange and road worker all over County Meath were vital in the poetry of Francis Ledwidge. His life and work in these years after 1903 when he escaped the career of grocer's boy in Dublin and Drogheda were lived in the places of his first love, the country, roads, fields, rivers of County Meath.

Hard work on the roads did not preclude an extensive social life for him. He supported the Slane Gaelic Football team. He attended their matches. He took part in local athletics being pre-eminent in the high jump. He acted in the Slane dramatic class. He attempted without success to persuade Sean MacNamee, a Navan teacher who taught Irish throughout County Meath on a voluntary basis, to instruct a class in Slane. It seems that Sean MacNamee was too busy to give Irish learners in Slane the benefit of his attentions. Francis Ledwidge struggled alone in the study of his native language.

His poetry was published in *The Irish Weekly Independent* from May 1909 and in the Drogheda Independent from January 1910. Poems unpublished in Lord Dunsany's *The Complete Poems of Francis Ledwidge* published in 1918 and in Alice Curtayne's *Complete Poems of Francis Ledwidge* published in 1972 have been unearthed thanks to the prodigious researches of Liam O'Meara. They have been published in *Francis Ledwidge The Poems Complete* in 1997. The theme at which we are at present looking, the pervasive influence of all things natural in his early writing is evident in the poems discovered by Liam O'Meara.

THE ROBIN IN TOWNLEY HALL

In joyous youth long, long ago
Beside the river Boyne,
Through lonely woods and sparkling streams
I've wandered many a time.
I love to scan those distant days
And sadly I recall
Each hour I sat near the red-breast bird

That piped in Townley Hall.
I knew the blackbird of Rossnaree
That joyous long ago;
I knew the finch of Carraghbawn,
The throstle of Dunmore.
No bird the more could cheer my heart
I heard them each and all,
Than the robin in the thorn
In the woods of Townley Hall.

By 1910, Francis Ledwidge had changed jobs from road worker to mine worker.

He was taken on as a labourer in a copper mine being developed at Beaupark, near Slane. Conditions were uncomfortable and dangerous. There was regular flooding. Francis Ledwidge was the worker's choice to confront management to improve conditions. He organised a strike. He was instantly dismissed. He returned to roadwork.

He was promoted to ganger. His wages were 24 shillings a week plus overtime. His job involved supervision rather than actual physical labour on the roads. It involved extensive cycling throughout County Meath. He took lodgings between Navan and Kells. He was employed on the roads of County Meath until he answered the call to war.

This brief review of the social and economic conditions under which Francis Ledwidge lived and worked and wrote his earlier poetry up to 1914 discloses circumstances which were hard and demanding. There was fun but no luxury in the Ledwidge household and in the life of Francis Ledwidge. There was poverty but not penury.

The social and economic background of his early life from his birth in 1887 up to his joining the British Army in 1914 had none of the misery, squalor and degradation apparent in the life of someone of humble means growing up in the poorest areas of Dublin, for example Sean O'Casey.

Sean O'Casey was born in Dublin in 1880. His mother, like Francis Ledwidge's mother, was left in poverty with six children. Mrs Ledwidge was living in a small house outside Slane; Mrs O'Cassidy, Sean O'Casey's mother, was living in a Dublin tenement.

Sean O'Casey, in the first volume of his Autobiography *I Knock at the Door* wrote of his own birth. 'In Dublin, sometime in the early eighties, on the last day of the month of March, a mother in child-pain clenched her teeth, dug her knees home into the bed, sweated and panted and grunted, became a tense living mass of agony and effort, groaned and pressed and groaned and pressed and pressed and pressed a little boy out of her womb … Down into a world that was filled up with the needs, ambitions, desires, and ignorances of others, to be shoved aside, pressed back, beaten down by privileges carrying god-warrants of superiority because they had dropped down into the world a couple of hours earlier.' … On his own near blindness, 'Then they all forsook him, saying, leave him to the pain, then, since he won't do the one thing that will do him good; he has been pampered too much for anyone to pity him. Only his mother harassed her mind for help; only she, with deep pity and unbreakable patience, stood between him and the chance that his sight might go, leaving him helpless in the hands of man and no nearer to God; only she raised the banner of fear for him in the face of everyone she met, and tried everywhere for assistance to save him from the evil of perpetual darkness … Then a nurse heavily bandaged his eyes, and his mother led him forth from the hospital, having finished his first day with an institution that was to know him so well in the future that the doors nearly opened of their own accord when they saw him coming.'

Accordingly, although as we have seen the circumstances of Francis Ledwidge's early life were financially stringent, there is nothing that we know about its conditions and certainly nothing in his poetry which suggest the misery and squalor of life in the poorer areas of Dublin which, making all allowances for Sean O'Casey's powerful literature on the subject of his early life, must have been quite horrific. Rather the reverse; the early life of Francis Ledwidge at home in Slane, whatever its social and economic limitations, prompted some of his loveliest poetry.

A SWAN'S SONG.

Whence comes this music bearing me adown?
Whither am I borne wave tossed along?
To be covered up in some bye-place
Where shallows are loud,
And the king-fisher washes his little face?
Or shall I find the end of my song
In the middle of wheels that toil for a town,
My sun in a cloud?

Whence comes this music? From Memory's shell,
Of Youth's and Beauty's pleasantry,
Of Love and summer water singing
     Of the wonders
     Of the thunder's
Dark unfathomable well.
Of the blackbird on the tree
Piping 'til the world is weary
Of its own pain,
And the lily stops its swinging
And offers him a bell of rain.

Rowing up the lonesome waters
Thro' the shadows of the spring,
All the lovely country daughters
Watched me dress my foamy wing.
Floating to the lonesomer waters
But the poets hear me sing.

Francis Ledwidge.

May 1916

A hitherto unpublished poem by Francis Ledwidge
from a private collection

TWO
MY NATIVE LAND

Breathes there the man with soul so dead,
Who never to himself hath said
This is my own, my native land!
Whose heart hath ne'r within him burned
As home his footsteps he hath turned
From wandering on a foreign strand!
If such there breathe, go, mark him well,
For him no minstrel raptures swell;
High though his titles, proud his name
Boundless his wealth as wish can claim;
Despite those titles, power and pelf,
The wretch, concerted all in self,
Living, shall forfeit fair renown,
And, doubly dying, shall go down
To the vile dust, from whence he sprung,
Unwept, unhonoured and unsung.

The Lay Of The Last Minstrel, Walter Scott

FRANCIS LEDWIDGE was the opposite of the wretch in *The Lay Of The Last Minstrel.* His native land was everything to him. Family, home, friends were vital sources of his joy and poetry. He dedicated his first book of poems *Songs Of The Fields* to 'My Mother the first singer I knew'.

His love for his mother sustained him through the years of war so that when in hospital in Egypt after the Gallipoli and Serbian campaigns he wrote in 1916 *My Mother*:

God made my mother on an April day,
From sorrow and the mist along the sea,
Lost birds' and wanderers' songs and ocean spray,
And the moon loved her wandering jealously.

Beside the ocean's din she combed her hair,
Singing the nocturne of the passing ships,
Before her earthly lover found her there
And kissed away the music from her lips.

She came unto the hills and saw the change
That brings the swallow and the geese in turns.
But there was not a grief she deemed strange,
For there is that in her which always mourns.

Kind heart she has for all on hill or wave
Whose hopes grew wings like ants to fly away.
I bless the God Who such a mother gave
This poor bird-hearted singer of a day.

Perhaps not surprisingly Francis Ledwidge was not alone among the slaughtered poets of the First World War for whom their mother was the greatest person in their lives. Who remembers now the poetry of the Honourable Wyndham Tennant, Grenadier Guards? He fell in the battle of the Somme, aged 19. He had written of his mother at the age of eight:

She is full of love and grace
A kind of flower in all the place
Even the trees give her salutes,
They seem to know who's near their roots
She is something quite divine,
And joy, of joy, this mother's mine.

Mrs Ledwidge was Anne Lynch when she married Patrick Ledwidge, a labourer, in 1872. She had always lived in Slane. She was deeply in love with her husband who

Meath Countryside as seen from Slane

CATHERINE FLANAGAN

worked then and until his death as a farm labourer. She was thin and dark-haired. She had bright brown eyes. Her happy personality was inherited by Francis Ledwidge as well as her luminous eyes. Francis Ledwidge was her eighth child born on the 19 August 1887, fifteen years after his parents married.

She lost her husband on 13 March 1892, when he was aged fifty-two. The feeding of a family of eight children on outdoor relief of a shilling a week per child was an undertaking of daunting proportions for Mrs Ledwidge. She refused to put any of her children into care. She took work in the fields of Slane at two and six per day. It was work of backbreaking exertion involving potato picking, haymaking and other agricultural activities more properly carried out by robust young men. If there was no work in the fields she took in laundry for washing and mending.

It is scarcely surprising that Francis Ledwidge adored his mother. As the elder children grew up they became earners. When Patrick started to earn Mrs Ledwidge was able to leave working in the fields and stay at home to look after her younger children full time. Patrick contracted tuberculosis and could not work. Mrs Ledwidge returned to working in the fields. Patrick died four years later. There was no money to pay for his coffin. The Guardians put the Parish to the expense. Francis Ledwidge later wrote 'I was seven years of age when my eldest brother died, and although I had only been to school on occasional days I was able to read the tombstones in a neighbouring graveyard and had written in secret several poems which still survive. About this time I was punished in school for crying and that punishment ever afterwards haunted the master like an evil dream, for I was only crying over Goldsmith's *Deserted Village* which an advance class had been reading aloud. It was in this same school that I wrote my first poem in order to win for the school a half-holiday. It was on a Shrove Tuesday and the usual custom of granting the half-holiday had not been announced at playtime. So when the master was at lunch I crept quietly into the school and wrote on a slate a verse to remind him, leaving it on his desk where he must see it. I remember it yet.'

> Our master is too old for sweets,
> Too old for children's play
> Like Aesop's what he can't eat
> No other people may.

So Francis Ledwidge was a scholar and a poet from an early age.

His mother was working in the fields while Francis Ledwidge and his younger brother were still at school. When the two brothers returned home they went straight into the fields and worked with her until the end of the day. After homework she told them stories or sang to them. Francis Ledwidge wrote 'These stories told at my mother's doorstep in the owl's light were the first things I remember, except perhaps the old songs she sang to me, so full of romance, love and sacrifice.' The family unit in County Meath had to struggle hard in 1900 against poverty but did not have to compete with television and video which between them have put an end to the family making its own entertainment, in many cases having put an end to family conversation.

We will see shortly that the myths of ancient Ireland were a significant inspiration for Francis Ledwidge's poetry. It seems that at least some part of that inspiration was prompted by his mother's stories and songs after a day in the fields.

In 1909, Francis Ledwidge, aged 22, was promoted a ganger on the roads. This involved his leaving home in Slane. He took lodgings at Martry, between Navan and Kells. He returned to Slane every Saturday. He had Sunday at home. But living Sunday to Saturday away from home was an exile to him. He was then and remained throughout his life totally home-loving. Home was one of the fountains of his joy. Home, apart from the small house and small garden, was his mother, his brother Joe, and the friends of Slane who collected around the Ledwidge family.

Home sustained his strength and inspired his poetry in the years of war. Shortly after joining the army he wrote to a Slane friend Bobby Anderson 'I hear the Russians are in Germany. God send they may bring this war to a hasty termination and let me home again. I am drifting far away from Slane, far, far. Does W Corbally still come in the morning and Jack McGuirk for his brown cake? I keep always remembering the little things.'

In February 1915, he wrote to Lizzie (Healy) 'When I come again I will do great things, there is very little chance here, I am always so lonesome I can think of nothing but Slane and the quiet peace of the home ways, and you.'

Again, in February 1915, he wrote to Lizzie 'When you have a minute to spare, drop me a few lines, as I watch for something from the old place every day.'

Shortly before going to France he wrote again to Lizzie 'I feel sure that I will return again safely and then and then! Yes, when the war is over, if I am not shot, I am coming back to Slane. I love it very much because from nowhere else have I ever had such calls to my heart. I love Stanley Hill and all the distances so blue around it. I love the Boyne and the fields through which it sings. I love the peace of it above all.'

Friends were an abiding source of joy to Francis Ledwidge. 'Think where man's glory most begins and ends. And say my glory was I had such friends.' [*The Municipal Gallery Revisited*, WB Yeats]

To My Best Friend is the first poem in *Songs Of The Fields*.

> I love the wet-lipped wind that stirs the hedge
> And kisses the bent flowers that drooped for rain,
> That stirs the poppy on the sun-burned ledge
> And like a swan dies singing, without pain.
> The golden bees go buzzing down to stain
> The lilies' frills, and the blue harebell rings,
> And the sweet blackbird in the rainbow sings.
>
> Deep in the meadows I would sing a song,
> The shallow brook my tuning-fork, the birds
> My masters; and the boughs they hop along
> Shall mark my time: but there shall be no words
> For lurking Echo's mock; an angel herds
> Words that I may not know, within, for you,
> Words for the faithful meet, the good and true.

Matty McGoona was his best friend.

The friendship was lifelong for Francis Ledwidge. On 22 July 1917, he wrote *To One Who Comes Now And Then:*

> When you come in, it seems a brighter fire
> Crackles upon the hearth invitingly,
> The household routine which was wont to tire
> Grows full of novelty.
>
> You sit upon our home-upholstered chair
> And talk of matters wonderful and strange,
> Of books, and travel, customs old which dare
> The gods of Time and Change.
>
> Till we with inner word our care refute
> Laughing that this out bosoms yet assails,
> While there are maidens dancing to a flute
> In Andalusian vales.
>
> And sometimes from my shelf of poems you take
> And secret meanings to our hearts disclose,
> As when the winds of June the mid bush shake
> We see the hidden rose.
>
> And when the shadows muster, and each tree
> A moment flutters, full of shutting wings,
> You take the fiddle and mysteriously
> Wake wonders on the strings.
>
> And in my garden, grey with misty flowers,
> Low echoes fainter than a beetle's horn
> Fill all the corners with it, like sweet showers
> Of bells, in the owl's morn.
>
> Come often, friend; with welcome and surprise
> We'll greet you from the sea or from the town;
> Come when you like and from whatever skies
> Above you smile or frown.

He never saw Matty McGoona again after he wrote that poem. He was dead by a German shell nine days later. It tells of the deepest friendship of his life. A friendship, which was vitally alive although they were separated by two years of war. It speaks through the images of the natural world around Slane.

Matty McGoona was Francis Ledwidge's closest friend but in no way his only friend. Francis Ledwidge was sociable. He was friendly with Paddy Healey who became principal of Slane School in 1912. They visited and enjoyed together many of the public houses in the Slane area. They supported the Slane Blues, the local football team. Francis Ledwidge was known and well liked by many of those who supported the dances, the public houses, the football matches in and around Slane. It is a mistake to imagine that he was sitting at home in a poetic haze gazing across the Boyne. He was a vibrant man living fully in the world which surrounded him.

One of the first poems, which Francis Ledwidge wrote after joining the Army but before serving abroad, is inspired by friendships at home. It was written about Christmas 1914. It is interesting as indicative of the maturing of his style. It is written about Jack Tiernan, a neighbour's son who used to drive cows past Francis Ledwidge's home early every morning:

A LITTLE BOY IN THE MORNING

He will not come, and still I wait.
He whistles at another gate
Where angels listen. Ah, I know
He will not come, yet if I go
How shall I know he did not pass
Barefooted in the flowery grass?

The moon leans on one silver horn
Above the silhouettes of morn,
And from their nest-sills finches whistle
Or stooping pluck the downy thistle.
How is the morn so gay and fair
Without his whistling in its air?

The world is calling, I must go.
How shall I know he did not pass
Barefooted in the shining grass?

Tie Dream.

I told my dream in a bird's nest
At the waning of the morn,
But the nest swayed over and over
Up in the scanty thorn.

And I went to the broken rushes
That swayed by the windy stream.
But I only heard my own voice
And the voices of my dream.

Then I went to the wise old woman
Who lives !mid the rocks of Crew,
And I crossed her hand with silver
At the falling of the dew.

And I am to marry a Princess
Who will come from the midst of the sea
On a horse as wite as the seasflakes
With t appings of filigree.

Oh, there's many a maid in Ireland
Who scorned me long ago
Will be coming with their dowries
To my home at Gurteen mo ,

And there's one whom I thought the fairest
Will be wanting to marry me
When I'm far away on the waters
With the Princess of the sea.

J. Eledwdee

A hitherto unpublished poem by Francis Ledwidge
from a private collection

THREE

THE HEART OUTRIGHT

Never give all the heart, for love
Will hardly seem worth thinking of
To passionate women if it seem
Certain, and they never dream
That it fades out from kiss to kiss;
For everything that's lovely is
But a brief, dreamy, kind delight.
O never give the heart outright,
For they, for all smooth lips can say,
Have given their hearts up to the play.
And who could play it well enough
If deaf and dumb and blind with love?
He that made this knows all the cost,
For he gave all his heart and lost.

Never Give All The Heart, WB Yeats

FRANCIS LEDWIDGE, like WB Yeats, gave all his heart and lost. His loss in love, like WB Yeat's passion for Maude Gonne, produced some of his finest poetry.

His first and great passion was for Ellie Vaughey. She was a beauty. She lived with her brothers in a cottage on the Hill of Slane. Her mother had died in 1908. Her father had died some years earlier. She worked as a milliner's apprentice in Drogheda.

She moved from Slane to Mornington to be nearer her work. She was message girl for some of Francis Ledwidge's earlier poems in the *Drogheda Independent*. She delivered them for him in Drogheda on returning after the weekend in Slane. She was an early follower of his poetry.

They started walking out together in 1912. He was twenty-five: she was twenty.

The problem was that romance could not, for Ellie Vaughey or her family, advance from the hills of love to the valley of marriage. The Vaugheys were landowners. At least they owned part of the Hill of Slane. Francis Ledwidge was a ganger working on the roads. The social barrier was impassable in Irish country life in 1912.

She inspired some of his loveliest early poems.

THE BROKEN TRYST

The dropping words of larks, the sweetest tongue
That sings between the dusks, tell all of you;
The bursting white of Peace is all along
Wing-ways, and pearly droppings of the dew
Emberyl the cobwebs' greyness, and the blue
Of hiding violets, watching for your face,
Listen for you in every dusky place.

You will not answer when I call your name,
But in the fog of blossom do you hide
To change my doubts into a red-faced shame
By'n by when you are laughing by my side?
Or will you never come, or have you died,
And I in anguish have forgotten all?
And shall the world now end and the heavens fall?

THOUGHTS AT THE TRYSTING STYLE

Come, May, and hang a white flag on each thorn,
Make truce with earth and heaven; the April child
Now hides her sulky face deep in the morn

Of your new flowers by the water wild
And in the ripples of the rising grass,
And rushes bent to let the south wind pass
On with her tumult of swift nomad wings,
And broken domes of downy dandelion.
Only in spasms now the blackbird sings.
The hour is all a-dream.

We are looking at the sources of Francis Ledwidge's inspiration separately; but of course they merge. These two love poems, written about Ellie Vaughey tell also of that first fountain of his joy, the world of natural beauty; in particular living beauty; as in so many of his poems the blackbird is a significant person in his world of nature.

The happiness of loving Ellie Vaughey inspired some further poetry before the clouds began to form around it.

EVENING IN MAY

The blackbird blows his yellow flute so strong,
And rolls away the notes in careless glee,
It breaks the rhythm of the thrushes' song,
And puts red shame upon his rivalry.
The yellowhammers on the roof tiles beat
Sweet little dulcimers to broken time,
And here the robin with a heart replete
Has all in one short plagiariséd rhyme.

Ellie Vaughey's withdrawal from the romance struck at Francis Ledwidge's heart.

BEFORE THE TEARS

You looked as sad as an eclipsed moon
Above the sheaves of harvest, and there lay
A light lisp on your tongue, and very soon
The petals of your deep blush fell away;
White smiles that come with an uneasy grace
From inner sorrow crossed your forehead fair,
When the wind passing took your scattered hair
And flung it like a brown shower in my face.

Tear-fringed winds that fill the heart's low sighs
And never break upon the bosom's pain,
But blow unto the windows of the eyes
Their misty promises of silver rain,
Around your loud heart ever rose and fell.
I thought 'twere better that the tears should come
And strike your every feeling wholly numb,
So thrust my hand in yours and shook farewell.

He did not abandon the struggle lightly. He continued to meet Ellie. The pain of
losing Ellie Vaughey stayed with him.

INAMORATA

The bees were holding levees in the flowers,
Do you remember how each puff of wind
Made every wing a hum? My hand in yours
Was listening to your heart, but now
The glory is all faded, and I find
No more the olden mystery of the hours
When you were lovely and our hearts would bow
Each to the will of each, but one bright day
Is stretching like an isthmus in a bay
From the glad years that I have left behind.

I look across the edge of things that were
And you are lovely in the April ways,
Holy and mute, the sigh of my despair. ...
I hear once more the linnet's April tune
Beyond the rainbow's warp, as in the days
You brought me facefuls of your smiles to share
Some of your new-found wonders. ... Oh when soon
I'm wandering the wide seas for other lands,
Sometimes remember me with folded hands,
And keep me happy in your pious prayer.

Within a very few years Francis Ledwidge was to wander the wide seas for other lands in circumstances far from his thoughts when he wrote this poem; wandering to the sound of gunfire and towards his death.

The losing struggle for Ellie Vaughey pervaded his entire personality for a period.

IN THE DUSK

Day hangs its light between two dusks, my heart,
Always beyond the dark there is the blue.
Sometime we'll leave the dark, myself and you,
And revel in the light for evermore.
But the deep pain of you is aching smart,
And a long calling weighs upon you sore.

Day hangs its light between two dusks, and song
Is there at the beginning and the end.
You, in the singing dusk, how could you wend
The songless way Contentment fleetly wings?
But in the dark your beauty shall be strong,
Tho' only one should listen how it sings.

It is not clear to what extent Ellie Vaughey was suffering. But the shutters came down on the active relationship when Francis Ledwidge visited Ellie Vaughey at Mornington. He failed to persuade her to come back to him or to stay with him as he struggled on to become a writer.

The last two verses of *A Memory* tell of the pain of the final parting at Mornington:

I feel the warm hand on my shoulder light,
I hear the music of a voice that words
The slow time of the feet, I see the white
Arms slanting, and the dimples fold and fill. ...
I hear wing-flutters of the early birds,
I see the tide of morning landward spill,
The cloaking maidens, hear the voice that tells
'You never know' and 'Soon perhaps again,'
With white teeth biting down the inly pain,
Then sounds of going away and sad farewells.

A year ago! It seems but yesterday.
Yesterday! And a hundred years! All one.
'Tis laid a something finished, dark, away,
To gather mould upon the shelves of Time.
What matters hours or æons when 'tis gone?
And yet the heart will dust it of its grime,
And hover round it in a silver spell,
Be lost in it and cry aloud in fear;
And like a lost soul in a pious ear,
Hammer in mine a never easy bell.

A hint of why he lost Ellie Vaughey comes into a poem written shortly afterwards.

A SONG

My heart has flown on wings to you, away
In the lonely places where your footsteps lie
Full up of stars when the short showers of day
Have passed like ancient sorrows. I would fly
To your green solitude of woods to hear
You singing in the sounds of leaves and birds;
But I am sad below the depth of words
That nevermore we two shall draw anear.

Had I but wealth of kind and bleating flocks
And barnfuls of the yellow harvest yield,
And a large house with climbing hollyhocks
And servant maidens singing in the field,
You'd love me but I own no roaming herds,
My only wealth is songs of love for you,
And now that you are lost I may pursue
A sad life deep below the depth of words.

These reflections on his lack of wide windy acres were the closest that Francis Ledwidge came to bitterness on the matter of why he lost Ellie. The line 'My only wealth is songs of love for you' tells us that the balance of his heart was still loving and not bitter towards Ellie even though he had given all the heart and lost. No doubt Ellie inspired his thoughts and poetry in the somewhat more romanticised *The Maid In Low-Moon Land.*

I know not where she be, and yet
I see her waiting white and tall.
Her eyes are blue, her lips are wet,
And move as tho' they'd love to call.
I see her shadow on the wall
Before the changing moon has set.

She stands there lovely and alone
And up her porch blue creepers swing.
The world she moves in is her own,
To sun and shade and hasty wing.
And I would wed her in the Spring,
But only I sit here and moan.

Francis Ledwidge's political sympathies were strongly pro-labour and strongly nationalist. We will have to examine in due course why, with such strongly held nationalistic sentiments, Francis Ledwidge joined the British Army in 1914. Notwithstanding the lines 'I'm wild for wandering to the far-off places Since one forsook me whom I held most dear', I will suggest that Francis Ledwidge's painful defeat in his pursuit of Ellie Vaughey had in fact, nothing to do with his decision to join the Army later in 1914. The final hammer blow on Francis Ledwidge's heart did not fall until after he had joined the Army. He was at Richmond Barracks in Dublin. He read in a local paper 'O'Neill and Vaughey on November 25 at St Patrick's RC Church, Slane, by the Rev. F Fagan, CC Slane, John J O'Neill, Rossin to Ellen Mary (Ellie) only daughter of the late John and Mrs Vaughey, Hill of Slane, Co. Meath.'

The finality of that notice launched Francis Ledwidge into depression. Hitherto although defeated, in love he was unbowed. He hoped that time and his achievements, particularly in writing, would bring Ellie and himself together again. It was not to be. He never saw her again. He wrote to Matty McGoona on 9 March 1915:

'I am glad we are going to the war, it will cheer me up, it will dispel these thoughts which are at war with me so long. Ellie Vaughey got married! That was a great blow, perhaps the greatest of all. I am going to try for a day home St Patrick's Day. If I manage it, could you come to Slane. I want to see you so badly.

How is your Pegasus? (bicycle). And how is the violin. Do you ever play sweet music now? Every time you play 'The Blackbird' think of me. I love that tune and snatches of it sing in my memory an odd time like ghosts haunting an old garden. My memory is no more than an old garden now full of the withered flowers of a dead summer.

Your old affectionate friend in trouble.'

We will see in due course the extent to which the memory of Ellie Vaughey inspired Francis Ledwidge in war.

In January 1914, Ledwidge had met Lizzie Healey, the younger sister of the local schoolmaster, Paddy Healy. She was twenty: Francis Ledwidge was twenty-seven. He began to enjoy her company. She read extensively. Francis Ledwidge wrote to her several letters, on 9 February 1914, 13 February 1914, 2 March 1914. On 9 March 1914, he wrote:

> I am delivering a lecture entitled: The Irishman Abroad in Manchester on the 21. I leave here on the 18, or perhaps the night of the 17. I want to see you before I go as I am longing for a chat with you. Could I see you in Slane on Saturday or Sunday next, or had I better go to Wilkinstown on Friday? Dear Lizzie, I very much appreciate your friendship and want to hold it forever. I won't say anything in future that would annoy you and hope you will not tire of me too soon.

It is apparent from his letters that Francis Ledwidge wrote as well in prose as in poetry. A romantic slant on life was never far below the level of his daily thinking.

We shall see that, as Francis Ledwidge recovered from the shock and hurt of Ellie Vaughey's marriage, Lizzie Healey grew in his affections and inspired his poetry. Some of his best poetry written after he joined the Army was written to and about Lizzie Healey. We will return to Lizzie Healey and Francis Ledwidge's enthusiasm for her after we have seen him into the colours.

There is no doubt that Francis Ledwidge was a passionate man. To what extent was he a religious man?

It is apparent that he was a God-fearing man. There are recurring references in his letters to D.V. – God willing. There is no reason to think that such references were merely conventional. The Christian message as articulated by the Roman Catholic Church in County Meath in the early twentieth century was active in his life and thoughts. But there is no hint in his poetry that the Christian message was the inspiring light of his poetic vision as it so clearly was for another Catholic poet, writing slightly earlier than Francis Ledwidge, Gerald Manley Hopkins. Francis Ledwidge's spiritual country was mystical and dreamy rather than overtly religious.

Songs Of The Fields draws to a close in melancholy. Francis Ledwidge was still only 27 in 1914.

GROWING OLD

We'll fill a Provence bowl and pledge us deep
The memory of the far ones, and between
The soothing pipes, in heavy-lidded sleep,
Perhaps we'll dream the things that once have been.
'Tis only noon and still too soon to die,
Yet we are growing old, my heart and I.

A hundred books are ready in my head
To open out where Beauty bent a leaf.
What do we want with Beauty? We are wed
Like ancient Proserpine to dismal grief.
And we are changing with the hours that fly,
And growing odd and old, my heart and I.

Across a bed of bells the river flows,
And roses dawn, but not for us; we want
The new thing ever as the old thing grows
Spectral and weary on the hills we haunt.
And that is why we feast, and that is why
We're growing odd and old, my heart and I.

FOUR

MYTHS & LEGENDS

FRANCIS LEDWIDGE'S POETRY discloses a deep and well-researched knowledge of Irish myths and legends. He had lived with them at least from his school-days in Slane. His master, Thomas Madden believed that a knowledge of Irish was essential to education. It was not then included in the official curriculum. He spent so much time learning Irish by candlelight at night that his eyesight was seriously damaged. Boys attending his school in Slane had to arrive half an hour early to be taught Irish. Madden was well informed of the significance in early Irish history of the legend of Slane and the surrounding areas such as the burial ground at Newgrange, a few miles from Slane and well worth a visit; Rosnaree, the Hill of Slane, and Tara.

Francis Ledwidge's fascination with Irish legend stayed with him to the end of his life. It sustained him through the years of war. One of the last poems he wrote was in France, dated 7 January 1917.

THE DEAD KINGS

All the dead kings came to me
At Rosnaree, where I was dreaming.
A few stars glimmered through the morn,
And down the thorn the dews were streaming.

And every dead king had a story
Of ancient glory, sweetly told.
It was too early for the lark,
But the starry dark had tints of gold.

I listened to the sorrows three
Of that Eire passed into song.
A cock crowed near a hazel croft,
And up aloft dim larks winged strong.

And I, too, told the kings a story
Of later glory, her fourth sorrow:
There was a sound like moving shields
In high green fields and the lowland furrow.

And one said: 'We who yet are kings
Have heard these things lamenting inly.'
Sweet music flowed from many a bill
And on the hill the morn stood queenly.

And one said 'Over is the singing,
And bell bough ringing, whence we come;
With heavy hearts we'll tread the shadows,
In honey meadows birds are dumb.'

And one said: 'Since the poets perished
And all they cherished in the way,
Their thoughts unsung, like petal showers
Inflame the hours of blue and gray.'

And one said: 'A loud tramp of men
We'll hear again at Rosnaree.'
A bomb burst near me where I lay.
I woke, 'twas day in Picardy.

Francis Ledwidge did not launch into the perils of the poetry of mythology until he had completed more than half of the poems published in *Songs Of The Fields*. His first poem in this difficult area was, curiously, not drawn from Irish mythology. It was *The Wife Of Llew,* taken from *Mabinogion,* a collection of fourteenth century Welsh romances. It is the most renowned and quoted of Francis Ledwidge's poems of mythology and historical romance, although deriving from Wales and not from Ireland.

THE WIFE OF LLEW

And Gwydion said to Math, when it was Spring:
'Come now and let us make a wife for Llew.'
And so they broke broad boughs yet moist with dew,
And in a shadow made a magic ring:
They took the violet and the meadowsweet
To form her pretty face, and for her feet
They built a mound of daisies on a wing,
And for her voice they made a linnet sing
In the wide poppy blowing for her mouth.
And over all they chanted twenty hours.
And Llew came singing from the azure south
And bore away his wife of birds and flowers.

This and other of Francis Ledwidge's poems based in mythology and romance are indicative of the very real scope of his poetic imagination. If he was inspired significantly by the country of the Boyne and his family and friends of Slane, he was by no means limited to them as sources of poetic joy.

The next poem of mythology in *Songs Of The Fields* shows Francis Ledwidge exploring one of the heroic themes of Ireland's past in lines worthy of Matthew Arnold's *Sohrab and Rustram.*

THE DEATH OF AILILL

When there was heard no more the war's loud sound
And only the rough corn-crake filled the hours,
And hill winds in the furze and drowsy flowers,
Maeve in her chamber with her white head bowed
On Ailill's heart was sobbing: 'I have found
The way to love you now,' she said, and he
Winked an old tear away and said: 'The proud
Unyielding heart loves never.' And then she:

'I love you now, tho' once when we were young
We walked apart like two who were estranged
Because I loved you not, now all is changed.'
And he who loved her always called her name
And said: 'You do not love me, 'tis your tongue
Talks in the dusk; you love the blazing gold
Won in the battles, and the soldier's fame.
You love the stories that are often told
By poets in the hall.' The Maeve arose
And sought her daughter Findebar: 'O child,
Go tell your father that my love went wild
With all my wars in youth, and say that now
I love him stronger than I hate my foes. ...'
And Findebar unto her father sped
And touched him gently on the rugged brow,
And knew by the cold touch that he was dead.

He does not return to Maeve and mythology until later in *Songs Of The Fields* and then gives us a number of intriguing details in the life and times of Maeve, in *Before The War Of Cooley*.

At daybreak Maeve rose up from where she prayed
And took her prophetess across her door
To gaze upon her hosts. Tall spear and blade
Burnished for early battle dimly shook
The morning's colours, and then Maeve said:
    'Look
And tell me how you see them now.'
    And then
The woman that was lean with knowledge said:
'There's crimson on them, and there's dripping red.'
And a tall soldier galloped up the glen
With foam upon his boot, and halted there
Beside old Maeve. She said, 'Not yet,' and turned
Into her blazing dun, and knelt in prayer
One solemn hour, and once again she came
And sought her prophetess. With voice that mourned
'How do you see them now? she asked.

'All lame
And broken in the noon.' And once again
The soldier stood before her.
        'No, not yet.'
Maeve answered his inquiring look and turned
Once more unto her prayer, and yet once more
'How do you see them now?' she asked.
        'All wet
With storm rains, and all broken, and all tore
With midnight wolves.' And when the soldier came
Maeve said, 'It is the hour.' There was a flash
Of trumpets in the dim, a silver flame
Of rising shields, loud words passed down the ranks,
And twenty feet they saw the lances leap.
They passed the dun with one short noisy dash.
And turning proud Maeve gave the wise one thanks,
And sought her chamber in the dun to weep.

This is followed, in *Songs Of The Fields*, by *The Sorrow Of Findebar*.

These and other of Francis Ledwidge's poems of mythology are a departure for him into the language and thoughts of war. Descriptions of the slain, hair red with blood, wounds, falls upon his shields, were unknown in Francis Ledwidge's poems of the Boyne, of home, of love. Did the study of Irish mythology and the terminology which he used to tell its tale prepare his mind in any way for the horrors of war which he was so shortly to meet at first hand. We do not know.

His poems of mythology also gave him the opportunity to write and experiment in the longer poem, in blank verse as opposed to rhyming lines and in the art of telling the story.

THE PASSING OF CAOILTE

'Twas just before the truce sang thro' the din
Caoilte, the thin man, at the war's red end
Leaned from the crooked ranks and saw his friend
Fall in the farther fury; so when truce
Halted advancing spears the thin man came
And bending by pale Oscar called his name;
And then he knew of all who followed Finn,
He only felt the cool of Gavra's dews.

And Caoilte, the thin man, went down the field
To where slow water moved among the whins,
And sat above a pool of twinkling fins
To court old memories of the Fenian men,
Of how Finn's laugh at Conan's tale of glee
Brought down the rowan's boughs on Knocnaree,
And how he made swift comets with his shield
At moonlight in the Fomar's rivered glen.

And Caoilte, the thin man, was weary now,
And nodding in short sleeps of half a dream:
There came a golden barge down middle stream,
And a tall maiden coloured like a bird
Pulled noiseless oars, but not a word she said.
And Caoilte, the thin man, raised up his head
And took her kiss upon his throbbing brow,
And where they went away what man has heard?

This poem introduces us to some new and fascinating characters hitherto unmentioned in Francis Ledwidge's mythological poetry; Caoilte, the thin man, pale Oscar and Finn. But more exciting than the new characters it discloses the breath of Francis Ledwidge's poetic imagination. At the start of the poem we are led to expect more of the same tale of war and death but by the end Coailte, the thin man, leaves the scene in a golden barge with a tall maiden coloured like a bird and 'took her kiss upon his throbbing brow.'

This is the last poem of mythology in *Songs Of The Fields*. But as we shall see Irish mythology was a sustaining source of strength and interest to Francis Ledwidge after he had gone to war and he returns to it almost on joining the Army.

Such then were the fountains of Francis Ledwidge's joys and sorrows. The beautiful country in which he grew up, his family, his home, his friends, his loves won and lost, his dreams and his interest in Irish mythology were the inspiration of his poetry before he went to war. It is time to move beyond Slane and County Meath to see to what extent Francis Ledwidge and his poetry were affected by the great events then taking place in politics and in literature in Ireland.

All Hallows Eve

The dreadful hour is sighing for a moon
To light old lovers to the place of tryst.
And old footsteps from blessed acres soon
On old known pathways will be lightly prest.
And winds that went to eavesdrop all the noon,
Kinking* at some old tale told sweetly brief,
Will give a cowlick+ to the yarrow's+ leaf,
And sling the round nut from the hazel down.

And there will be old yarn balls and old spells
In broken lime-kilns, and old eyes will peer
For constant loves in old spidery wells,
And old embraces will grow newly ~~fondly~~ dear.
And some may meet old lovers in old dells,
And some in doors ajar** in ~~and~~ towns light lorn —
But two will meet beneath a gnarly thorn
Down in the bosom of the windy fells.

** Maidens throw balls of yarn (which must be black) over their shoulders into old lime-kilns & winding it up till they feel it caught somehow expect to see in the darkness the face of their lover. + Also they look for his face in old wells

* A tuft of hair thrown back from the forehead is called a cowlick

+ Trying to hold in a laugh that bursts out — Shatter the outburst of laugh held-back

+ Maidens on hallowe'en pull leaves of yarrow & saying over it certain words put it under their pillows & so dream of their true-loves.

3.

Then when the night slopes home & white-faced day,
Yawns in the east there will be sad farewells.
& many feet will tap a lonely way
Back to the comfort of their chilly cells.
& eyes will backward turn & long to stay
Where love first found them in the clover bloom—
But one will never seek the lonely tomb
& Two will linger at the tryst alway.

The original handwritten version of *All Hallow's Eve* (p 129) by Francis Ledwidge
with annotation by Lord Dunsany, from a private collection

FIVE

TWILIGHT
OF THE EMPIRE

A husband that had sold his wife
And after that betrayed;
But stories that live longest
Are sung above the glass,
And Parnell loved his country,
And Parnell loved his lass.

Come, Gather Round Me, Parnellites, WB Yeats

THE YEARS WITH WHICH WE ARE PARTICULARLY CONCERNED are the years 1900–1914 during which Francis Ledwidge was writing poetry before he went to war. To what extent, if at all, was his poetry influenced by the great political events unfolding then in Ireland?

The problem in attempting to trace political influence on any particular life in Ireland is to know where to begin; to a greater or lesser extent no doubt we have all been influenced by the campaigns of Cromwell, the Act of Union, Catholic Emancipation, the Famine and the whole tale of happy and unhappy events which go to make up Irish History. At the risk of appearing arbitrary I do not propose to go any further back than the fall of Parnell, an event of awesome significance inspiring Yeats' famous panegyric set out above.

The dominant figure in the early days of the Home Rule Party had been Isaac Butt. Isaac Butt, born in 1813, was the son of a County Donegal clergyman. He graduated from Trinity College, Dublin where he stayed on as a don. He was called to the Bar.

He defended young Irelanders arrested in 1848, became a Member of Parliament and, in 1868, he was prominent in his defence of Fenians arrested following the 1867 Fenian rising. His solution to the Irish problem was federalism which he advanced from 1870 onwards. Federalism meant the establishment of an Irish Parliament with full control over Irish affairs but leaving to the Imperial Parliament at Westminster authority for defence, foreign affairs and certain taxation matters. In pursuit of his Federal aims he formed the Home Government Association attempting to attract Conservatives, Liberals, constitutional Nationalists and Fenians. The idea was that the Home Government Association would be a pressure group for federal ideas, not a political party as such. At this stage therefore, in the years immediately following 1870, Home Rule meant federalism. The Home Government Association became in 1873 the Home Rule League. The subscription was £1 per year, 1 shilling for associate membership. In 1874 fifty-nine MPs were elected on a Home Rule platform.

One of the most vociferous of the new MPs elected was JG Biggar, a Belfast merchant. In 1875 he used the rules of the House of Commons to compel the Prince of Wales to withdraw from the public gallery. He was indifferent to his unpopularity at Westminster consequent to this somewhat churlish gesture. He converted to Catholicism. He joined the Irish Republican Brotherhood. He believed in the tactics of obstruction rather than conciliation as more likely to advance Ireland's needs at Westminster. Biggar was too plebeian to lead the Home Rule Party, many of whom were from Southern landowning and professional backgrounds.

But in April 1875 a new force broke upon the Irish political firmament. Charles Stewart Parnell was elected to Parliament in a County Meath by-election. He was a Protestant landowner. He lived and enjoyed the life of a country gentleman in County Wicklow. He was reserved. He was a natural leader with a mighty self-confidence. His mother was American, the daughter of an Admiral who fought against England in 1812; from her Charles Stewart Parnell inherited strong anti-English sentiments which grew within him into a driving political inspiration. He had not enjoyed Cambridge. An Irish aristocrat, he deeply resented English superiority and indifference to the affairs of Ireland.

Parnell supported Biggar's obstructionist activities in the House of Commons. He met Fenians in England. In 1877 he became President of the Home Rule Confederation of Great Britain. In May 1877 Isaac Butt, the leader of the Home

Rule Party died against a background of declining health, personal debts and falling popularity in the Party.

Parnell became leader of the Home Rule Party. In 1879 he became President of the Irish National Land League whose aims were to preserve tenants from being rack-rented and unjustly evicted; and in due course to make them owners of their farms. Land tenure was at the heart of Irish politics in 1879 and was to remain so for many years. It was an important subsidiary allegiance for Parnell whose driving aim was for political independence for Ireland from England. The Land League grew in importance and was supported by many parish clergy, some Bishops, Home Rule Members of Parliament and a variety of newspapers. In the 1880 General Election Parnell stormed to success. He was returned for three seats. He was extensively supported by newly elected Home Rule MPs. He was made Chairman of the Home Rule Parliamentary Party.

The activities of the Land League were now central to politics. There had been an escalating sequence of evictions for non-payment of rent followed by outrages and violence in the years 1878–1880. Parnell was accordingly extensively concerned in seeking redress for evicted tenants. A Bill to award compensation to evicted tenants was defeated in the House of Lords leading to significant financial and membership support for the Land League, including substantial support from America. Agrarian outrages multiplied. A Coercion Bill and the Protection of Person and Property Bill were introduced in the House of Commons. Parnell led the Parliamentary opposition with the maximum disruption to House of Commons business causing one sitting to last over 40 hours. Parnell and over thirty Home Rulers were suspended and then ejected from the House of Commons. Consideration was given by the Home Rule Party as to whether it should withdraw entirely from the House of Commons and pursue revolutionary rather than constitutional methods of achieving its aims; its aims at this stage being just treatment for tenants and in the longer term political independence from England. Parnell received divergent advice but decided firmly for a constitutional and not an extra constitutional or revolutionary path. He believed that he could achieve more for the Irish tenantry by constitutional rather than violent means. He was correct. The Land Act of 1881 established fair rents, fixity of tenure and free sale; a massive advance for the tenantry although the complexity of the Act led to extensive litigation and many were excluded from its operation.

Parnell thereafter made a number of speeches highly critical of the Act and of the Prime Minister, Mr Gladstone. It seems that he so enraged the British Government that in October 1881 he was arrested under the Coercion laws and lodged in Kilmainham jail where he was joined by other leaders of the Land League. Parnell's imprisonment added extensively to his support in Ireland and provoked even greater agrarian outrages. He was released in May 1882 after extensive negotiations with the British government in which both sides made concessions; the British Government over details in the operation of the Land Act, Parnell in accepting the Land Act and undertaking to use his influence against intimidation and outrage.

In 1882 the Land League was succeeded by the Irish National League. Parnell's concentration on the achievement of his greatest political end, namely, independence for Ireland by constitutional means, was gathering momentum. In the 1885 elections the Home Rule Party won every seat in Ireland apart from Trinity College, Dublin and in eastern Ulster. The Home Rule Party now numbered eighty-six; it was firmly behind Parnell's leadership. It was supported by the Irish clergy and hierarchy.

In June 1885 Parnell and the Home Rulers voted with the Conservatives to defeat and topple the Liberal Government. Parnell had therefore created a political force of crucial power which could, with eighty-six votes, dependent on the balance of British parties, at Westminster, topple Liberal or Conservative governments in furtherance of Ireland's best interests. The result of the 1885 election gave the Liberals a majority of eighty-six over the Conservatives. The Home Rule Party led by Parnell was eighty-six strong. Parnell was on a pinnacle of political power and influence.

In December 1885 Herbert Gladstone, the Prime Minister's son, let it be known by way of public hint in the press that his father was moving towards Home Rule. Accordingly the stage was set for momentous events in the story of Ireland's struggle for independence.

Gladstone's Home Rule Bill of 1886, the year before Francis Ledwidge was born, provided for an Irish Parliament of two orders who would, or at least could, vote separately and have a suspensory power of veto over each other's legislation. An Irish executive would be responsible for this legislation. Reserved to the Westminster Parliament were the Crown, defence, war, foreign and colonial affairs, trade, post office and coinage. There would be a right of appeal from the Irish Court of Appeal to the Judicial Committee of the Privy Council.

These proposals of limited Home Rule were opposed by those who were not prepared to hand over Ulster and Unionists to a nationalist Parliament which they rejected. Opposition on this ground was articulated in particular by Lord Randolph Churchill with his famous 'Ulster will fight and Ulster will be right' speech delivered in the Ulster Hall, Belfast. It was massively supported in Ulster.

The proposals in Gladstone's Home Rule Bill of 1886 were for a final solution to the issue of Irish independence. Did Parnell accept them as a final solution or as a stepping stone on the way to total serverance? Parnell said that he did. He stated 'I accept this Bill as a final settlement of our national question and I believe the Irish people will accept it.' He had earlier in 1885 stated in his most famous words 'No man has the right to set a boundary to the onward March of a nation. No man has a right to say 'Thus far shalt thou go and no farther'.'

The Bill was defeated. The Conservatives were joined by defecting Liberal Unionists. Gladstone resigned. The best chance for a peaceful resolution of Ireland's independence was lost. Turmoil and blood were to follow. These momentous events occurred one year before Francis Ledwidge was born. They constitute something of the political background of his early years.

In the consequent election a Conservative and Liberal Unionist majority was elected. Lord Salisbury became Prime Minister. Thereafter Parnell and the Home Rule Party were entirely dependent on the Liberals, reduced in numbers certainly so far as Home Rule and Irish independence were concerned.

Parnell's eminence grew with the failure to discredit him in The Times' articles, 'Parnellism and crime' appearing from March 1887. The articles suggested a link between Parnell and terrorism; a link alleged in a letter purporting to have been written by Parnell in May 1882 suggesting that he expressed his regret for having to denounce the Phoenix Park murders in which the Chief Secretary, Lord Frederick Cavendish and the Under-Secretary, TH Burke had been stabbed to death by assassins in the Phoenix Park. It is difficult to imagine a more shocking libel against a public man. Parnell denounced the letter as a forgery and demanded a Select Committee of the House of Commons to investigate the authority of the letters. It was refused. But a commission was set up to investigate the charges made by The Times against Parnell and the Home Rule Party. The commission sat in 1888 and 1889 and investigated the charges. The crucial matter was whether the letters alleged to have been written by Parnell were genuine or forgeries. A Dublin journalist, Richard Pigott, admitted under cross-examination forging the letters, fled and shot himself in Spain. Parnell was vindicated. The Report, published later, cleared Parnell and the Home Rule leaders from the charges but said they had promoted agrarian agitation in which crime and outrage had been committed. The failure to discredit Parnell left him in a more pre-eminently popular position. Hopes were high for a new Home Rule alliance between the Gladstonian liberals and the Home Rule Party. Parnell visited Gladstone at his home at Hawarden.

Parnell believed that the Liberal alliance was the best hope for Home Rule; the alliance was a means to an end and not an end in itself. He said in 1889 'Suppose that it turned out that Home Rule could not after all be won in Parliament. I for one would not continue to remain for twenty-four hours in the House of Commons at Westminster … The most advanced section of Irishmen, as well as the least advanced, have always understood that the Parliamentary policy was to be a trial and that we did not ourselves believe in the possibility of maintaining for all time an incorruptible and independent Irish representation at Westminster.'

It was in 1889, two years after the birth of Francis Ledwidge, that disaster struck Parnell. He had been in love with Katherine O'Shea, the wife of Captain O'Shea, since he met her in 1880. In 1880 the O'Shea's marriage had been a façade for some years. In 1881 Parnell and Katherine O'Shea started to live together for short periods; she gave birth to their child in 1882 at a time when Parnell was in Kilmainham jail. He was allowed out to see his daughter before she died. In 1883 and 1884 two further children were born to them. In 1886 they were living together continuously. O'Shea's divorce petition was not brought until 1889. It seems incredible that O'Shea did not know that his wife was living with Parnell or that he was deceived by either of them. In 1886 Parnell had supported him strongly as MP for Galway City against the strongest opposition from some members of the Home Rule Party. He was elected but achieved no position in the Home Rule Party and indeed declined to vote for the Home Rule Bill.

Neither Parnell nor Mrs O'Shea defended the petition. But details horrendously damaging to Parnell became public; the trivia of matrimonial deception was extensively ventilated.

The pressure mounted upon Gladstone to discontinue any form of political alliance with Parnell or with the Home Rule Party while led by Parnell. The Liberal Party drew significant support from the non-conformist element in society. Nonconformist sensibilities were seriously outraged by the details of Parnell's adulterous love affair with Katherine O'Shea. Gladstone ensured that the impossibility of a continuing close alliance between the Liberal Party and the Home Rule Party unless Parnell withdrew from ...

Shortly after ...
the political sce...
party was in igno...
elected him. Parnel...
resigning.

Parnell was a proud ...
The Home Rule Party ...
Bishops intervened against ...
by forty-five against him, twe...
up his own candidates at by-elec...
against Parnell was the fear that if ...
was dead. So long as Gladstone led t...
would be withdrawn if Parnell became...

fought on in Ireland to recover the leadership. He refused to accept any deal based on his temporary retirement.

In fact the strain of politics had ravaged his health; and with his struggle to recover the leadership of the Home Rule Party in full swing he died in October 1891, still only forty-five.

So the very early years of Francis Ledwidge's life were spent in the political shadow of the fall of the uncrowned King of Ireland. For many years after Parnell's fall and death the Home Rule Party and movement were debilitated by the split between Parnellites and anti-Parnellites. The driving force for Home Rule lost in the years following Parnell's death at least some of its purpose and momentum. So the last years of the century in which Francis Ledwidge was growing up were not as politically dynamic as the years 1880–1890 nor as politically vibrant as the years from 1912 onwards.

Gladstone's second Home Rule Bill was killed off in the House of Lords. Gladstone retired from politics. Parnell was dead. Home Rule was on the back burner in the closing years of the century. But although the pursuit of Home Rule over the years 1890–1912 was significantly less in the public domain than previously important advances in the cause of improving Irish, particularly agricultural Irish, life were made.

Sir Horace Plunkett, the uncle of Lord Dunsany, who features so prominently in Francis Ledwidge's life and in his poetic development, launched in 1889 and built up over the following years his co-operative societies for the improvement in the production and marketing of Irish agriculture. The Irish Agricultural Organisation Society was formed in 1894; by 1904 it had expanded to over eight hundred Societies. Prominent in the work of the Irish Agricultural Society and editor of its journal 'The Irish Homestead' was George Russell, who became famous, or at least widely known, under the name of AE He was a mystic, a poet and a painter, one of the few prominent men in the Dublin literary scene with whom Francis Ledwidge was to become acquainted. Notwithstanding AE's pervasive influence in the world of Dublin letters in the years up to 1914, Ledwidge's contact with him, as we shall see in due course, did nothing to advance his career or poetic development.

But apart altogether from AE's literary and artistic eminence he was an important man in an important development in Irish public life over the turn of the century, namely Sir Horace Plunkett's co-operative agricultural movement, which set out to improve, and succeeded in improving, methods of production and marketing in Irish agriculture through techniques of co-operation between landlords, tenants and farmers.

It was in matters relating to land rather than Home Rule as such that the years from 1890–1903 were so significant. The Land Act of 1896 increased the amount of land available under the Land Act 1891 and rendered it easier for peasants to purchase land.

In 1898 the Irish Local Government Act introduced a system of local government analogous to the British system bringing into Ireland a system of local government operating through county councils, urban district councils and rural district councils to be elected on a wide franchise, including women. These councils had the right to impose their own rates; they could receive Treasury grants and were allotted administrative duties. This was an Act of far reaching significance in the development of attitudes in self-government, as it allocated to those elected to the councils very real powers of local government.

In 1899 the Department of Agriculture and Technical Instruction for Ireland was created. Sir Horace Plunkett became Vice-President. Among many other functions it took on responsibility for agricultural instruction. By 1914 it had a staff of over three hundred; and many institutions, such as the Royal College of Science were brought under its control. It maintained a staff of lecturers giving instruction throughout Ireland on agriculture, horticulture, poultry breeding and butter manufacturing. It carried out other important functions directed to the improvement of agricultural performance throughout Ireland which, consequent to its activities and efforts, undoubtedly did improve significantly, leading to at least some increase in crop yields.

If the new century opened on a quiescent note in relation to the politics of Home Rule, the politics of land ownership were again on the boil. Agitation for the buying out of the landlords by compulsory purchase had been on the increase towards 1900. In 1900 George Wyndham became Chief Secretary. He quickly put his very astute mind to a resolution of the land problem. His proposed Bill for compulsory purchase did not go forward in 1902.

Under the initiative of Captain Shaw-Taylor, Lady Gregory's nephew and a country gentleman acclaimed in some of Yeats' poetry, a Land Conference between representatives of landowners and of tenants to settle differences between the two classes, was convened. The Duke of Abercorn and other invited landowners did not attend; but in due course the Land Conference got under way chaired by the Earl of Dunraven. The Chief Secretary was strongly supportive. The Land Conference rapidly produced a unanimous report covering extensive areas of agrarian concern. In particular it recommended a massive scheme of land purchase by the Government. The Report of the Conference was the basis of Lord Wyndham's Act of 1903. It vastly extended the principle and fact of land purchase. It encouraged landlords to sell entire estates. Sales would proceed if three quarters of the tenants agreed. The prices to be paid were based on varying years of purchase. The money for purchase was to be advanced by the British Government to be repaid over 68^1/2 years at the rate of 3^1/2 percent. The effect of this Act was to generate a massive land transfer from landowners, compensated by the British Government, to small farmers who had hitherto been tenants or labourers. By 1920 nine million acres had changed hands. A great step forward was achieved in effecting peace on the land. So that as Francis Ledwidge was growing into his poetic years in County Meath his joy in natural beauty was not marred by war on the land.

A significant feature in the background of Irish political life in these years was the launching of the Gaelic League in 1893. Its most powerful driving force was Douglas Hyde, the son of a Church of Ireland rector, born in Sligo in 1863. He grew up in County Roscommon. He learned Irish from the Irish speaking community living around his home. He wrote poems in Irish. He had joined with Yeats in forming the Irish Literary Society in London in 1891. In 1892 they founded the National Literary Society in Dublin. We will look in the next Chapter, *Celtic Twilight*, at the powerful contribution to Irish poetry and literature made by WB Yeats in these years.

The purposes of the Gaelic League were the preservation of Irish as the national language of Ireland and the extension of its use as the spoken language; and the study and publication of Gaelic literature and the development of a modern literature in Irish. It did not seek to be identified with any specific political group or allegiance. It was an appeal to all Irishmen.

It grew significantly in Francis Ledwidge's early years. It was founded in 1893, six years after he was born. By 1908, by which time Francis Ledwidge was writing poetry, the Gaelic League had six hundred branches. It had achieved the introduction of the teaching of Irish in the Primary School curriculum. In 1909 Irish was included as a compulsory subject for matriculation in the National University in Dublin. These endeavours brought the Gaelic League into the political arena but not into party political life.

The fall and death of Parnell in 1890 and the consequent divisions within the Home Rule Party undoubtedly led to a lacuna in the pressure for independence by way of Home Rule. However in 1906 the Liberals won a landslide victory in the Imperial Parliament. Home Rule for Ireland was by then official party policy. The drive for Home Rule accordingly rose in public and political importance from 1906 onwards.

But while the focus on independence as carried on by the parliamentary party went quite lame after the death of Parnell and the consequent divisions in the Home Rule Party the impulse for independence did not die. Some at least of its energies were channelled into more extreme endeavours.

The most significant force outside the Home Rule Party was Sinn Fein. The most significant inspiration behind the rise of Sinn Fein was Arthur Griffith. He was born in 1871; by 1899 he had become Editor of the United Irishman. His life's work was to pursue complete political independence for Ireland from England and to achieve an Ireland governed by Irishmen for Irishmen.

He launched a savage attack on Queen Victoria's visit to Ireland in 1900. WB Yeats' critical comments on this visit had prompted Percy French to write in *The Queen's After-Dinner Speech* (*The World of Percy French 180*).

> 'Now Maud 'ill write,' sez she,
> 'That I brought the blight,' sez she,
> 'Or altered the saysons,' sez she,
> 'For some private raysins,' sez she,
> 'An' I think there's a slate,' sez she,
> 'Off Willie Yeats,' sez she.
> 'He should be at home,' sez she,
> 'French polishin' a pome,' sez she,
> 'An' not writin' letters,' sez she,
> 'About his betters,' sez she,
> 'Paradin' me crimes,' sez she,
> 'In the Irish Times,' sez she …

Griffith's United Irishman suggested that Queen Victoria had been sent over 'in her dotage to seek recruits for her battered army' (then fighting in the Boer War). He set out to and succeeded in raising the political temperature of anti-English feeling.

Griffith's aim was an Irish Republic; accordingly the purposes of the Home Rule Bill fell significantly short of what he was pursuing. He called in 1902 for the withdrawal of Irish members of Parliament; he asserted that the British Parliament's right to legislate for Ireland should not be recognised and that Members of Parliament should remain in Ireland to promote Ireland's interest. He advocated the establishment in Ireland of a Council of three hundred charged with making policy for Ireland to be carried out by locally elected bodies. He pressed for Irish industry to be protected. He was adamant that independence must be economic as well as political.

By 1903 his efforts were being channelled through the National Council which was originally concerned to protest against the visit of King Edward VII to Ireland. Edward Martyn was Chairman; Maud Gonne was active. WB Yeats supported. A massive public meeting took place in Dublin in protest against the visit.

In 1905 the National Council changed its name to Sinn Fein into which merged a variety of elements inspired into existence by Arthur Griffith's energetic prorogation of national self-reliance and his pursuit of economic and political independence. By 1908 the principal forces for independence outside the Home Rule Party had joined under the banner of Sinn Fein. Griffith's central and driving aim was the independence of Ireland. This was expressly set out in the constitution of Sinn Fein as the 'creation of a prosperous, virile and independent nation' with all the political and economic institutions of an independent state such as a national bank, a national stock exchange, and many other institutions of the modern state.

The advance of Sinn Fein in terms of support after initial enthusiasms was limited. By 1909 the Home Rule Party, led by Redmond, had succeeded in getting Home Rule up and running. It still commanded majority support in Ireland outside Ulster notwithstanding the cutting edge which Arthur Griffith and Sinn Fein had established in the minds of the politically conscious.

Redmond was a country gentleman. He was a Parnellite. The anti-Parnellites accepted him as leader. The divisions occasioned by the fall of Parnell were substantially healed. Redmond was a formidable parliamentarian and a powerful advocate. He developed into a prominent political leader of the Home Rule Party and carried it far towards the fulfilment of its cherished aim of independence.

The Liberal landslide of 1906 gave the Home Rule Party high hopes. Their massive majority of course meant that the Irish Party could not in any way hold them to ransom in order to stay in office. The House of Lords veto was not fragmented until the Lloyd-George Finance Bill crises of 1909–1910. The Conservative majority in the House of Lords was wholly opposed to Home Rule. The Liberal Party was no longer led by Gladstone. He had made Home Rule for Ireland the means by which he hoped to achieve one of his greatest ambitions, 'to pacify Ireland'. So the progress of Home Rule in the years following the great Liberal landslide was that of the tortoise rather than the hare.

Political progress on Home Rule was slow but there were important social and economic Bills in the years following the Liberal victory of 1906. Advances were made to the Wyndham Land Act of 1903. The Irish Universities Act of 1908 established Queen's College in Belfast as Queen's University from which it went on to achieve great intellectual eminence, particularly in the field of medicine. It also established the Colleges of Dublin, Cork and Galway as the new University of Ireland. All three have prospered.

The crises over the Finance Bill and the House of Lords powers of veto led to the general election of 1910. It was crucial in the life and progress of the Home Rule

Party. The Liberal leader, HH Asquith, gave a public undertaking that the problem of Ireland would only be solved 'by a policy which, while safeguarding the supremacy and indefeasible authority of the Imperial Parliament will set up in Ireland a system of full self-government in regard to purely Irish affairs.' This was a very firm commitment to further advance for Home Rule.

The result of the election advanced the negotiating power of the Home Rule Party immeasurably; Liberals 275, Conservatives 273, Labour 40, Irish Party 71. Accordingly, the Liberals could not survive in power against the determined voting opposition of the Irish Party if they could ever bring themselves to vote with the Conservatives; an unlikely event since the Conservatives were closely allied with Ulster Unionism and would have buried Home Rule if given half a chance. A second general election in 1910 gave the Liberals 273, the Conservatives 273, Labour 42, the Irish Party 83. Redmond was therefore in a numerically commanding position. One of the major consequences of the turmoil was the Parliament Act of 1911 which reduced the absolute veto of the House of Lords on House of Commons legislation to a delaying power of two years. The scene was set for Home Rule to run.

It was a run whose first and continuing hurdle was the determination of Ulster Unionism to have no part of Home Rule; and if it found its way on to the Statute Book of Westminster to ensure that Ulster had no part of it.

The reduction of the power of the House of Lords in 1911 ensured that the alarm bells in Ulster's constitutional sensibility kept ringing. Ulster Unionists had been alerted to the perils of their position since Home Rule had been formulated by Parnell and the English liberals in 1880. As from time to time over the years from 1885 to 1911 the progress of Home Rule grew stronger so the intensity of Ulster Unionist opposition increased to an iron determination to fight an independent Ireland at every turn and at least to ensure that Ulster was excluded from it.

The Ulster Unionists did not stand alone in their fierce opposition to Home Rule. They struck a powerful alliance with the Conservative party in opposition to a separation between the United Kingdom and Ireland, or at the very least Ulster, which struck, argued the Unionist and Conservative advocates, at the integrity of the British Empire. The Home Rule-Ulster crisis therefore spread far beyond Irish shores in its implications for British Dominions overseas.

Supporters of Ulster Unionism organised energetically from 1885 onwards when the body of the Home Rule movement gathered flesh and force. They organised through Orange lodges, which moulded and controlled Protestant opinion on the ground. They organised politically through the Ulster Loyalist Anti-Repeal Union formed in 1886; they had the support of important areas of the press, particularly the *Belfast Newsletter*. They made full use of important politicians in England, in particular Lord Randolph Churchill who saw in the 'Orange' card a welcome rod with which to thrash the Liberals. Rioting in Belfast and other places caused thirty-two deaths. Rioting and violence featured again in 1893 on the occasion of Gladstone's second Home Rule Bill passing through the House of Commons. The Ulster Unionist Council was formed in 1906 to advance and defend the interests of Ulster Unionism. It is still in existence today.

The election of Sir Edward Carson as leader of the Irish Unionists in 1910 guaranteed that the cause of Unionism had a protagonist of massive weight and persuasion. He was a dominating figure at the English Bar and sat in Parliament as a member for Trinity College, Dublin.

The temperature of Irish politics was rising to the boil from 1912 onwards when Home Rule was again on the march towards the Statute Book and reality. Carson spoke to Unionist supporters of the need to resist 'the most nefarious conspiracy' to bring in Home Rule; if need be, by taking over the government in areas controlled by Unionists. He joined with James Craig and the Ulster Unionist Council in framing a Constitution for a Provisional Government of Ireland, in the event of Home Rule.

The leader of the Conservative Party as from 1911 was Bonar-Law. He was of Ulster origin. He was vehemently opposed to Home Rule. He was determined that if he could not stop Home Rule Ulster would be excluded from it. The third Home Rule Bill introduced in 1912 contained no safeguards for Ulster. Political tension was rising to explosion point.

Unionists made clear that, whatever the price to be paid, they would not accept Home Rule and independently Bonar-Law stated publicly that the Conservatives, in their opposition to Home Rule, would not be bound by the restraints which would influence them in an ordinary constitutional struggle. Ulster Unionists were fortified in their resistance to Home Rule by Bonar-Law's public exhortation 'that if any attempt were made to deprive Ulster Protestants of their birthright they would be justified in resisting such an attempt by all means in their power including force.' He could imagine, he said, 'no length of resistance to which Ulster could go in which he would not be prepared to support them and in which, he believed, they would be supported by the overwhelming majority of the British people.' Words, which, although spoken in England, did not go unnoticed in Ulster. Words, which, although coming from the leader of the party traditionally holding itself out as the party of law and order, appeared in fact and in spirit to be counselling rebellion.

The Liberal government regarded Ireland as one country and were determined that Home Rule would apply to all Ireland. Carson and the Unionists were determined that Ulster would be excluded. Partition came into the language of Irish politics. The introduction of Home Rule was scheduled for 1914. The closer it approached, the greater the chances of clash appeared. In September 1912 Carson led the signing of the Solemn League and Covenant by which each who signed vowed to use all necessary means 'to defeat the present conspiracy to set up a Home Rule Parliament in Ireland. And in the event of such a Parliament being forced upon us we further solemnly and mutually pledge ourselves to refuse to accept its authority.'

Thousands of Unionists signed. Thousands began to drill and train in arms in support of their signatures. In January 1913 the Ulster Volunteer Force was formed at the instigation of the Ulster Unionist Council. The force was limited to one hundred thousand men. One hundred thousand men on the ground is a lot of men. The one hundred thousand Ulster Volunteers had the assistance of returned British army officers to guide their training.

Carson and the Unionists were adamant on Partition and the exclusion of the nine or at least six of the nine counties of Ulster. Redmond and the Irish nationalists were equally adamant that the Irish nation could not be mutilated by Partition. The scene was set for the next seventy-five years of infighting on Partition.

By 1913 Home Rule was grounded in political deadlock, again the shape of things to come in British-Irish relations. The Liberal Government, led by Asquith, became increasingly convinced that some form of Partition was inevitable. The Irish nationalists would not yield.

It was not immediately clear to what extent Ulster Unionist opposition to Home Rule might contain an element of bluff. But as arms and ammunition were secretly imported into Ulster in quantities for supply to the Ulster Volunteer Force it became clear that Ulster Unionist opposition was for real, and with hardware in support.

Irish Nationalists did not sit idly by while Ulster armed. In November 1913 the Irish Volunteers were established.

With armies gathering north and south of the Border, although dignified by the name of Volunteers, it is scarcely surprising that Asquith and the Liberal Government were pursuing any realistic compromise. Asquith proposed that individual counties could opt out of Home Rule for six years. Redmond agreed with this concession, concerned that Home Rule might flounder again for the third time. Carson would have none of it, rejecting it in the House of Commons with the high rhetoric 'that Ulster could not accept a sentence of death, with a stay of execution for six years.'

The drama of politics spread to the Armed Forces. The Army stationed in the Curragh made it known to the Government in the clearest terms that it might not be counted on to coerce Ulster if Ulster resisted Home Rule. Fifty-eight officers offered to resign rather than be put in the position of marching against Ulster if Ulster revolted against Home Rule.

In April 1914 large consignments of arms were secretly landed from Germany in County Down and extensively distributed.

While tension on the ground mounted by the day political deadlock showed no sign of easing. Provisions for the exclusion of Ulster for six years, totally unacceptable to Carson, were introduced into the Commons. The House of Lords altered them from six years to an indefinite period which could not be accepted by Redmond and the Irish Nationalists.

In the hope of breaking the deadlock a conference was held at Buckingham Palace on 21 July 1914. The Liberal-Irish Nationalist team was represented by Asquith, Lloyd-George, Redmond and Dillon. The Union team was represented by Bonar-Law, Lord Lansdowne, Carson and James Craig. There was no agreement on which parts of Ulster were to be excluded. Nothing was finalised when the conference broke down on 24 July 1914.

On 26 July the Irish Volunteers caught up at least some of the armed ground gained by the Ulster Volunteers on their recent major arms importation from Germany. They unloaded a large quantity of arms at Howth in daylight.

No compromise agreement on the exclusion of Ulster had been reached by August 1914. The momentous events unfolding to crisis in Ireland were overtaken by the outbreak of war between Great Britain and Germany. Home Rule was not on the Statute Book. It had not been achieved. Redmond promised Ireland's support for the war. Asquith agreed to put the Government of Ireland Act on the Statute Book provided it did not come into operation until after the war and until provision was made for Ulster by further legislation. The deadlock over Partition was far from ended by the outbreak of the 1914–1918 war.

To what extent were Francis Ledwidge's life and thoughts affected by the great events unfolding in Ireland's political affairs between the fall of Parnell and the outbreak of the Great War? In particular to what extent was his poetry concerned with those momentous affairs?

Francis Ledwidge was a committed Nationalist. He was a founder member of the Slane Corps of the Irish Volunteers formed in November 1913. He was their first secretary. He went to Manchester where his brother and sister were living to help start a branch of the Irish Volunteers in Manchester and to raise funds. He delivered a lecture at the John Redmond Club. The success of this trip to Manchester is not clear. He wrote a poem about Manchester (see page 11).

He devoted a significant proportion, if not all, of his free time to the Irish Volunteers. He drilled two evenings a week and on Sunday. He went on lengthy route marches. He cannot have known that this neo-military training was the shape of things to come for him.

In early 1914 he was elected to the Navan Rural District Council and Board of Guardians. This was a forum concerned with local affairs, in particular matters affecting the workhouse. Francis Ledwidge's election was a significant achievement for him; it was a foundation step on a ladder which could have led him to prominence on at least local and possibly national politics. He attended and spoke on 1 July 1914 against the proposed Arms Proclamation aimed by the Government against the Irish Volunteers.

On 14 August 1914 England declared war on Germany, Germany having declared war on Russia on 1 August and on France on 3 August.

On 15 August there was a rally of the Irish Volunteers in Slane. Two thousand five hundred men were on parade, including Francis Ledwidge. Among distinguished local figures in the rally were the Marquis Conygham, Viscount Gormanston and Lord Trimelstown. The Corps were inspected by the Earl of Fingal and Lord Dunsany. God Save the King was played. At this stage, mid 1914, the role envisaged by its members for the Irish Volunteers was to defend Ireland from foreign invasion as British troops were withdrawn. This envisaged role was to change dramatically as the war wore on.

Redmond, the leader of the Irish Party in Parliament, strongly and publicly supported the war. He invited the Irish Volunteers to train and hold themselves in readiness for service on behalf of Great Britain, if necessary, outside Ireland. This led to a serious split in the Irish Volunteers. Redmond and his supporters became known as the National Volunteers. Eion MacNeill and those in opposition to Redmond's pro-British position continued to be known as Irish Volunteers. The Slane Corps opted to support Redmond. Francis Ledwidge was one of six who disagreed with the pro-Redmond resolution. The Meath Volunteer force declared for Redmond. Francis Ledwidge ceased to be a member. Accordingly, his politics continued to be firmly Nationalist.

On 10 October 1914 the Navan Rural Council considered whether to pass a Vote of Congratulations to Mr Redmond and the Irish Parliamentary party in their success in placing Home Rule on the Statute Book. The resolution for debate continued. 'Now a militant organisation had got up in the County and people who had no control wanted to take control of the Volunteer movement. These dissidents were just the same as the officers of the Curragh; they seceded from the governing body and he held they were rebels.' This was a reference to the Irish Volunteers led by Eion MacNeill.

Francis Ledwidge was at the meeting. He took a strongly Nationalist, strongly anti-Redmond, and strongly pro-Irish Volunteer position. At an early stage in the debate Francis Ledwidge said 'The proper men to follow were the men who started the movement and not Mr Redmond, who, after the movement had been organised, tried to get hold of it. So far as Home Rule was concerned they were as far of it today as ever.' The resolution was passed. Francis Ledwidge said 'I dissent from the resolution. The county will know more about it. I have seen people passing such resolutions unanimously and accepting Mr Redmond's policy, and when the motor cars came next day for them to join the army, I did not see them go.'

On 19 October at a meeting of the Navan Board of Guardians to discuss the placing of advertisements in the 'Volunteer', a paper issued by the Irish Volunteers or the 'National' or the 'National Volunteer', a paper issued by the National (Redmond) Volunteers Francis Ledwidge took a consistently anti-Redmond position.

In the course of an acrimonious debate one speaker said 'What was England's difficulty was now Ireland's difficulty and what was England's downfall would also be Ireland's. What was England's uprise would also be Ireland's uprise. He wondered at Mr Ledwidge or any other man calling himself an Irishman to stand up in that room and give expression to what he had said.' Francis Ledwidge said 'England's uprise had always been Ireland's downfall.' In answer to the question 'Was he an Irishman or a pro-German', Francis Ledwidge replied that he was an anti-German and an Irishman.

On 24 October 1914 Francis Ledwidge joined the Royal Inniskilling Fusilliers. We will look in due course in detail at the forces which drove him to that momentous and in the event fatal decision. No one listening to his talk on 10 and 19 October would have expected it.

There are fifty poems edited by Lord Dunsany of *Songs Of The Fields*, poems which Francis Ledwidge wrote before he went to war in 1914. None of the poems in *Songs Of The Fields* are overtly political. None of them are impliedly political. There is not a political concept in them. They are simply not about, or apparently influenced in any way, by the momentous political events taking place around Francis Ledwidge.

This is not to suggest that he was not deeply interested in politics. It is simply that politics were not an inspiration for his writing, as they undoubtedly were, for example, to *WB Yeats*. The total absence of any political content in his poetry before he went to war may reflect the strength of the other fountains of his inspiration at which we have looked in detail. It may be that as he was only 27 when he went to war in 1914 he had not developed an interest in politics sufficient to inspire or activate his writing.

The only influence of public affairs on his writing before 1914 was the rise and spread of the Gaelic League, with its concentration on all things Irish, Irish language, Irish history. It may well have guided him into the rich areas of Irish mythology which, as we have seen, was a significant inspiration of his poetry. It is of interest that all his poems of Irish mythology fall in the second and last half of *Songs Of The Fields*. The longer and more important of the mythological poems were the last ten. Accordingly inspirations specifically from native Irish culture, if not from Irish politics, were assuming a place of greater importance in his poetic consciousness before the war.

A branch of the Gaelic League was started in Slane; initially it did not prosper and died out. Francis Ledwidge tried to resuscitate it by engaging the support of a Navan schoolmaster, Sean MacNamee. It seems that Sean MacNamee was extensively engaged in other work for the Gaelic League and did not consider Slane sufficiently interesting for his attentions. A somewhat acrimonious correspondence ensued between Francis Ledwidge and Sean MacNamee carried on through the columns of the *Drogheda Independent.*

In fact no branch of the Gaelic League was started in Slane so that Francis Ledwidge had to educate himself in Irish. The Irish mythological poems in *Songs Of The Fields* pay a high tribute to Francis Ledwidge's devotion to Irish unassisted by the support which a branch of the Gaelic League might have given him.

He was a member of the Slane Gaelic Football club. He was not chosen to play, but supported Slane enthusiastically from the sidelines. On one occasion he landed a punch on one of the Navan Harp supporters who had taken to slandering the Slane Blues team after a match in Slane. The punch sent the Navan man to the ground; unhappily the Navan Harp supporters were about in force. Francis Ledwidge came off the worst with a black eye. His comment on the Navan Harps in a letter to the *Drogheda Independent* is forcefully expressed. 'They should only be allowed to play football in their bare feet and with blocks on their necks like vicious dogs.'

Labour became an organised force in Irish life significantly later than in England. The driving energy for reform in Ireland was channelled to politics, namely the pursuit of independence rather than into improved working conditions for the poor, terrible as they were. Outside Ulster there was no industrial proletariat to generate a labour movement as developed in England. It was not until 1894 that an Irish Trades Congress was formed.

The pusillanimous nature of the Irish labour movement received an injection of power in 1897 by the arrival of James Connolly from Scotland to become organiser of the Dublin Socialist Society. He founded the Irish Socialist Republican party in 1897, supported by a newspaper, the Workers Republic. The aims as ventilated through these two institutions were the establishment of an Irish Socialist Republic and the public ownership of land and the instruments of production, distribution and exchange. His politics were therefore far to the left of the Home Rule Party. His nationalist aspirations were not far removed, if at all, from Sinn Fein. He was vehemently opposed to all forms of private ownership. How this was to be reconciled with the split up of the great estates effected by Lord Wyndham's Act of 1903 and the consequent ownership of land by small farmers is not clear.

Intensity on the labour scene arose further by the arrival in Dublin in 1908 of Jim Larkin. Jim Larkin grew up in Liverpool, born of Irish parents. He was a strike-organiser of formidable ability. The shocking poverty and degradation of life for the Dublin poor were the backdrop to Larkin's efforts to improve conditions for the very poor. By 1900 the mansions of Georgian Dublin had become slums of horrendous proportions; many had no light, no heat, no indoor water and outdoor sanitation of the most lurid kind. Infant mortality was rampant; tuberculosis was a feature of everyday life.

Larkin's hope was to organise Dublin labour, particularly dockers, to strike for improved conditions. In 1908 he organised three strikes successfully. He founded the Irish Transport and General Workers Union.

Larkin fell foul of the Home Rule Party because he re-established the Dublin branch of the Independent Labour Party. He fell foul of Sinn Fein because Arthur Griffith considered that he was modelling the Irish Trade Union movement on the much better established English Trade Union movement. Nothing good came out of England for Arthur Griffith.

By 1911 the two great labour leaders of Ireland, Connolly and Larkin had come together. Connolly, who had emigrated in 1903 because of poverty, had returned from America and become an organiser for Larkin's union. He was based in Ulster. 1911, 1912 and 1913 were successful years with extensive gains for Dublin workers effected by Larkin's bargaining with employers.

However, 1913 as it wore on was less happy. The Dublin United Tramways Company, owned by a rich and powerful man, William Martin Murphy took issue with Larkin. He stated that his Company would not recognise Larkin or his Union. Larkin called out the tramway men during the Dublin Horse Show; an act calculated to inflict at least inconvenience on the rich and privileged who enjoyed Dublin's foremost social event of the year. The strike spread to other areas of Murphy's commercial empire. Murphy and the employers replied savagely. The Employers Federation locked out all employees belonging to Larkin's Union. Twenty-five thousand men were out of work within a month. This involved a massive deprivation to the families involved. At one meeting being addressed by Larkin the police broke up the attendant crowds with fearsome baton charges which provoked mob rioting.

Two men were killed; many were wounded including many police. Dublin by 1913 had become an embattled and bitter city. The lockout continued. Misery and starvation multiplied despite significant support from the British Trade Union movement. It did not however back Irish labour with any strike action in England which enraged Larkin who believed that the aggressive road was the true one for all genuine trade unionists.

Sean O'Casey describes the lockout in *Drums Under The Window.* 'The employers gathered their forces together too, to harass the workers and stamp their menace out. William Martin Murphy, their leader, who owned the Dublin Tramways, Clery's huge stores, and God knows what else besides, determined to get the employers to refuse to give work to any man who was a member of Larkin's Union. Let them submit or starve. Jacob's the biscuit makers, Shackleton's the millers, Eason's the newspaper and magazine distributors, along with coal factories, timber merchants, and steam ship owners came to Martin Murphy and said 'We're with you old boy. What thou doest, we will do; what thou sayest, we will say; thy profits shall be our profits; and thy gods, ours too.' And so it was. Catholic, Protestant, Quaker and pagan employer joined hand and foot, flung their money into one bag, and with bishop and priest, viceroy and council, infantryman and cavalry trooper, and bludgeon-belted policeman, formed a square, circle, triangle and crescent to down the workers …'

On a bright and sunny day, while all Dublin was harnessing itself into its best for the Horse show, the trams suddenly stopped. Drivers and conductors left them standing wherever they happened to be at a given time in the day when the strike commenced, to be brought to their sheds by frightened inspectors and the few scabs and blacklegs who saw in Martin Murphy another God incarnate. And the employers kept on locking out all who refused to abandon their Union – mill men, men and women from the factories, from the docks, from the railways, and from the wholesale warehouses of the cities and towns. They came out bravely, marching steadily towards hunger, harm and hostility, just to give an answer for the hope that was burning in them. … The dust and mire in which the people lived and died were being sprinkled everywhere through the gallant, aristocratic streets; it drifted on the crimson or away through a crowd of ragged women, and ragged children, bootless as well as ragged, carrying jugs, saucepans and even kettles to collect their ration of stew, cooked in the Daglan, down in the damp and dreary basement; he had never seen the Countess doing anything any one could call a spot of work. He often had a share of the stew, and sometimes snapped up a chance to bring some home to his mother, who welcomed it when it came, but said nothing when he came home without any; but never once did he see the Countess bearing up in the burden and heat of the day. Whenever a reporter from an English or an Irish journal strayed into the Hall and cocked an eye over the scene, there was the Countess in spotless bib and tucker, standing in the steam, a gigantic ladle in her hand, busy as a beebessee, so that a picture of the lady of the ladle might brighten the papers of the morrow; and significant enough, though many months belied the myth of her devotion to the poor, Orpen sketch of the eskitchen doesn't show sign or light of the good-natured dame anywhere near. The myth, it would seem appeared in a vision to those who wanted to see it so.

Neither did the Countess understand Ireland, even when she was green costumed in her own selective uniform of the citizen army. She differed from Captain White in while she never understood the workers, and never tried to, he, though never understanding them either, failed, I imagine, by trying too ardently to do so. Gaelic Ireland she never even glimpsed; and the English-speaking world she ran about in was seen as in a wonderland looking glass, darkly, so different from Alice Milligan who saw it clear, and was able to fondle it with both her clever hands. Countess Markiewicz lagged far behind Maud Gonne in dignity, character and grace, and could not hold a candle to her as a speaker. Her passionate speeches always appeared to be strained and rarely had any sense in them; and they always threatened to soar into a stillborn scream. Ideas of order she had little and looked rather contemptuously at any mind that had. She usually whirled into a meeting, and whirled out again, a spluttering Catherine-wheel of irresponsibility. Although he had often seen her handling a gun, he had never seen her fondling a book and he thought that odd. In her young days she could hardly have been a Cathleen Ni Houlihan, and when she grew old she had no resemblance to the old woman of Beare. She grew very thin and bony, and in spite of all her irritating and fantastic liveliness, there was invariably a querulous look on her face. No part of her melted into the cause of Ireland, nor did she ever set a foot in the fold of Socialism. She looked at the names over the doors and even thought she was one of the family. But the movements to her were no more than the hedges over which her horses jumped. She wanted to be in everything and to be everything and to be everywhere. She rushed into Arthur Griffith arms, near knocking the man down; she danced to the Republicanism of the Irish Brotherhood; she stormed into the Gaelic League, but quickly slid out again, for the learning of Irish was too much like work; she bounded into the Volunteers one night, and into the Citizen army the next. Then she bounced on Connolly and dazzled his eyes with her flashy enthusiasm. She found it almost impossible to reason out a question, and smothered the reasonable answer of another with a sequel. She seemed never to be able to make any golden or silver thing out of the ore of experience. She tried verses and failed; she tried painting and could not do any better; and yet she never reached the rank of failure, for she had not the constitution to keep long enough at anything in which, at the end, she would see a success or a failure facing her.

One thing she had in abundance – physical courage: with that she was clothed as with a garment. She was not to be blamed, for she was born that way, and her upbringing in which she received the ready. Av. Av. madame, your right of the Sligo peasants, stiffened her belief that things just touched were things well done. So she whirled about in her scintillating harlequin suit, lozenged with the colours of purple, old gold, and virgin green, bounding in through windows and dancing out through doors, striking, as she went by, her cardboard lath of thought against things to make them change, verily believing that they did, but never waiting to see if they did or not. Well, well, may she rest in peace at last".

And later in 1916 "He had no ties at the moment. He had left the Citizen Army over a difference with Madame Markiewicz, moving a motion that she should either give up her connection with the army or the Irish Volunteers. The vote had gone against him in a curious way. She had voted for herself: a strange thing to do, but typical, thought Sean, for her to do. Tommy Fran, President of the Union who had never attended one meeting of the Committee, put in an appearance at this, and, of course, gave his vote of confidence in Madame. Even with Tommy's vote and her own, she had but a majority of one: and had she refrained from voting for herself, as Sean did, like a fool, the vote would have been an even one. But Madame on this result built up a demand for an apology, and Sean obliged by resigning, and leaving the Army for good.

Clearly the Countess Markiewicz upset Sean O'Casey. WB Yeats remembers her former beauty.

ON A POLITICAL PRISONER

She that but little patience knew,
From childhood on, had now so much
A grey gull lost its fear and flew
Down to her cell and there alit,
And then endured her finger's touch
And from her fingers ate its bit.

Did she in touching that lone wing
Recall the years before her mind
Became a bitter, an abstract thing,

Her thought some popular enmity:
Blind and leader of the blind
Drinking the foul ditch where they lie?

When long ago I saw her ride
Under Ben Bulben to the meet,
The beauty of her country-side
With all youth's lonely wildness stirred,
She seemed to have grown clean and sweet
Like any rock-bred, sea-borne bird:

Sea-borne, or balanced on the air
When first it sprang out of the nest
Upon some lofty rock to stare
Upon the cloudy canopy,
While under its storm-beaten breast
Cried out the hollows of the sea.

It is doubtful whether the terrible price of the strike in poverty and suffering were worth the gains which were few. The Union was not destroyed. By early 1914 men were working again but on terms distinctly unfavourable to Larkin's Union. Many were refused their jobs unless they left the Union and agreed not to join sympathetic strikes.

The lockout of 1913–14 produced as a by-product the Irish Citizen Army. It started as a small group committed to protect the locked out men in clashes with the police. It was the protégé of James Connolly. In its reborn state in 1914 it was inspired largely by Sean O'Casey. It was socialist in principle and totally committed to public ownership. It had attracted the passionate support of the Countess Markiewicz who by 1914 had abandoned the aristocratic leisure of Lissadel to fight the battles of the poor in the streets of Dublin. The Citizen Army was to feature significantly in the life of Connolly. It was at the heart of the awesome events of the Easter Rising in 1916.

It is probable that the events of the Dublin lockout of 1913–14 made a greater impression on Francis Ledwidge than the political developments which we have considered briefly above.

His early career had disclosed a strong inclination to take the part of the worker. While employed at the Beauparc Copper Mine in 1909 he led strike action in pursuit of safer working conditions. There was serious flooding in the copper mine.

The men had to work in soaking clothes in conditions of sodden slush. Ledwidge's efforts with the management on behalf of the men were ignored. Dreadful conditions continued. Francis Ledwidge organised a strike. He was dismissed and returned to roadwork. The strike failed. In 1912 the mine was flooded. It had to close down temporarily. In 1914 it closed down permanently.

None of this activity as strike leader is reflected in any of Francis Ledwidge's poetry.

He was a founder member of the Slane branch of the Meath Labour Union in 1906. By 1912 he had been elected to the Committee of Management. In 1913 he designed the medal for Union members to wear. He failed narrowly to be elected paid secretary of the Union in November 1913; but he agreed to stand in for the candidate, TP Kelly, who had defeated him and who was unable to take up the job immediately. Accordingly Francis Ledwidge left his job as road ganger and became a Union official. It was the first and only office job he ever had. The office was in Navan. He lived at home and cycled every day to Navan. He taught himself typing and shorthand.

In the course of a series of articles on the Boyne Valley written for the *Drogheda Independent*, Francis Ledwidge wrote, 'Cast your eyes around the ranches of Meath and see pride in her poverty. The sighing of the unlaboured fields are pronouncing a severe judgment on the air; ay, are sending our able-bodied across the sea in dozens, and to the lunatic asylums in scores. We are the greatest idlers in the world, we Meathians. But we must shortly mend our ways or leave the country, as the dawn of an era of labour is in the sky. We must be prepared to strip off our collars and ties and wear frieze once more and make a friend of the spade instead of the broken down aristocrat, or else the rising generation will evacuate us. We must till our fields instead of letting them to the men of cattle, and we must not think our sons and daughters too grand for a trade. It is easy for us now who breathe on the verge of freedom, and have full liberty to air our political feelings to hold out our hands and say 'To-morrow it comes'.'

W.B. YEATS.

N.J. '87

HEAD-BOY

TO IRELAND IN THE COMING TIMES

Know, that I would accounted be
True brother of a company
That sang, to sweeten Ireland's wrong,
Ballad and story, rann and song;
Nor be I any less of them,
Because the red-rose-bordered hem
Of her, whose history began
Before God made the angelic clan,
Trails all about the written page.
When Time began to rant and rage
The measure of her flying feet
Made Ireland's heart begin to beat;
And Time bade all his candles flare
To light a measure here and there;
And may the thoughts of Ireland brood
Upon a measured quietude.

Nor may I less be counted one
With Davis, Mangan, Ferguson,
Because, to him who ponders well,
My rhymes more than their rhyming tell
Of things discovered in the deep,
Where only body's laid asleep.
For the elemental creatures go
About my table to and fro,
That hurry from unmeasured mind
To rant and rage in flood and wind;
Yet he who treads in measured ways
May surely barter gaze for gaze.
Man ever journeys on with them
After the red-rose-bordered hem.
Ah, faeries, dancing under the moon,
A Druid land, a Druid tune!

While still I may, I write for you
The love I lived, the dream I knew.
From our birthday, until we die,
Is but the winking of an eye;
And we, our singing and our love,
What measurer Time has lit above,
And all benighted things that go
About my table to and fro,
Are passing on to where may be,
In truth's consuming ecstasy,
No place for love and dream at all;
For God goes by with white footfall.
I cast my heart into my rhymes,
That you, in the dim coming times,
May know how my heart went with them,
After the red-rose-bordered hem.

So wrote WB Yeats in *To Ireland In The Coming Times*, published in 1893 in his Book of Poems *The Rose*.

George Moore had very clear ideas about where leadership of the Irish Celtic Revival lay.

She, (Lady Gregory) would never have written a play if she had not met Yeats, nor would Synge who is looked upon as an artist as great as Donatello or Benevenuto Cellini and perhaps I should not have gone to Ireland if I had not met Yeats.

So all the Irish movement rose out of Yeats and returned to Yeats. He wrote beautiful lyrics and narrative poems from twenty till five and thirty, and then he began to feel that his mission was to give a literature to Ireland that should be neither Hebrew or Greek, nor French, nor German nor English – a literature that should be like herself, that should wear her own face and speak with her own voice, and this he should do only in a theatre. We have all wanted repertory theatres and art theatres and literary theatres, but these words are vain words and mean nothing. Yeats knew exactly what he wanted; he wanted a folk theatre, for if Ireland were ever to produce any literature he knew that it would have to begin in folk, and he has his reward. Ireland speaks for the first time in literature in the Abbey Theatre.

Hail And Farewell, Volume 2, George Moore

1893, year of the publication of *The Rose*, was shortly before Francis Ledwidge began to write his earlier poetry. By 1893 Ireland's literary heart had begun to beat. Over the coming years the heartbeat was to flower into one of the great periods of Irish poetry, drama and literature. It was a heartbeat which inspired the writing of WB Yeats himself, John Synge, Lady Gregory and many others. To what extent was Francis Ledwidge and his poetry influenced by the renaissance of Irish letters unfolding about him? It was in full flight by the time that Francis Ledwidge was establishing himself as a poet in the years immediately before the war in 1914.

The Celtic Renaissance was led by WB Yeats. He worked unsparingly to establish an Irish Theatre. Yeats wrote in *Autobiographies* 'The Young Ireland poets created a mass of obvious images that filled the minds of the young – Wolfe Tone, King Brian, Emmet, Owen Roe, Sarsfield, the Fishermen of Kinsale – answered the traditional slanders on Irish character and entered so into the affections that it followed men on to the scaffold. The ethical ideas implied were of necessity very simple, needing neither study nor unusual gifts for their understanding. Our own movement thought to do the same thing in a more profound and therefore more enduring way.'

The Yeats family had moved from Dublin to London in 1887. WB Yeats made a mass of literary contacts in London including Oscar Wilde who asked him for Christmas dinner on his first London Christmas. He thought Yeats was on his own. He was equally generous in his reviews of some of Yeats' earlier poetry, particularly *The Wanderings Of Oisin*.

After dinner Oscar Wilde commented to Yeats 'Ah Yeats, we Irish are too poetical to be poets; we are a nation of brilliant failures.' Yeats had no intention of being a brilliant or any other kind of failure. In addition to extensive contributions to literary publications to finance himself Yeats cultivated his fascination with séances and the occult, more particularly as practised by Madame Blavatsky. In 1886 Yeats joined the Esoteric Section of her lodge devoted to occultism. He left in 1890. He joined the Hermetic Order of the Golden Dawn in 1890 which studied among other subjects ritual magic and astrological and alchemical symbolism. In 1889 Yeats met Maude Gonne. She inspired his poetry and haunted his passions for many years. He was a founder member of the Rymers Club in 1890 through which he met a number of significant poets including Lionel Johnson and Ernest Dowson. The Club met in the Cheshire Cheese in Fleet Street where they read poetry aloud and drank wine.

In 1891 he initiated with John O'Leary the Young Ireland League to unite Irish literary societies. In January 1892 he was a party to setting up the Irish Literary Society in London. In May he founded the National Literary Society in Dublin. It was to involve a travelling theatre company and an Irish library. It was added joy for Yeats that Maud Gonne was involved.

In addition to his other activities Yeats was writing plays. In 1892 he published *The Countess Cathleen*, inspired at least in part by Maud Gonne. In 1894 he wrote *The Land of Heart's Desire*. It was produced in London at the Avenue Theatre. It ran from 21 April – 12 May in conjunction with Shaw's *Arms And The Man*. In late 1894 he returned to Sligo to write *The Shadow Waters*, which did not in fact appear in print until 1900. He started work on a novel called *The Speckled Bird*. It was never finished. He wrote a series of stories called *The Secret Rose*, which he described as 'An honest attempt towards that aristocratic esoteric Irish literature, which has been my chief ambition. We have a literature for the people but nothing yet for the few.' This is an interesting foretaste of some of Yeats later thinking, which developed, at the very least, elitist tendencies. A number of the stories concentrate on the Rose as a symbol; some derive from Irish history and myth.

While staying at Tulira Castle, the home of Edward Martyn, in 1986, Yeats visited the Aran Islands. He had incensed Edward Martyn, a committed Catholic, by indulging in lunar invocations in a room above the chapel. The reason for Martyn's fury, it seems, was that Yeats' séances may have interfered with the path of prayer from the chapel below to higher places.

Lady Gregory visited Tulira Castle and invited Yeats to stay at Coole Park. This was the beginning of the greatest friendship of Yeats' life.

Yeats' visit to the Aran Islands of Inishmaan and Inishmore was momentous. In

Inishmaan he met the oldest man on the island. He informed Yeats 'If any man has done a crime, we'll hide him. There was a gentleman that killed his father, and I had him hid in my own house six months till he got away to America.' The story did not inspire Yeats to literature. But, when in December 1896, he went to Paris he met John Millington Synge, then aged 25. Synge was an upper class Dublin Protestant in rebellion against his own class and background, training to be a musician but more keen to be a writer. Yeats persuaded him to go to the Aran Islands and to base his writing on the people of the West.

WB Yeats later wrote 'I had met John Synge in 1896. Somebody had said 'There is an Irishman living on the top floor of your hotel. I will introduce you.' I was very poor, but he was much poorer. He belonged to a very old Irish family and, though a simple courteous man, remembered it and was haughty and lonely. With just enough to keep him from starvation and not always from half starvation, he had wandered about Europe, travelling third-class or upon foot, playing his fiddle to poor men on the road or in their cottages. He was the man that we needed, because he was the only man I have ever known incapable of a political thought or of a humanitarian purpose. He could walk the roadside all day with some poor man without any desire to do him good or for any reason except that he liked him. He was to do for Ireland, though more by his influence on other dramatists than by his direct influence, what Robert Burns did for Scotland. When Scotland thought herself gloomy and religious, Providence restored her imaginative spontaneity by raising up Robert Burns to commend drink and the Devil. I did not however see what was to come when I advised John Synge to go to a wild island off the Galway coast and study its life because that life had never been expressed in literature. He had learned Greek at College and I told him that, as I would have told it to any young man who had learned Gaelic and wanted to write. When he found that wild island he became happy for the first time, escaping, as he said 'from the nullity of the rich and the squalor of the poor.' He had bad health, he could not stand the island hardship for long, but he would go to and fro between there and Dublin:

> And that enquiring man John Synge comes next,
> That dying chose the living world for text
> And never could have rested in the tomb
> But that, long travelling, he had come
> Towards nightfall upon certain set apart
> In a most desolate stony place,
> Towards nightfall upon a race
> Passionate and simple like his heart.

Accordingly persuaded by Yeats, Synge went to the Aran Islands from which *The Playboy Of The Western World* and other great drama emerged.

In 1897 Yeats made the first of his many long visits to Lady Gregory at Coole Park. The beauty of the place, its physical comfort, its aristocratic code suited Yeats admirably. Lady Gregory's husband, a former governor of Ceylon and 33 years older than her, had died in 1892. She had a passionate interest in the people and literature of the land, particularly in County Galway. 'She made the people a part of her soul' wrote Yeats. She became a guiding light in Yeats' life. She took Yeats out visiting cottages 'to gather folk-belief, tales of the faeries, and the like and wrote down herself what we had gathered, considering that this work in which one lets others talk, and walked about the fields so much, would lie, to use a country phrase 'very light upon the mind' *WB Yeats – Autobiographies.*

It was at Coole Park with Lady Gregory that Yeats' dreams of an Irish Theatre formalised: 'I wanted a theatre – I had wanted it for years but knowing no way of getting money for a start in Ireland, had talked to Florence Farr, that accomplished speaker of verse, less accomplished actress, of some little London hall, where I could perform plays. I first spoke to Lady Gregory of my abandoned plan for an Irish Theatre, if I can call anything so hopeless a plan, in the grounds of a little country house at Duras, on the sea-coast, where Galway ends and Clare begins. It was the house of Count Florimonde de Basterot, a friend of Lady Gregory. In his garden under his friendly eyes the Irish National Theatre was born.'

It was Lady Gregory's inspiration that Yeats, Edward Martyn and she should form the Irish Literary Theatre. George Moore, Martyn's cousin whom he despised, was brought in as co-director. The first two plays to be produced were *The Countess Cathleen* by Yeats and *The Heather Field* by Edward Martyn. *The Countess Cathleen* is the drama of the Countess who sells her soul for gold to save her starving people. The theme was not to the liking of the Roman Catholic hierarchy. Cardinal Logue condemned it.

Yeats wrote later in connection with *The Countess Cathleen* 'Did that play of mine send out, Certain men the English shot.'

The Irish National Theatre Company was by 1902 producing plays in London and Dublin. Miss Horniman, a lady of means and friend of Yeats through his spiritualist activities was becoming interested in supporting the theatre financially. It was fortunate that his days were occupied with theatrical and literary pursuits because on 21 February 1908 Maud Gonne married John McBride in Paris. He had fought against the British in South Africa in the Transvaal Irish Brigade. It was a bitter blow to Yeats.

In 1904 Miss Horniman offered Yeats £5000 part of which was to construct the

Abbey Theatre out of two adjoining buildings. Miss Horniman would not have declined an invitation to become Mrs Yeats. But she did not like Ireland, she did not like Lady Gregory; Yeats was a long way from having recovered from the trauma of Maud Gonne's marriage. He had not the slightest idea of marrying Miss Horniman. He was highly grateful for her substantial funding of the Abbey Theatre in its early years.

The National Theatre became a limited company with Yeats, Lady Gregory and Synge as Directors; they were also its principal dramatists. Miss Horniman, who so substantially financed it in its early years, designed the costumes for Yeats' '*On Baile's Strand*', performed in December 1904. In November 1906 Yeats' '*Deirdre*' was staged. The scenery was painted by Robert Gregory, Lady Gregory's son.

Public temperature surrounding the Abbey rose in January 1907 with the production of the '*Playboy Of The Western World*', certainly Synge's most celebrated play. The Abbey audiences, or some of them, regarded the play as a slur on the Irish character, more particularly its central theme that an Irish community would welcome as a hero someone who arrived among them announcing that he had murdered his Da. Some regarded the use of the word 'shift' to describe a girl's undergarment as indelicate. Yeats returned from a lecture tour in Scotland. He invoked the assistance of the Royal Irish Constabulary to keep the peace in the theatre. Nationalists in the audience regarded that action of Yeats as provocative and indicative of Yeats' arrogant hauteur towards the common people. On 4 February Yeats himself addressed the audience in the Abbey. He asserted in powerful advocacy the importance of freedom of expression and the right of the theatre to put on the play and have it judged on its merits without being interrupted. His poem *On Those That Hated 'The Playboy Of The Western World*, isolates his contempt for the crowd.

> Once, when midnight smote the air,
> Eunuchs ran through Hell and met
> On every crowded street to stare
> Upon great Juan riding by:
> Even like these to rail and sweat
> Staring upon his sinewy thigh.

He was particularly incensed since when he had visited Inishmaan in 1896 the oldest man on the island told him of the gentleman who had killed his father whom he had hidden for six months 'till he got away to America'. Yeats was furious with the Abbey audiences who did not accept Synge as the writer of genius acclaimed by Yeats. Yeats had advised and inspired Synge to go to the West of Ireland and use its people and language as the basis of his literature.

By 1908 Synge was in charge of the Abbey. He became ill. Yeats took over working control from him. Synge died in March 1909. Yeats was deeply affected. He wrote extensively about Synge in his Diary kept in 1909, published in 1928 as part of Yeats' *Autobiographies* under the heading *The Death Of Synge* – Paragraph 12, 24 March. 'Synge is dead.' In the early morning he said to the nurse 'It is no use fighting death any longer,' and he turned over and died.'

DETRACTIONS

He had that egotism of the man of genius which Nietsche compares to the egotism of a woman with child. Neither I nor Lady Gregory ever had a compliment from him. After *Hyacint* Lady Gregory went home the moment the curtain fell, not waiting for the congratulations of friends, to get his supper ready. He was always ailing and weakly. All he said of the triumphant *Hyacinth* was 'I expected to like it better.' He had under charming and modest manners, in almost all things of life, a complete absorption in his own dream. I have never heard him praise any writer, living or dead, but some old French farce writer. For him nothing existed but his thought. He claimed nothing for it aloud. He never said any of those self-confident things I am enraged into saying, but one knew that he valued nothing else. He was too confident for self-assertion. I once said to George Moore 'Synge has always the better of you, for you have brief but ghastly moments during which you admit the existence of other writers; Synge never has.' I do not think he disliked other writers They did not exist. One did not think of him as an egotist. He was too sympathetic in the ordinary affairs of life and too simple. In the arts he knew no language but his own. I have often envied him his absorption as I have envied Verlaine his vice. Can a man of genius make that complete renunciation of the world necessary to the full expression of himself without some vice or some deficiency. You were happy or at least blessed, 'blind old man of Scio's Rocky isle'.'

Conal O'Riordan took over management at the Abbey which continued to produce drama approved by Yeats and Lady Gregory. In 1910 Yeats' *The Green Helmet* was successfully staged. In August 1910 the Abbey produced *The Showing Up Of Blanco Posnet* by Shaw. The play was banned in England. Its production annoyed Miss Horniman, the Abbey's English financial backer. In 1910 she offered to sell the theatre to Yeats and Lady Gregory for £1000. He kept the theatre open on the day of Edward VII's funeral. Other theatres closed. Mis Horniman was upset. Her subsidy was withdrawn.

She moved her area of patronage to Manchester. She invited Yeats to write for her new theatrical enterprise there. He declined on the basis that he was too old to change his nationality. It is doubtful whether he or his poetic drama would have been at home in Manchester.

Other financial support was sought by Yeats and Lady Gregory which included a tour of America. Yeats lectured extensively. There were riots in the theatre in New York but riots in the production of plays by the Abbey Theatre were not new to Yeats or Lady Gregory or the players.

It is difficult to assess the impact which the great theatrical renaissance led by Yeats, Lady Gregory and Synge had on Francis Ledwidge and his writing in the years up to 1914.

The influence of the Abbey theatre spread throughout Ireland, including County Meath and Slane. In Slane a dramatic class was formed. Francis Ledwidge joined. He had a leading part in their first play, Handy Andy. He continued to act in the Slane dramatic class.

It seems therefore that Francis Ledwidge enjoyed the theatre, acted in theatre on a local basis, attended the Abbey theatre when opportunity offered and considered writing drama. It is quite clear that he was fully alive to the great adventure in theatre led by the Abbey. The Celtic renaissance in theatre was part of the background and general stimulus to his life and thought. However it was not, it appears, one of the fundamental sources of his inspiration as was the Boyne, the country, his family, his loves, and his friends which inspired his early, and as we shall see his later poetry.

Yeats had become the dominant poet of Ireland by the time he set himself the task of establishing a national Irish Theatre. His early poems published as *The Crossways* in 1889 might have cast him simply as a lyricist and dreamer.

THE FALLING OF THE LEAVES

Autumn is over the long leaves that love us,
And over the mice in the barley sheaves;
Yellow the leaves of the rowan above us,
And yellow the wet wild-strawberry leaves.

The hour of the waning of love has beset us,
And weary and worn are our sad souls now;
Let us part, ere the season of passion forget us,
With a kiss and a tear on thy drooping brow.

But Yeats was concerned with sterner intellectual things than lyrical dreaming. It is unlikely that any one poem establishes a poet in the ranks of the great. However in 1893 the collection of poems published under the title *The Rose* contained *The Lake Isle Of Innisfree.* It acclaimed his pre-eminence.

> I will arise and go now, and go to Innisfree,
> And a small cabin build there, of clay and wattles made:
> Nine bean-rows will I have there, a hive for the honey-bee,
> And live alone in the bee-loud glade.
>
> And I shall have some peace there, for peace comes dropping slow,
> Dropping from the veils of the morning to where the cricket sings;
> There midnight's all a glimmer, and noon a purple glow,
> And evening full of the linnet's wings,
>
> I will arise and go now, for always night and day
> I hear lake water lapping with low sounds by the shore;
> While I stand on the roadway, or on the pavements grey,
> I hear it in the deep heart's core.

It was written by Yeats in 1889 in London. It isolates to perfection the dreams of thousands of Irishmen living in British cities. The actual lake Isle of Innishfree on Lough Gill is curiously disappointing. It can be reached at the end of a long, narrow and winding road in County Sligo. It is attractive to see but has none of the high perfection of the poem.

Yeats' hopeless and unfulfilled passion for Maud Gonne inspired his great love poems many of which were published in 1889 under the title *The Wind Among The Reeds.*

A POET TO HIS BELOVED

> I bring you with reverent hands
> The books of my numberless dreams,
> White woman that passion has worn
> As the tide wears the dove-grey sands,
> And with heart more old than the horn
> That is brimmed from the pale fire of time:
> White woman with numberless dreams,
> I bring you my passionate rhyme.

HE GIVES HIS BELOVED CERTAIN RHYMES

Fasten your hair with a golden pin,
And bind up every wandering tress;
I bade my heart build these poor rhymes:
It worked at them, day out, day in,
Building a sorrowful loveliness
Out of the battles of old times.

You need but lift a pearl-pale hand,
And bind up your long hair and sigh;
And all men's hearts must burn and beat;
And candle-like foam on the dim sand,
And stars climbing the dew-dropping sky,
Live but to light your passing feet.

He Thinks Of Those Who Have Spoken Evil Of His Beloved, published in *The Wind Among The Reeds* in 1899:

Half close your eyelids, loosen your hair,
And dream about the great and their pride;
They have spoken against you everywhere,
But weigh this song with the great and their pride;
I made it out of a mouthful of air,
Their children's children shall say they have lied.

This is followed shortly by *He Wishes For The Cloths of Heaven*.

Had I the heavens' embroidered cloths,
Enwrought with golden and silver light,
The blue and the dim and the dark cloths
Of night and light and the half-light,
I would spread the cloths under your feet:
But I, being poor, have only my dreams;
I have spread my dreams under your feet;
Tread softly because you tread on my dreams.

In 1910 Yeats published a collection of poems under the title *The Green Helmet And Other Poems*.

He was still haunted by Maud Gonne.

NO SECOND TROY

Why should I blame her that she filled my days
With misery, or that she would of late
Have taught to ignorant men most violent ways,
Or hurled the little streets upon the great,
Had they but courage equal to desire?
What could have made her peaceful with a mind
That nobleness made simple as a fire,
With beauty like a tightened bow, a kind
That is not natural in an age like this,
Being high and solitary and most stern?
Why, what could she have done, being what she is?
Was there another Troy for her to burn?

Yeats' passion for Maud Gonne was for a very brief period, physically fulfilled in Paris. The joy inspired *Reconciliation.*

Some may have blamed you that you took away
The verses that could move them on the day
When, the ears being deafened, the sight of the eyes blind
With lightning, you went from me, and I could find
Nothing to make a song about but kings,
Helmets, and swords, and half-forgotten things
That were like memories of you – but now
We'll out, for the world lives as long ago;
And while we're in our laughing, weeping fit,
Hurl helmets, crowns and swords into the pit.
But, dear, cling close to me; since you were gone,
My barren thoughts have chilled me to the bone.

According to Maude Gonne, Yeats had said to her one day 'O Maud, why don't you marry me and give up this tragic struggle and live a peaceful life? I could make such a beautiful life for you among artists and writers who would understand you.' 'Willie, are you not tired of asking that question? How often have I told you to thank the Gods that I will not marry you. You would not be happy with me.' 'I am not happy without you,' 'Oh yes you are, because you make beautiful poetry out of what you call your unhappiness and you are happy in that. Marriage would be such a dull affair. Poets should never marry. The world should thank me for not marrying you.'

Maud Gonne married John McBride in Paris on 21 February 1903. He had fought in the Irish Brigade against England in the Boer War. She later said that she got married 'in a sudden impulse of anger.' Their son Sean McBride in due course became a prominent Nationalist politician in the Republic of Ireland. John McBride, estranged from Maud Gonne, was executed by firing squad after the Easter Rising.

These were still early days for the great poet. He continued to write poetry until his death in 1939. The poetry inspired by the terrible times of civil war in Ireland, by his political views, by his friendship with Lady Gregory and his fascination with the land and people of Galway and the West of Ireland, and by old age were all to come. But the briefest look at his poetry up to 1910, by which time Francis Ledwidge was writing poetry, indicates its massive scope. In addition to the lyrical and romantic poems mentioned above, Yeats, by 1910, was writing extensively of Irish mythology, of mystical and fairy people, of real people who excited his curiosity, and in some cases a combination of many of his inspirations.

THE SONG OF WANDERING AENGUS

I went out to the hazel wood,
Because a fire was in my head,
And cut and peeled a hazel wand,
And hooked a berry to a thread;
And when white moths were on the wing,
And moth-like stars were flickering out,
I dropped the berry in a stream
And caught a little silver trout.

When I had laid it on the floor
I went to blow the fire aflame,
But something rustled on the floor,
And someone called me by my name:
It had become a glimmering girl
With apple blossom in her hair
Who called me by my name and ran
And faded through the brightening air.

Through I am old with wandering
Through hollow lands and hilly lands,
I will find out where she has gone,
And kiss her lips and take her hands;
And walk among long dappled grass,
And pluck till time and times are done
The silver apples of the moon,
The golden apples of the sun.

It is one of the sadnesses of Irish literature that Francis Ledwidge never met Yeats. In answer to an enquiry from Professor Lewis Chase of the University of Wisconsin, requesting biographical information and poems to include in a series of lectures on contemporary poets, Francis Ledwidge wrote from France on 6 June 1917, eleven days before he was killed, a long letter detailing the poets whom he had read and studied. They included poets from Chaucer to Swinburne, the Elizabethans, ballads before the Renaissance, Shelley and Byron. He emphasised in particular the appeal of Keats for him. He mentioned somewhat unenthusiastically Longfellow and Tennyson. On Yeats he wrote:

> My taste, I think, became extremely acute and was inclined to blow warm and cold over such works as Yeats than sit to admire as I do now. I have never met Yeats but I hope to one day for I have much to say to him. I do not think he has quite ever reached the hearts of the people and if any of his works live it will be his early poems on Maeve and Cuchulain. If you remember his early works you will agree with me in saying that the revisions which he made on them in later years have robbed them of much enchantment. I agree that many of his far-fetched metaphors require elucidation, but, in attempting this, he has not always been successful. Take for example, two lines which appeared in the first version of the *Wandering Of Oisin*.
>
> > Empty of purple hours as a beggar's cloak in the rain
> > As a grass seed crushed by a pebble, or a well sucked under a weir.
>
> I have always pointed out these similes as the most ludicrous of Yeats. They do not illustrate his meaning, and were probably written in a rainstorm in a moment certainly happy for rhyme, not for reason. In the revised edition it reads 'As a haycock out on the fiord etc' which is better because it gives you a picture of things adrift, of loneliness and the beauty of a cataclysm. This is the single exception in his work of where his second thoughts were better than his first.

This letter suggests that Francis Ledwidge's attitude to Yeats' poetry fell far short of idolatry. His confident assertion in relation to Yeats at least discloses none of the arrogance of what James Joyce is alleged to have said on meeting Yeats 'We have met too late; you are too old to be influenced by me.' According to Yeats this conversation went as follows:

> Presumably he got up to go – and as he was going out, he said 'I am twenty, how old are you.' I told him but I was afraid and said I was a year younger than I am. He said with a sigh 'I thought as much – I have met you too late – you are too old.

… It appears from the letter to Professor Chase that if the poetry of Yeats did in any way influence the writing of Ledwidge it was a hidden rather than an express influence. But it is equally clear that he had studied closely and followed carefully Yeats' writing. Alice Curtayne (page 112) says in terms that Ledwidge's *Bound To The Mast* is an imitation of Yeats. In *The Bounty of Sweden* Yeats wrote 'I have seen so much beautiful lyric poetry pass unnoticed for years, and indeed at this very moment a little book of exquisite verse lies upon my table, by an author who died a few years ago, whom I knew slightly and whose work I ignored, for chance had shown me only that part of it for which I could not care.' Yeats does not say to whom he refers; who can doubt that if he had known Francis Ledwidge and read his work closely he would have given him the firmest hand of friendship.

All that can be said for certain is that Francis Ledwidge did not model his poetry on Yeats or adopt Yeats' style. His poetry has none of the detachment, the hint of coldness evident in some of Yeats earlier poetry and pronounced in his later writing. It is unlikely that his subject matter was influenced by Yeats. Although their poetry covers some of the same country, such as unfulfilled passion, and Irish mythology, our study of the sources of Francis Ledwidge's early poems in *Songs Of The Fields* shows very clearly that the fountains of his joy were strongly inherent and highly personal to himself. The degree to which, if at all, the writing of Yeats may have influenced the poetry of Francis Ledwidge in a way which he himself may not have recognised is impossible to assess. What can be said for certain is that Francis Ledwidge read, marked, learned and inwardly digested Yeats' poetry closely.

The letter of 6 June 1917 to Professor Lewis Chase is fascinating as indicative of Francis Ledwidge's ability to cope with war and his attitude to it. He says 'You will, of course, understand that I am writing this under the most inept circumstances between my watches, for I am in the firing line and may be busy at any moment in the horrible work of war. I am on active service since the spring of 1915, having served in the Dardenelles and in the first British expeditionary force to Serbia and after a brief interval at home came to France in December 1916.'

It is fascinating as indicative of his continuing interest in political developments in Ireland and his continuing openness of mind after the Easter Rising of 1916. His letter continues:

> I am sorry that party politics should ever divide our own tents but am not without hope that a new Ireland will arise from her ashes in the ruins of Dublin, like the Phoenix, with one purpose, one aim and one ambition. I tell you this that you may know what it is to me to be called a British soldier while my own country has no place among the nations but the place of Cinderella.

It is fascinating as indicative of his method of work. 'Of myself: I am a fast worker and very prolific. I have long silences, often for weeks, then the mood comes over me and I must write and write no matter where I be or what the circumstances are. I do my best work in the spring. I have had many disappointments in life and many sorrows but in my saddest moment song came to me and I sang. I get more pleasure from a good line than from a big cheque.'

AN ENQUIRING MAN

JOHN MILLINGTON SYNGE came from a family of distinction, particularly eminent in its production of Anglican bishops. In the 18th century, the life of the spirit was eased by the families' extensive ownership of land, particularly in County Wicklow where the family seat was Glanmore Castle, neighbour estate to the Parnells of Avondale. Synge's mother was the daughter of the Reverend Robert Traill, a member of the well-known Ulster family from Bushmills who owned an electric railway running from Portrush to the Giant's Causeway until its unhappy demise. He did not advance to the purple since, he said 'the bishop, who is well-known as the enemy of all evangelical piety, objects to me on account of my religious sentiments.'

Synge was born in 1871. His father died of smallpox in 1872. He and his brother and sisters were brought up in the most stringent financial circumstances in Rathgar. His mother as a daughter of the Rectory encouraged Synge in evangelical devotions against which in due course he reacted totally.

He studied at Trinity College, Dublin and thereafter travelled extensively in Europe. By December 1896 he was in France when by good chance Yeats took a room at the same hotel. Yeats describes the meeting in his Preface to Synge's *Well Of The Saints.* 'Six years ago I was staying in a student's hotel in the Latin quarter, and

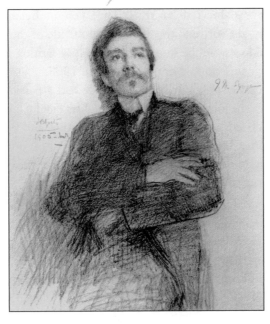

John Millington Synge
by John Butler Yeats

somebody whose name I cannot recollect introduced me to an Irishman, who, even poorer than myself, had taken a room at the top of the house. It was JM Synge, and I, who thought I knew the name of every Irishman who was working at literature, had never heard of him. He was a graduate of Trinity College, Dublin, too and Trinity College does not as a rule produce artistic minds. He told me that he had been living in France and Germany, reading French and German literature, and that he wished to become a writer. He had, however, nothing to show but one or two poems and impressionistic essays, full of that kind of morbidity that has its root in too much brooding over methods of expression, and ways of looking upon life, which come not out of life but out of literature, images reflected from mirror to mirror. He had wandered among people whose life is as picturesque as the middle ages, playing his fiddle to Italian sailors, and listening to stories in Bavarian woods, but life had cast no light into his writings. He had learned Irish years ago, but had begun to forget it, for the only language that interested him was that convention language of modern poetry which has begun to make us all weary … I said 'Give up Paris, you will never create anything by reading Racine, and Arthur Symons will always be a better writer of French literature. Go to the Aran Islands. Live there as if you were one of the people themselves; express a life that has never found expression. I had just come from Aran and my imagination was full of those gray islands, where men must reap with knives because of the stones'

Synge did exactly as directed by Yeats. The West of Ireland was his road to Damascus. The joys, the sorrows, the dramas and the life of the people of the West of Ireland and Wicklow were the sources of his creative writing and the raw material upon which his genius worked until his death in 1908.

Synge, like Francis Ledwidge, from an early age had a passionate love of nature and country. In 1886 he joined the Dublin Naturalists Field Club. He collected butterflies, moths and beetles. His love of all natural things and beings was, as it was with Francis Ledwidge, one of the driving inspirations of his poetry. Synge's poetry, in its concentration on natural beauty, was closer to Francis Ledwidge's poetry than any other poet writing over the same period.

PRELUDE

[Collected Works of J M Synge]

Still south I went and west and south again,
Through Wicklow from the morning till the night,
And far from cities, and the sites of men
Lived with the sun-shine and the moon's delight.

I knew the stars, the flowers and the birds,
The grey and wintry sides of many glens
And did but half remember human words,
In converse with the mountains, moors, and fens.

Synge and Francis Ledwidge had in common a relationship towards nature so that they both felt and wrote about natural and all living things as if about a living person.

SAMHAIN

Though trees have many a flake
Of copper, gold and brass,
And fields are in a lake
Beneath the withered glass;

Though hedges show their hips
And leaves blow by the wall
I taste upon your lips
The whole years Festival.

Like Francis Ledwidge, Synge had no heart for the city although when active in the Abbey Theatre much of his life was spent in Dublin.

THE FUGITIVE

I fled from all the wilderness of cities,
And nature's choristers my art saluted,
Chanting aloud to me their tunes and ditties
And to my silent songs their joys imputed.

But when they heard me singing in my sorrow,
My broken voice that spoke a bosom breaking,
They fled afar and cried I Hell did borrow
As through their notes my notes fell discord waking.

Synge and Francis Ledwidge loved and wrote about the joy of friends enjoying themselves.

BEG-INNISH

Bring Kateen-beug and Maurya Jude
To dance in Beg-Innish;
And when the lads (they're in Dunquin)
Have sold their grabs and fish,
Wave fawny shawls and call them in,
And call the little girls who spin,
And seven weavers from Dunquin,
To dance in Beg-Innish.

I'll play you jigs, and Maurice Kean,
Where nets are laid to dry,
I've silken strings would claw a dance
From girls are lame or shy;
Four strings I've brought from Spain and France
To make your long men skip and prance,
Till stars look out to see the dance
Where nets are laid to dry.

We'll have no priest or peeler in
To dance in Beg-Innish;
But we'll have drink from M'riarty Jim
Rowed round while gannets fish
A keg with porter to the brim;
That every lad may have his whim,
Till we upsails with M'riarty Jim
And sail from Beg-Innish.

Love and passion inspired Synge's poetry as they inspired the writing of Francis Ledwidge.

THE MEETING

We met and the furze in golden mist,
Watching a golden moon, that filled the sky,
And there my lips your lips young glory kissed
Till old high loves, in our high love went by.

Then in the hush of plots with shining trees
We lay like gods disguised in shabby dress,
Making with birches, bracken, stars and seas,
Green courts of pleasure for each long caress;
Till I found in you and you in me
The crowns of Christ and Eros – all divinity.

IN GLENASMOLE

We reached the Glen of Thrushes where Usheen
Lost all his youth and turned diseased and grey
And there your lips – such lips few men have seen –
With one long kiss took my dead years away.

And then your young girl's voice grew wide and deep,
With happy words in love's long wisdom planned,
And with all the glen grew dim with sunny sleep,
While brow met brow and hand met happy hand.

Synge's first love was Cherry Matheson. Her father was a leader of the Plymouth Brethren. Cherry was closely directed in the ways of salvation. Synge's faith was far from active. The relationship never blossomed even though Cherry leant Synge religious books. He was not converted. He proposed to her from Paris. She refused which induced a state of some depression in Synge. His mother recorded in her diary, 'I got a sad, sad letter from my Johnie in Paris.'

He was friendly with Marie Zdanowsha and Margaret Hurden in Paris. By 1899 he asked Margaret Hurden to marry him. She refused him. It appears that unrequited love was as much a feature of Synge's life as it certainly was of Francis Ledwidge's life.

Synge's last and greatest love was Molly Allgood. He met her when she was 19. She acted for the Abbey Theatre under the name of Maire O'Neill. She acted a number of parts in Synge's plays including Cathleen in *Riders To The Sea* and Nora Burke in *In The Shadow Of The Glen*. She inspired the delightful addition to his poem *Dread*, written when his rooms in Rathgar Road, Dublin, overlooked a chapel.

> Beside a chapel I'd a room looked down,
> Where all the women from the farms and town,
> On Holy-days and Sundays used to pass
> To marriages, and Christenings and to Mass,
>
> Then I sat lonely watching score and score,
> Till I turned jealous of the Lord next door …

His love for Molly developed into a passion. He added the lines:

> Now by this window, where there's none can see
> The Lord God's jealous of yourself and me.

Synge was fifteen years older than Molly Allgood. She was Roman Catholic. Her father was working class. She had been employed as a sales girl before coming on to the stage; all incidents which were not calculated to endear her to Synge's mother as a potential wife for Synge. It was an emotional relationship not to the liking of Yeats and Lady Gregory; not for the incidents of Molly Allgood's background but because they were not keen on love affair between director and actress. They considered such an affair as not conducive to good order and discipline in the life of the growing theatre.

In 1906 Synge was living at his mother's house, Glendalough House. He was working on his most famous play *The Playboy Of The Western World*. He spent

Sundays with Molly Allgood, usually walking in the hills near Bray in County Wicklow. He wrote to her every evening. If he was working in the theatre, they walked together before or afterwards in the Phoenix Park.

Synge and Molly Allgood were discussing their married life together before he had told his mother and family that they were engaged. Molly's career as an actress prospered.

Synge eventually wrote to his mother of his love for Molly. She had suspected it for some time. Her comment to Synge was that it would be a good thing if it made him happier but that they would be very poor with his £100 a year. Shortly afterwards he wrote to Molly 'I can say now that I have never loved anyone but you, and I am putting my whole life now into this love … My mother enquired quite pleasantly about our walk and where we had been. She is coming round to the idea very quickly, I think, but still it is better not to hurry things.' He wrote on 27 December 1907 'I am growing sure of one thing and that is that we are not going to destroy the divine love that God has put between us by the wretched squabbles and fightings that seemed to threaten us at first.'

Molly Allgood had the leading female role in the first production of *The Playboy Of The Western World* as Pegeen Mike. Some of the stronger lines were omitted including the lines in which Pegeen Mike accuses the Widow Quinn of having reared a black ram at her breast 'so that the Lord Bishop of Connaught felt the elements of a Christian, and he eating it after in a kidney stew.' However the lines 'Its Pegeen I'm seeking only and what'd care if you brought me a drift of chosen females, standing in their shifts itself, maybe, from this place to the eastern world', were too much for the sensibilities of the audience. Some regarded them as a slur on Irish womanhood and at the end of Act 3 erupted into hissing. One well-known theatre goer wrote in his diary that 'Synge is the evil genius of the Abbey and Yeats his able lieutenant. Both dabble in the unhealthy.' Synge wrote to Molly the day after the first night 'It is better any day to have the row we had last night, than to have your play fizzling out in half-hearted applause. Now we'll be talked about. We're an event in the history of the Irish stage.'

'Dearest treasure you don't know how you have changed the world to me. Now that I have you I don't care twopence for what anyone else in the world may say or do. You are my whole world to me now, you that is, and the little shiny new mouse and the showers of the earth. My little love how I am wrapped up in you. I went to my heart to desire you last night, but I could not get away from Lady Gregory.'

He also wrote *The Curse* to the sister of an enemy of the author's who disapproved of the *Playboy*.

Lord, confound this surly sister
Blight her brow with blotch and blister
Cramp her larynx, lung and liver,
In her guts a galling give her.
Let her live to earn her dinners
In Mountjoy with seedy sinners;
Lord this judgement quickly bring,
And I'm your sure servant, JM Synge.

On Monday 31 January police were present. The uproar at the end was worse than on the opening night. Yeats appeared later in the week and delivered a spirited peroration to the Abbey audience of the necessity for freedom of expression ending with the fighting words 'And I promise you that if there is any small section in this theatre that wish to deny the rights of others to hear what they themselves don't want to hear we will play on, and our patience will last longer than their patience.'

The play has come to be accepted as one of the greatest pieces of Irish literature. It was adapted into a lovely musical called *The Heart's A Wonder*, which was unkindly reviewed under the title 'Synge can't be sung.'

Synge was ill with influenza in the months following the *Playboy* disturbances. On 1 March he wrote to Molly 'Then in my bed I cannot even see a bit of sky or a cloud. That's what comes when you are as weak as I am, and as wretched. I can't live any longer without you.' Shortly afterwards he wrote, 'My mother was enquiring about your temper today. She says my temper is so bad, it would be a terrible thing to marry a bad tempered wife. If only she knew.'

As his love for Molly grew stronger, his physical health deteriorated. Synge's doctor advised that the glands in his neck, which were enlarging, should be removed before his marriage. Plans for the marriage did not finalise. They were in London when *The Playboy Of The Western World* was staged at the Great Queen Street Theatre in June 1907. The play was a success. Synge's reputation as a playwright was established in London. He wrote to Molly 'You were capital last night in almost all of it and everyone is speaking well of you, Yeats especially. He says also that you were excellent in *The Shadow Of The Glen* and that he withdraws all his former criticism of you. My poor pet, I am sick of being shut away from you like this and I fear it will get worse as the week goes on, as I am being asked to go to all sorts of teas and things.'

Synge was due to be operated on in September for the removal of a gland in the back of his neck. He wrote to Molly the night before he went into hospital 'By this time tomorrow of course I'll be pretty flat. Now Goodbye for a few days my own pet, treasure, life, love, light and all that's good.' He was home by 25 September. He left Dublin for Kerry on 12 October minded to write a new play. His asthma played up and he returned to Dublin on 16 October. He started to write *Deirdre Of The Sorrows*. On 6 December Synge wrote to Molly 'I had not been quite well this week with queer pains in a portion of my inside.' On 8 December he wrote again 'It seems years since you went away. I feel like a blind man, a deaf man, or something queer and horrible ever since. I can't live now without you.'

In January 1908 their marriage plans were under extensive discussion. Synge proposed to take a flat in Upper Rathmines until they were married when they would both live in it. He moved into 47 York Road, Rathmines on 2 February. He continued actively in the management of the Abbey with Yeats, directing plays other than his own. Pain and a lump developed in his side. He was operated on 4 May 1908. He wrote to Molly, 'My dearest love, – this is a mere line for you my poor child, in case anything goes wrong with me tomorrow, to bid you good bye and ask you to be brave and good, not to forget the good times we've had and beautiful things we've seen together. Your old friend.' He marked the envelope 'To be sent in cover in case of death to Miss M Allgood.' He recovered sufficiently to write to Molly on 11 June. He left hospital on 6 July.

He wrote to Molly on 24 July. 'My God if we could only be well again and out in the hills for a long summer day and evening, what heaven it would be! I feel ready to cry, I am getting better so slowly.' His health throughout the summer was indifferent. He was working on his last play *Deirdre Of The Sorrows*.

In August he sent Yeats a collection of his poetry for advice. 'I do not feel very sure of them yet enough of myself has gone into them to make me sorry to destroy them, and I feel at times it would be wise to print them while I am alive, than to leave them after me to go God knows where.' He wrote to Molly 'I don't know how I'll ever show them to Yeats, but it will have to be done, God help me.'

On 27 September he asked Molly as a joke if she would come to his funeral, which prompted his poem.

A QUESTION

I asked if I got sick and died, would you
With my black funeral go walking too,
If you'd stand close to hear them talk or pray
While I'm let down in that steep bank of clay.

And, No, you said, for if you say a crew
Of living idiots pressing round that new

Oak coffin – they alive, I dead beneath,
That board – you'd run and rend them with your teeth.

By December his stomach pains had returned. His doctor recommended castor oil. His energy was in serious decline. He returned to hospital on 1 February. Doctors decided not to operate. Molly visited him every day. On 13 February he made his will leaving Molly an annuity of £80 a year for life. Molly left on 13 February for a tour of Manchester. He was too weak to write to her. She returned on 22 February. She visited priests seeking to have a Mass offered for Synge's recovery. But the priest, she said, had asked how she was seeking to have a Mass offered for a Protestant. She was distraught and incoherent. He died on 24 March and was buried in Mount Jerome. He and Molly had never married.

This brief review of Synge's poetry establishes quite clearly that in many ways the inspirations of his poetry, in particular his passion for all things of nature, are analogous to the inspirations which stimulated Francis Ledwidge. But, although living less than thirty miles apart, they never met. If they had met, it is doubtful if a close friendship would have developed as it did between Francis Ledwidge and Lord Dunsany. If Yeats is correct, Synge was not interested in other writers. But more important, Francis Ledwidge was joyful and an extrovert. Synge was melancholic and an introvert.

EXECRATION

I curse my bearing, childhood, youth
I curse the sea, sun, mountains, moon,
I curse my learning, search for truth,
I curse the dawning, night and noon.

Cold, joyless I will live, though clean,
Nor, by my marriage, mould to earth
Young lives to see what I have seen
To curse – as I have cursed – their birth.

Francis Ledwidge could not have written this poem.

TO THE OAKS OF GLENCREE

My arms are round you, and I lean
Against you, while the lark

Sings over us, and golden lights, and green
Shadows are on your bark.

There'll come as a season when you'll stretch
Black boards to cover me:
Then in Mount Jerome I will lie, poor wretch,
With worms eternally.

Synge was a superb essayist. In Wicklow, West Kerry and Connemara is the most beautiful and sensitive study of rural Ireland written in this century.

THE VAGRANTS OF WICKLOW

In the middle classes the gifted son of a family is always the poorest – usually a writer or artist with no sense for speculation – and in a family of peasants, where the average comfort is just over penury, the gifted son sinks also, and is soon a tramp on the roadside.

In this life, however, there are many privileges. The tramp in Ireland is little troubled by the laws, and lives in out-of-door conditions that keep him in good-humour and fine bodily health. This is so apparent, in Wicklow at least, that these men rarely seek for charity on any plea of ill-health, but ask simply, when they beg: 'Would you help a poor fellow along the road' or, 'Would you give me the price of a night's lodging, for I'm after walking a great way since the sun rose'?

'(31) Among the country people of the East of Ireland the tramps and tinkers who wander round from the West have a curious reputation for witchery and unnatural powers. 'There's great witchery in that country', a man said to me once, on the side of the mountain to the east of Aughavanna, in Wicklow. There's great witchery in that country, and great knowledge of the fairies. I've had men lodging with me out of the West – men who would be walking the world looking for a bit of money – and every one of them would be talking of the wonders below in Connemara. I remember one time, a while after I was married, there was a tinker down there in the glen, and two women along with him. I brought him into my cottage to do a bit of a job, and my first child was there lying in the bed, and he covered up his chin with the bed-clothes. When the tallest of the women came in, she looked around at him, and then she says – 'That's a fine boy, God bless him.' 'How do you know it's a boy', says my woman, 'when its only the head of him you see'? 'I know rightly', says the tinker, 'and it's the first one too.' 'Then my wife was going to slate me for bringing in people to bewitch her child, and I had to turn the lot of them out to finish the job in the lane.'

FROM A LANDLORD'S GARDEN IN COUNTY WICKLOW

Everyone is used in Ireland to the tragedy that is bound up with the lives of farmers and fishing people; but in this garden one seemed to feel the tragedy of the landlord class also, and of the innumerable old families that are quickly dwindling away. These owners of the land are not much pitied at the present day, or much deserving of pity; and yet one cannot quite forget that they are the descendants of what was at one time, in the eighteenth century, a high-spirited and highly-culti-vated aristocracy. The broken greenhouses and mouse-eaten libraries, that were designed and collected by men who voted with Grattan, are perhaps as mournful in the end as the four mud walls that are so often left in Wicklow as the only remnants of a farmhouse

The Shadow Of The Glen, one of Synge's earliest plays, was set in Wicklow. The degree to which climate and the nuances of place affect character is not easy to assess. It is not possible to know if the sadness evident in the hardships of life in Wicklow where Synge spent so much time increased his disposition to melancholy; or was he drawn to spend so much time in Wicklow because of that very sadness. Similarly one cannot help feeling that the lightness and openness of County Meath at least contributed to Francis Ledwidge's joyful and extrovert nature; or did he love and stay in County Meath at least partly because the very country was itself full of joy.

Synge also travelled extensively in West Kerry and wrote about it.

IN WEST KERRY

As far as I could see there were little groups of people on their way to the chapel in Ballyferriter, the men in homespun and the women wear-ing blue cloaks, or, more often, black shawls twisted over their heads. This procession along the olive bogs, between the mountains and the sea, on this grey day of autumn, seemed to wring me with the pang of emotion one meets everywhere in Ireland – an emotion that is partly local and patriotic, and partly a share of the desolation that is mixed everywhere with the supreme beauty of the world.

West Kerry is a land of momentous beauty as well as a land of story tellers and porter drinkers. It was the inspiration of one of Synge's few joyful poems, *Beg-Innish*. Francis Ledwidge never spent time in the West of Ireland. He did not have Synge's enquiring mind which prompted him to spend long periods in the most humble of peasant cottages. Francis Ledwidge had significant family obligations, particularly to his mother to hold him to County Meath. His finances did not afford him the luxury of holidays in the West of Ireland extensively enjoyed by the more prosperous in Ireland.

Synge walked in, lived in and wrote extensively about Connemara, the nearest place to heavenly beauty in all Ireland. He was not a rich man. His travels in West Kerry and Connemara were possible because of a modest degree of financial independence which allowed him to travel and write.

Francis Ledwidge's travels were limited to travelling around County Meath on a bicycle as a ganger. It is impossible to doubt that he would have been deeply stimulated by the loveliness of Connemara if he had ever got there.

ERRIS

In the poorest districts of Connemara the people live, as I have already pointed out, by various industries, such as fishing, turf-cutting, and kelp-making, which are independent of their farms, and are so precarious that many families are only kept from pauperism by the money that is sent home to them by daughters or sisters who are now servant-girls in New York. Here in the congested districts of Mayo the land is still utterly insufficient – held at least in small plots, as it is now – as a means of life, and the people get the more considerable part of their funds by their work on the English or Scotch harvest, to which I have alluded before. A few days ago a special steamer went from Achill Island to Glasgow with five hundred of these labourers, most of them girls and young boys. From Glasgow they spread through the country in small bands and work together under a ganger, picking potatoes or

weeding turnips, and sleeping for the most part in barns and outhous-
es. Their wages vary from a shilling a day to perhaps double as much
in places where there is more demand for their work.

It is apparent that Synge had a highly developed social conscience and a deep
awareness of the hardship of life for country people in Ireland, particularly in the
West of Ireland. Social and economic conditions in Ireland is another area in which
Synge and Francis Ledwidge, if they had ever met, would have had a substantial
community of interest. This brief look at Synge's poetry and essays show quite clearly that notwithstanding the significant differences in temperament and background
between Synge and Francis Ledwidge that their poetry, their sympathies and attitudes disclose the most striking similarities. If Francis Ledwidge had known Synge
his horizons would have been deepened and broadened.

Synge's genius was poured into his plays. His energies for the last years of his life
were extensively engaged in writing and for and in the theatre. By 1905 he had
become a Director of the Irish National Theatre Society with Yeats and Lady
Gregory. By 1906 he was managing it. His own plays were an important part of the
diet. It is not useful here to enter into the details of the politics, personalities and
troubles surrounding the Abbey Theatre in its early life. Yeats was the guiding spirit. Lady Gregory was the moderating and controlling spirit. But Synge's contribution in its early life and growth was positive and significant. He wrote *In The Shadow
Of The Glen* and *Riders To The Sea,* and the first draft of *The Tinker's Wedding* in
1902 while staying with his mother in Wicklow. He followed these in 1903 with
The Well Of The Saints. So that by the time Synge came to write *The Playboy Of The
Western World* he had become an established dramatist of the Irish literary movement.

Yeats had persuaded Synge to seek his inspiration in the Aran Islands.
Undoubtedly, life on the Aran Islands and his travels in Kerry and Connemara
where he lived among the country people were the inspiration for the language and
drama of much of his writing.

His first visit was in 1898, by which time his career as a writer had been a total
failure. It was on this first visit that he came by the theme stories for *In The Shadow
Of The Glen* and *The Playboy Of The Western World,* transferred by Synge to Wicklow
and Mayo. The language of Aran, the actual English as spoken by the people of
Aran, sometimes described as Western Anglo-Irish, gave to Synge's dramatic writings
a life force quite unknown in contemporary drama.

He commented on the girls of Aran 'I have noticed many beautiful girls whose
long luxuriant lashes lend a shade to wistful eyes.' As to the language of Aran he

wrote 'There exists yet in lonely places, the unlettered literature which was the real source of all the art of words. In the Gaelic speaking districts of Ireland, for instance recitation is of extraordinary merit.'

He visited Aran again in 1899. He wrote 'Last year when I came here everything was new and the people were a little strange to me, but now I am familiar with them and their way of life so that their qualities strike me more forcibly than before.'

He went for a third visit to Aran. A man's body had been found floating off the coast of Donegal and his clothes were sent to Innishman. There was a debate whether the returned clothes belonged to a man from Innishman or to a man from another island. Synge noted 'The loss of one man seems a slight catastrophe to all except the immediate relatives. Often when an accident happens a father is lost with his two eldest sons, or in some other way all the active men of a household die together.' Synge created *Riders To The Sea* from the incident.

His fourth and last visit was in October 1902 after staying with Lady Gregory at Coole Park.

On these four visits Synge wrote extensive notes from which he produced his masterpiece *The Aran Islands*.

Lady Gregory wrote to Synge that she had been reading the manuscript of his book aloud to Yeats and that they both liked it. 'It is extraordinarily vivid and gives an imaginative and at the same time convincing impression of the people and their life, and it ought, we think to be very successful. I have called Mr Yeats to say what he thinks – but I may speak with his authority – and he thinks, and I agree with him that the book being so solid and detailed, as it is, would lose nothing, but would rather gain by the actual names of the islands and of Galway not being given. Burrow always left his localities vague in this way, which gives a curious dreaminess to his work. It would be sufficient to say that they are islands off the West of Ireland. Leave the three heads distinct as they are – in fact there may be no change except leaving out the names. The book would be greatly improved by the addition of some fairy belief, and if you could give some of the words of the keens, and of the cradle songs you allude to, however few, the passages in which you touch on them would be greatly improved, as an important section of your readers will be students of these things.'

In fact Synge did not take her advice. But this letter is a fascinating example of the way in which Lady Gregory, Yeats and Synge co-operated in literary endeavour; how they helped each other and of how much Francis Ledwidge missed by not being part of this literary triumphvirate.

Lady Gregory
HULTON ARCHIVE/GETTY IMAGES

GRANDE DAME

FRANCIS LEDWIDGE NEVER MET LADY GREGORY, the lynch-pin of the whole literary revival. She wrote extensively and worked tirelessly in the cause of the Irish National Theatre. Her home, Coole Park, County Galway, was a centre of literary activity to which she attracted many of the greatest writers of the times. Many were persuaded to carve their initials on one of Coole Park's fine trees. That tree and the initials of great writers is almost all that remains physically of the glory that was Coole Park. The Forestry Commission bought the estate and demolished the house, Yeats wrote prophetically.

> I meditate upon a swallow's flight,
> Upon an aged woman and her house,
> A sycamore and lime-tree lost in night
> Although that western cloud is luminous,
> Great works constructed there in nature's spite
> For scholars and for poets after us,
> Thoughts long knitted into a single thought,
> A dance-like glory that those walls begot.
>
> There Hyde before he had beaten into prose
> That noble blade the Muses buckled on,

There one that ruffled in a manly pose
For all his timid heat, there that slow man,
That meditative man, John Synge, and those
Impetuous men, Shawe-Taylor and Hugh Lane,
Found pride established in humility,
A scene well set and excellent company.

They came like swallows and like swallows went,
And yet a woman's powerful character
Could keep a swallow to its first intent;
And half a dozen in formation there,
That seemed to whirl upon a compass-point,
Found certainty upon the dreaming air,
The intellectual sweetness of those lines
That cut through time or cross it withershins.

Here, traveller, scholar, poet, take your stand
When all those rooms and passages are gone,
When nettles wave upon a shapeless mound
And saplings root among the broken stone,
And dedicate-eyes bent upon the ground,
Back turned upon the brightness of the sun
And all the sensuality of the shade –
A moment's memory to that laurelled head.

Coole Park, WB Yeats

George Moore wrote of Lady Gregory in *Hail And Farewell (Vol 2, 310)*

'It is difficult to imagine Synge writing about the middle classes and their tea parties, or the upper classes and their motor cars, and we may exercise our wits trying to discover the turn his talent would have taken, but it is more practical to tell how Lady Gregory came to the rescue of the Abbey Theatre and saved it after the secession of the Fays.

She could write easily and well, and had shown aptitude for writing rural anecdotes in dialogue, and it is an open secret that she was Yeats's collaborator in the *Pot Of Broth* and in *Cathleen Ni Houlihan*, and feeling that the fate of the movement depended upon her, she undertook the great responsibility of keeping the theatre open with her pen, writing play after play, three or four a year, writing in the space of ten years something like thirty plays. And is there one among us who would undertake such a job of work and accomplish it as well as Lady Gregory? The plays that flowed from her pen so rapidly are not of equal merit, nor is there any one that compares with the *Playboy*, but all are meritorious, all are conceived and written in the same style. She is herself in her little plays, a Galway woman telling rural anecdotes that amuse her woman's mind, and telling them gracefully, never trying to philosophise, to explain, but just content to pick her little flower, to place it in a vase for our amusement, and to go on to another flower.'

George Russell (AE)
by John Butler Yeats
NATIONAL GALLERY OF IRELAND

SAGE

THE ONLY ONE OF THE GOOD AND THE GREAT of the Celtic twilight whom Francis Ledwidge did meet was George Russell (AE). It was not a happy acquaintanceship.

AE was the Sunday centre of the Celtic twilight. He held regular Sunday evening soirées attended by Yeats, George Moore and many other distinguished men of letters. He was an Ulsterman, a protestant, a mystic, a poet, a painter, an essayist and a man of firm views. By way of occupation he worked for the Irish Agricultural Organisation Society under Sir Horace Plunkett, Lord Dunsany's uncle. From 1905–1923 he edited the *Irish Homestead*, from 1923–1935 he edited the *Irish Statesman*. He published three of James Joyce's Dubliners stories in the Irish

Homestead; he features in *Ulysses*; he attended the Art School in Dublin in 1885 and painted extensively throughout his life. He exhibited with Count Markievicz. His paintings can be seen at Glenveigh Castle, County Donegal, the home of the late Henry McIlhenry, now open to the public. He was a poet and encouraged young poets. Padraic Colum and James Stephens were among his particular protégés. He was a pamphleteer, writing on many subjects, particularly the spiritual renewal of Ireland. He encouraged Irishmen to seek spiritual inspiration from Celtic heroes and to defy the might of the church to dictate to them. He believed that Celtic myths were an inspiration older than Christianity.

His poetry was closely inspired by his visions. His first volume of poetry *Homward* was published in 1913, and his selected Poems in 1935. His poetic position is evidenced in *The Great Breath*:

> Its edges foamed with amethyst and rose,
> Withers once more the old blue flower of day:
> Then where the ether like a petal glows
> Its petals fade away.
>
> A shadowy tumult stirs the dusky air;
> Sparkle the delicate dews, the distant snows;
> The great deep thrills for through it everywhere
> The breath of Beauty blows.
>
> I saw how all the tumbling ages past,
> Moulded to her by deep and deeper breath
> Neared to the hour when Beauty breathed her last
> And knows herself in death.

He wrote to Katherine Tynan. 'The greatest pleasure I find in life is discovering new young poets.' He met Francis Ledwidge but the bonds of admiration never grew strong between them.

He was a playwright of distinction. His play *Deirdre* was performed by the Irish Literary Theatre on 2, 3 and 4 April 1902 with Yeats' *Cathleen Ni Houlihan*. The double bill with Maud Gonne as Cathleen and Maire Quinn as *Deirdre* was a significant stimulus to the Irish Literary Theatre in its early years on its journey to becoming The Irish National Theatre and the Abbey Theatre.

AE was a visionary. He received instruction in Theosophy. He wrote of his experiences in the *Candle Of Vision*. It was from his visions, many of them of Celtic gods and heroes, that he created much of his poetry and painting. Francis Ledwidge attended a few of AE's Sunday night literary gatherings. In September 1914 he borrowed £5 from AE In November 1914 when Francis Ledwidge was training at Richmond Barracks Lord Dunsany wrote to ask permission for Ledwidge to have an occasional use of a room at the Co-operative Movements, Plunkett house, for writing. AE declined Lord Dunsany's request. He said there was no room available for use by Francis Ledwidge. He told Lord Dunsany that Ledwidge had borrowed £5 from him in September and had not returned it. He thought that Lord Dunsany should know his protégé's little ways. It is difficult to imagine a more uncharitable communication. The £5 clearly rankled with AE He wrote to JC Squire 'The new Irish poet has gone into the van. I heard vaguely that he had enlisted. I have not seen him for four months but that may be because he borrowed £5 from me on a promise to return it the next day. This singular silence has made me think that his verse will lack something or other. However, I believe it has been set up and Dunsany had the proofs. The poet is very young but regret to say that in common with many Irish poets they borrow money and never mention it again. I would share my possessions with a fellow poet cheerfully but I object to them telling me a little tale about their ship coming in the next day when they might have had what they wanted without straining an imagination better employed in their art.' The juxtaposition of the outstanding £5 and verse lacking something is difficult to fathom. Lord Dunsany paid AE the £5. AE undoubtedly had extensive connections and some influence in literary Dublin; for example among the people whom Francis Ledwidge met on his Sunday evening visits was George Roberts who had founded the publishing firm of Maunsels in 1905. He took five years to make up his mind whether or not to publish James Joyce's Dubliners. He rejected it. AE was a man who provoked in those who knew him the strongest sentiments of loyalty or loathing.

The magic of AE did not get through to Sean O'Casey. He mentions him first in his Autobiography *Drums Under The Window.*

Yeats, the poet, wandered, lonely as a cloud, through the streets, singing his lovely songs into his own ear, wailing at times to his own Psyche, 'Romantic Ireland's dead and gone, it's with O'Leary in the grave'; the wind for ever rustling the reeds under his feet; wild white swans for ever flying in a blue sky over his head. He would not kindle a flame in the eyes of the common people, though he had kindled one in the eyes of Cathleen, the daughter of Houlihan; though in a strange deep way he loved the common people more than Griffith, MacNeill or DeValera did or ever could. Hard at his heels followed the stout, lumbering George Russell, watching figures, featured with fire issuing out of their pituitary glands streaming from every chimney top and every smokers pipe; jumping hilariously, when on a holiday, from peak to peak of the Wicklow mountains, the planets for ever chiming the advent of an avatar who would lead Eire back to her old gods; believing that the world was buried in a purple glow; staring fixedly at every person newly presented to him, so that he might see if a red, a blue, or a golden aura bathed the body, telling him on what plane of spiritual achievement the newly presented person stood.

In his next volume of the Autobiography *Pictures In The Hallway*, Sean O'Casey's lack of enthusiasm for AE gathers momentum; (at 150) 'He realised that Lady Gregory, in the midst of her merriment and mourning, was ever running round, a sturdy little figure in her suit of solemn black, enlivened by gleaming eyes and dancing smile; ever running in and out of Yeats's Celtic twilight which she could never fully understand; turning his Rose Achemica into a homely herb; and turning the wildness of his Red O'Hanrahan into the serious, steady dancing of a hornpipe on the Abbey stage.

In her humorous and critical moods, swinging a critical latern, she trespassed into AE's amethystine no man's-land where AE became delirious with quivering, peacock-tinted visions, seeing things innumerable and unmentionable, being plumen, from petuity gland to backside, with red, white, green, blue and orange flames, Then he sat, with notebook in hand, taking down divine orders of the day from brotherserfs, master souls, ancient beauties, elfs and faeries, a rigodoon, a dad, a derry.'

In a chapter called *Dublin Gods and Half Gods* he wrote 'Sean was now walking tiptoe among the gods, but he had begun to doubt the divinity of most of them. His reference for the opinions of AE had begun to decline.'

In the chapter *Dublin's Glittering Guy* he wrote, 'AE's getting a little bent in the back' said Edwin D. Grey' and he looked old passing by us in O'Connell Street today. Curious guys. Curious guy – Dublin has her gods, her half-gods and her guys', said Donal. Dublin's boyos, the world final in painting, literature, poetry, philosophy, rural science, dreams and religion. He's the fairest and brightest humbug in Ireland. There's a genuine humility in Yeats's arrogance, but there's a deeper arrogance in AE's humility.

And the other day, said Edwin, Dunsany called AE the poet of the century. It's incomprehensible how Dunsany could overlook Yeats to hand the poetry to AE What a mass of glittering monotony his poems are. All paralysed with a purple glow. Swing exultation in them all. They make a mind dizzy. It's too much of a thing to be friends with the Ancient of Days; too big a thing to be the rocker of the infant suns; or to dip a forefinger into the fiery fountains of the stars; or to put on the mantelshelf of your room the Golden Urn into which all the glittering spray of planets fall. AE thinks he's God's own crooner.

Listen
When the breath of twilight blows to flame the misty skies,
With its vaporous sapphire, violet glow, and silver gleam
With their magic flood me through the gateway of the eyes
I am one with the twilight's dream.

On AE's Sunday night soirées. 'Sean strolled after the other two, thinking of how astonished he had been the first night he had gone to an AE 'at home'. When the room filled, desultory chat ended, and each settled himself for ordeal or treat. AE was climbing into his throne. This was a chair placed on his platform, and those present sat in a humble semi-circle round his royal seat. AE climbed heavily, hoisting himself into it, the rotund belly and big backside, eclipsing the throne for the rest of the evening. He ceremoniously lighted his pipe, while he waited for someone to start the talk rolling along like ole man river. It seemed plain to Sean that AE used the talk and the comments as a vocal rehearsal for what he would say in his Journal during the coming week. When he spoke, he did so as if his mind was the only one in harmony with the spheres. He became the policeman on point duty directing the way through the avenues and lanes of this life and those of the life to come. He had no music in him, for like Yeats and Gogarty, he was tone deaf. He poured out words in a steady, colourless torrent, full of sound, destitute of fury, signifying very little. It had struck Sean as strange how this man, so voluble in his own den, on his own throne could be so silent when he was in Yeats's parlour.

Sean had seen him there, sitting back in a fat settee, occasionally lighting his pipe with a casual air, as if to show an indifference he did not feel. There he sat, silent, as if this talk did not matter for importance and immensity were with him only who sat upon the fat settee. That AE uneasily felt that Yeats was beyond and above his rivalry was a sure thought to Sean, as he listened to the one and watched the other.'

It is not clear how many of AE's 'at homes' were attended by Francis Ledwidge when he was training at Redmond Barracks in Dublin. What is clear is that his poetry was totally unaffected either by AE's mystical posturing or AE's writing.

And O'Casey writes later in *Dublin's Glittering Guy* at James Stephens' flat 'Suddenly those present clapped their hands when James Stephens called on AE to join the crowd by reciting one of his poems, and in a fine burst of enthusiasm Sean called louder than the rest. AE murmured that it wasn't easy, after talking to O'Cassidy about things material for so long, to summon up the Divine Applatus. The hands clapped again, a little more impatiently, either to give AE encouragement, or to show advanced appreciation of the beauty that was to come. AE was pleased, taking long breathes, puffing himself out, breathing solemnity and power into his psyche, amid a hush of awed silence. In the midst of the awed hush, Tom McCreevy's voice, like a thunderclap, was heard saying, Give the poor man a chance – he has to pump himself up.

A titter, chokingly modified, rippled round the room, silenced altogether by Stephens's warning murmur of disapproval, and by the sudden rage of AE He rose roughly from his seat, snarling out that he wouldn't stay to be insulted; broke through the circle of friends by shoving his chair violently backwards, and rushed swiftly from the silent room. No one spoke, till McCreevy added to the given insult by saying: *There goes the most conceited man in Ireland.*

George Moore's admiration for AE is strongly supported by Oliver St John Gogarty, probably the most balanced man in the Celtic Twilight.

TO AE GOING TO AMERICA

Dublin transmits you, famous, to the West.
America shall welcome you, and we,
Reflected in that mighty glass, shall see,
In full proportion, power at which we guessed:
We live too near the eagle and the nest
To know the pinion's wide supremacy:
But yours, of all the wings that crossed the sea,
Carries the wisest heart and gentlest.
It is not multitudes, but Man's idea
Makes a place famous. Though you now digress,
Remember to return as, back from Rome,
Du Bellay journeyed to his Lyré home;
And Plutarch, willingly, to Chaeronea
Returned, and stayed, lest the poor town be less.

AE features in Gogarty's Autobiography *As I Was Going Down Sackville Street* 'I was expecting to hear his cheery knock at any moment now. Five or six taps and we know that it was George Russell the mystic, the poet and the economist (economics being more fanciful than poetry). Had not Sir Horace, his chief, wired to a friend – I am quoting Hone 'We men of affairs keep a poet in our office?' His pen name came about when he was devoted to Theosophy, and AE was short for Aeon. Anyone who heard his knock in my house could have told that it was Friday evening. He never failed us. I felt that he would not fail us now, though it was not safe to be out after nine when the firing began (177)' ... 'It has been said of AE that he is one of those rare spirits who bring us to a realisation of our own divinity and intensify it. He enlarges the joy that is hidden in the heroic heart. He is a magnifier of the moods of the soul; and he communicates them more naturally by music and murmuring sound than by the messages or points. Don't forget what Robert Louis Stevenson said about geniuses like AE 'Such are the best teachers. A spirit communicated is a perpetual possession. These best teachers climb beyond teaching to the plane of art. It is themselves, and what is more, the best in themselves, that they communicate. That is the secret of AE. He is an artist. He teaches nothing. He communicates himself, and the best in himself, which consists of poetry, loving kindness, and a passion for beauty more than anything else. So you see he is more like Plato than like the Tolstoi whom I saw that his appearance suggested at first sight.'

With such support from the most generous of men perhaps we should conclude that Sean O'Casey's judgement on AE is harsh; or would Francis Ledwidge have agreed with O'Casey having regard to AE's pettiness over the borrowed £5.

James Stephens
by Patrick Tuohy
NATIONAL GALLERY OF IRELAND

JAMES STEPHENS

ONE OF AE'S MOST ILLUSTRIOUS PROTÉGÉS was James Stephens. George Moore writes in *Hail And Farewell* (Vol II, 338) 'and recognising at once a new songster, AE put on his hat and went away with his cage, discovering him in a lawyer's office. A great head and two soft brown eyes looked at him over a typewriter, and an alert and intelligent voice asked him who he wanted to see. AE said he was looking for James Stephens, a poet, and the typist answered I am he.

James Stephens's novel *A Crock Of Gold* was acclaimed and lives on. It is without doubt the most delightful Irish fairy tale of the century. James Stephens, who met Francis Ledwidge in Dublin after Lord Dunsany introduced him to literary society, was critical of him. He wrote of Francis Ledwidge 'He is only a beginner and must digest his ancestries before we know what he really is like. Meanwhile he has a true singing faculty, and his promise is, I think, greater than any young poet now writing.

I do not believe, however, that he will ratify this promise by an almighty performance. I don't believe that his thought will equal his faculty for utterance ... A man is a mind and so is a poet and they are man and poet only to the extent of that. This is the croaking of the crow. I do not know Ledwidge at all well ... He is what we call here a hump of a lad and he was panoplied in all those devices, or disguises, which a countryman puts on when he meets the men of the town. Country people and children are all play actors.'

It is impossible to assess how Francis Ledwidge would have reacted if he had been introduced to AE's magic circle of Sunday night poetry on a regular basis; perhaps with readings of his poetry by AE I suspect that Francis Ledwidge was too straightforward and unsophisticated to have appreciated the mystical atmosphere circulating between AE and Yeats however fascinated he would have been by the undoubted heights which they inhabited.

James Stephens was twelve years older than Francis Ledwidge. He was a significant poet in the early decades of this century, a position he would have had to share with Francis Ledwidge if he had not been killed.

Oliver St John Gogarty also places James Stephens high in the poetic batting order.

TO JAMES STEPHENS

Where are you, Spirit, who could pass into our hearts and all
Hearts of little children, hearts of trees and hills and elves?
Where is the pen that could, sweetly deep and whimsical,
Make old poets sing again far better than themselves?

You passed through all our past worst time, and proved yourself
    no caitiff.
America then listened to a voice too dear for wealth;
Then you went to London, where I fear you have 'gone native';
Too long in a metropolis will tax a poet's health:

It's not as if you had no wit, and cared for recognition;
A mind that lit the Liffey could emblazon all the Thames,
But we're not ourselves without you, and we long for coalition;
Oh, half of Erin's energy! What can have happened James?

James Stephens had a diversity of inspirations. He was a poet of the country.

THE SNARE

I hear a sudden cry of pain!
There is a rabbit in a snare:
Now I hear the cry again,
But I cannot hear from where.

But I cannot tell from where
He is calling out for aid!
Crying on the frightened air,
Making everything afraid!

Making everything afraid!
Wrinkling up his little face!
As he cries again for aid;
And I cannot find the place.

And I cannot find the place
Where his paw is in the snare!
Little One! Oh Little One
I am searching everywhere!

The Easter Rising left its mark on his poetry.

FROM SPRING

Be green upon their graves, O happy Spring!
For they were young and eager who are dead!
Of all things that are young, and quivering
With eager life, be they remembered!
They move not here! They have gone to the clay!

They cannot die again for liberty!
Be they remembered of their land for aye!
Green be their graves, and green their memory!

He was a poet of mood and atmosphere, particularly as expressed through people.

SOFT WINGS

I saw a beggar woman bare
Her bosom to the winter air,
And into the tender nest
Of her famished mother-breast
She laid her child;
And him beguiled,
With crooning song, into his rest.

With crooning song, and tender word,
About a little singing bird,
That spread soft wings about her brood!
And tore her bosom for their food!
And sang the while,
Them to beguile,
All in the forest's solitude!

And hearing this, I could not see
That she was clad in misery!
For in her heart there was a glow
Warmed her bare feet in the snow!
In her heart was hid a sun
Would warm a world for everyone!

The only other significant Ulster contribution to the Celtic Twilight came from Alice Milligan. She grew up in County Tyrone. She wrote for the Abbey Theatre. She made her home in Dublin. Her sentiments were strongly nationalist and republican. Her poetry owed at least something to her Ulster origins.

WHEN I WAS A LITTLE GIRL

[Oxford Book of Irish Verses]

When I was a little girl,
In a garden playing
A thing was often said
To chide us delaying:

When after sunny hours,
At twilight's falling,
Down through the garden walks
Came our old nurse calling,

'Come in! for it's growing late
And the grass will wet ye!
Come in! or when it's dark
The Fenians will get ye'

Then, at this dreadful news,
All helter-skelter,
The panic-struck little flock
Ran home for shelter.

And round the nursery fire
Sat still to listen,
Fifty bare toes on the hearth,
Ten eyes a-glisten.

To hear of a night in March,
And loyal folk waiting,
To see a great army of men
Some devastating.

An army of Papists grim,
With a green flag o-er them,
Red-coates and black police
Flying before them.

But God (Who our nurse declared
Guards British dominions)
Sent down a fall of snow
And scattered the Fenians

But somewhere they're lurking yet,
Maybe they're near us'
Four little hearts pit-a-pat
Thought 'Can they hear us?'

Then the wind-shaken pane
Sounded like drumming;
Oh! 'they cried' tuck us in,
The Fenians are coming!'

Four little pair of hands
On the cots where she led those,
Over their frightened heads
Pulled up their bedclothes.

But one little rebel there
Watching all with laughter,
Thought, 'When the Fenians come
….. and go after.'

Wished she had been a boy
And a good deal older ..
Able to walk for miles
With a gun on her shoulder.

Able to lift aloft
The Green Flag o'er them
(Red-coates and black police
Flying before)

And as she dropped asleep,
Was wondering whether
God, if they prayed to Him,
Would give fine weather

AN EIGHTEENTH-CENTURY MAN

THE CHARMER OF THE CELTIC TWILIGHT was Oliver St John Gogarty. But as well as having wit and charm he was a distinguished surgeon, a scholar, a poet, an essayist, and a public man of high repute.

Francis Ledwidge first met Gogarty at Dunsany Castle. Gogarty was a close friend of Lord Dunsany and a visitor to Dunsany Castle. News of Francis Ledwidge's unhappy love affair with Ellie Vaughey reached Gogarty via Lord Dunsany. Gogarty composed some doggerel on the poet's emotional disaster. Gogarty followed Francis Ledwidge's life and times with interest and a cutting edge after he joined the army in 1914. He wrote to Lord Dunsany on 4 November 1914. 'Ledwidge, your harper whom you bring with you, met a friend of mine and said he hoped to preserve some individuality, but three weeks of discipline took it all away.' It seems that Francis Ledwidge showed at least some of his poetry to Gogarty. In an undated letter he wrote to Lord Dunsany:

Dear Lord Dunsany

I enclose herewith a copy of the poem which you liked so much and two rather interesting letters concerning it. Doctor Gogarty 'lain' where it is bad English and will require turning. I came at once for aid here to you … Fancy that little thing I wrote here with my pen causing a sensation in the Gogarty school. But I knew it was good when you said so.

Francis Ledwidge raised a significant mention in Gogarty's famous autobiography *As I Was Going Down Sackville Street*.

I must go down to Dunsany and see how the playwright is getting on. Dunsany Castle is about 25 miles from Dublin, and the journey takes about three quarters of an hour in a useful car. The great gates are seldom opened, so you go through a short drive through a gateless Gothic ruin, a 'reproduction' as Sir Thomley Stoker, the connoisseur would say. Sheer up from the dark gravel rises the great pile. The square tower beyond the door is half-covered with ivy. The hall is filled with armour and the trophies of the chase.

'His Lordship is not at home, Sir.' I well knew the difference between not being at home and not being in. 'Are you sure that he is not on top of the tower composing?' 'If you just say:' 'He is not in, Sir', 'Then, where is he?' 'He has been arrested, Sir, by the Black and Tans.' It was Maunder, the major-duomo, speaking. He could be relied upon, with such a master, carefully to frame his sentences, and to chose his words. By the Black and Tans, Well, of all the countries.

But what the devil was Dunsany doing to be arrested by the Black and Tans? Was he after all a rebel at heart, following in the footsteps of his ancestor, the Blessed Oliver Plunkett, who was condemned on a trumped up charge and hanged, drawn and quartered in 1681? If so, it is a surprise to me. I thought I knew a good deal about his points of view in literature, criticism and politics. I have it. He has been comforting Ledwidge, the Bard of Slane. That he had been supporting and educating him I knew. And now the master is arrested for the man. And there was in my mind the memory of a poem which Ledwidge broke off, dissatisfied. 'I got weary' he said as it was no good. Let me see how it went. I can never remember prose – but I cannot forget verse if it is smooth.

> What rumours filled the Atlantic sky,
> And turned the wild geese back again;
> When Plunkett lifted Balor's eye,
> And broke Andromedia's strong chain?
> Or did they hear that Starkie, James,
> Among the gallipots was seen,
> And he who called her sweetest names,
> Was talking to another queen?
>
> Now all the wise in quick lime burn,
> And all the strong have crossed the sea;
> But down the pale roads of Ashbourne,
> Are heard the voices of the free.
> And Jemmy Quigley is the boy,
> Could say how queenly was her walk,
> When Sackville Street went down like Troy,
> And peelers fell in far Dundalk.

They probably found a copy of that when raiding Dunsany Castle and were sure that Lord Dunsany was the Plunkett who lifted something. So they lifted the Plunkett. They had to lift something. But it was the wrong Plunkett. The Plunkett who died in 1681 had but one 'T' in his name.

Gogarty does not dignify the poem as anything more than smooth. But it was sufficiently smooth for him to remember and to include it in his Autobiography as part of the Dunsany saga. It does not feature in Lord Dunsany's Collected Edition of Ledwidge's poetry first published in 1918. Liam O'Meara says that it was dedicated to Oliver St John Gogarty so it is not surprising that he could remember it.

It seems therefore by the time that Francis Ledwidge had joined the army and was training in Dublin that Gogarty was taking an interest in him and in his poetry. If Ledwidge had survived the war it is likely that he would have become a friend; and what a friend for a young man with aspirations for a life in literature.

Gogarty was a man with a quite extraordinary diversity of talents. He was a surgeon by profession. He was a scholar. He had attended Trinity College, Dublin in the time of the great classical scholar John Pentland Mahaffy. Some of Mahaffy's excitement in the classics must have got through to Gogarty.

CHORIC SONG OF THE LADIES OF LEMNOS

STR I

Who will marry Hercules?
Tell me if you can.
Who will catch his eye, and please
The strong silent man?

Who will make a happy home,
For duty and desire:
In Summer tend the honey-comb,
In Winter, tend the fire?...

ANTIS II

O look at him with his club,
And his lion's fell!
That's the lad who made hub-
Bub below in Hell!

That which is the pirates' quest
May be Hercules's:
To carry off the buxomest,
And marry whom he pleases!

EPOS II

Praise him for his shoulder's breadth,
Him who took the Town of Death,

Took the triple Dog therefrom,
And Alcestis to her home.

Praise him, for he carries through
All he sets himself to do;
No one ever saw him chuck
Anything he undertook;

Softly talk of marriage, he
Might embrace the colony;
And if he were duly roused
Who would then be unespoused?

Gogarty was a playwright. He was a poet. In his introduction to the *Oxford Book of Modern Verse 1893–1935* Yeats described him as one of the great lyric poets of our age. His lyricism could be thoughtful, and also light.

GOLDEN STOCKINGS

Golden stockings you had on
In the meadow where you ran;
And your little knees together
Bobbed like pippins in the weather,
When the breezes rush and fight
For those dimples of delight,
And they dance from the pursuit,
And the leaf looks like the fruit.

I have many a sight in mind
That would last if I were blind;
Many verses I could write
That would bring me many a sight.
Now I only see but one,
See you running in the sun,
And the gold-dust coming up
From the trampled butter-cup.

His lyricism could be sad.

DEATH MAY BE VERY GENTLE

Death may be very gentle after all:
He turns his face away from arrogant knights
Who fling themselves against him in their fights;
But to the loveliest he loves to call.
And he has with him those whose ways were mild
And beautiful; and many a little child.

His lyricism was particularly inspired by all things natural.

FRESH FIELDS

I gaze and gaze when I behold
The meadows springing green and gold.
I gaze until my mind is naught
But wonderful and wordless thought!
Till, suddenly, surpassing wit,
Spontaneous meadows spring in it;
And I am but a glass between
Un-walked-in meadows, gold and green.

He was also a poet of the city.

LIFFEY BRIDGE

I gazed along the waters at the West,
Watching the low sky colour into flame,
Until each narrowing steeple I could name
Grew dark as the far vapours, and my breast
With silence like a sorrow was possessed.
And men as moving shadows went and came.
The smoke that stained the sunset seemed like shame,
Or lust, or some great evil unexpressed.
Then with a longing for the taintless air,
I called that desolation back again,
Which reigned when Liffey's widening banks were bare:
Before Ben Edair gazed upon the Dane,

Before the Hurdle Ford, and long before
Finn drowned the young men by its meadowy shore.

He was an athlete; an airman; a countryman with a particular passion for the West of Ireland, where he had a lovely home at Renvyle, County Mayo.

CONNEMARA

West of the Shannon may be said
Whatever comes into your head;
But you can do, and chance your luck,
Whatever you like West of the Suck.
There's something sleeping in my breast
That wakens only in the West;
There's something in the core of me
That needs the West to set it free…

…The very light above the bay,
The mountains leaping far away,
Are hands that wave through homely air,
To make me shout 'I'll soon be there!'

It is not everyone gets on
Where dwell the Seaside Sons of Conn;
It is not everyone that's wanted
Where things are apt to be enchanted …

… It's here that I get out to walk;
The Shannon's there for you that talk;
But I can only work my will
Where mountains leap and clouds lie still.

He was a wit with an ever bubbling sense of fun. When an American friend arrived in Dublin and informed Mrs Gogarty that on his trip from Queenstown to Killarney to Dublin he had seen Muckross Abbey and considered it the most beautiful ruin in Ireland, he heard Dr Gogarty walk into the room behind him saying 'Ah but you haven't seen …' a famous beauty whose loveliness had faded.

He was a man of faith. His faith overflowed into his poetry.

TO DEATH

But for your Terror
Where would be Valour?
What is Love for
But to stand in your way?
Taker and Giver,
For all your endeavour
You leave us with more
Than you touch with decay!

He was a public man. He became one of the first senators of the Irish Free State in 1922. He became increasingly disenchanted with the new State. His home, Renvyle, had been burnt down by the IRA. The story is told in his autobiography, *As I Was Walking Down Sackville* Street,

> Renvyle House is burned by the IRA. The long, lone house in the ultimate
> land of the undiscovered West. Why should they burn my house. Because
> I am not an Irishman? Because I do not flatter fools? If the only Irishman
> who is to be allowed to live in Ireland must be a bog trotter, then I am not
> an Irishman. And I object to the bog-trotter being the ideal exemplar of all
> Irishman. I refuse to conform to that type.
>   So Renvyle House, with its irreplaceable oaken panelling, is burned
> down. They say it took a week to burn. Blue china fused like a solder.

It is no consolation to know that it has been rebuilt as an excellent and happy family hotel, particularly attractive for children.

He was himself kidnapped. He escaped by swimming the Liffey. He promised the Liffey that if it landed him in safety from the gun shots of his kidnappers which followed him into the icy December water that he would present it with two swans.

TO THE LIFFEY WITH THE SWANS

Keep these calm and lovely things
And float them in your clearest water;
For one would not disgrace a King's
Transformed, beloved and buoyant daughter.

And with her goes this sprightly swan,
A bird of more than royal feather,
With alban beauty clothed upon:
O keep them fair and well together!

As fair as was that doubled Bird,
By love of Leda so besotten,
That she was all with wonder stirred
And the Twin Sportsmen were begotten.

Gogarty's disenchantment with the Ireland that developed out of the Free State is clear in *As I Was Walking Down Sackville Street.*

The old landlords betrayed their country; so the popular rumour has it. But nobody can betray Ireland; it does not give him the chance; it betrays him first. The landowners merely fell between two stools and two railway stations – Kings Cross and Euston. Since Lord Dunraven died and Horace Plunkett, they have not left a notable name in their club, save that of their last comer Yeats, and he will be about as sib to them as Daniel O'Connell's memory to the masonic Lodge round the corner in Molesworth Street, where his regalia is still preserved ... Ireland at present is parallel to what Greece was in the age of myths. We never had, as England had, the Roman schoolmaster to teach us logic. Therefore fairy tales are our politics. I am not anxious to compose fairy tales. I can always send out for a daily paper.
Suddenly the thought struck me, Irishmen like to be melancholy. It is the national pastime to brood full of blackbile. I remembered the dark figures in the Connemara pub. Even their drink is black. They chew on melancholy as a cow on the cud. Shane Leslie attributes it to 'hushed hate'. It is more than that. It is independent of external circumstances. They take pleasure in darkening with melancholia God's sweet air. (169)

Ireland's a free country, shoot whoever you please. We have too much liberty.

Lord Granard was a Senator too and it was a Senator's privilege to be escorted. Unescorted so much the less Senator he ... You know my Galway house is burned. They have exploded a bomb in the hall of Castle Forbes. I do not yet know how much damage has been done. We were partners in affliction. Our country was afflicting itself in a republic of ruin where all that is outstanding is levelled to the ground.'

He was a public man in the widest sense of the word. In addition to being a Senator he is said to be the foundation for Buck Milligan in *Ulysses*. Gogarty, James Joyce, and a friend called Trench (Haines in *Ulysses*) had lived together in the Martello Tower rented by Gogarty for nine pounds a year. The scope of Gogarty's talents and achievements was enormous. Poetry was his greatest achievement. It was an achievement at least stimulated by his friendship with Yeats whom he greatly admired. He wrote in *As I Was Walking Down Sackville Street* 'Yeats is the greatest poet of this and of most of the last generation. Tennyson, his predecessor, built a world of song on ready made foundations. Yeats had to create it all from Airy – nothing; and to protect it from maurading hands.'

AE was as admiring of Gogarty as Gogarty was of AE He wrote of Gogarty's poetry 'I take so much pleasure in my friend's poetry because it is the opposite of my own. It gives to me some gay and gallant life which was not in my own birthright. He is never the passionate poet made dull by the dignity of recognised genius. He has never made a business of beauty: and because he is disinterested in his dealings with it, the Muse has gone with him on his walks and revealed to him some airs and graces she kept secret from other lovers who were too shy or too awed by her to laugh and be natural in her presence.'

Gogarty's great admiration for Yeats was detailed in his poetry.

ELEGY ON THE ARCHPOET
WILLIAM BUTLER YEATS LATELY DEAD

> Now that you are a Song
> And your life has come to an end
> And you wholly belong
> To the world of Art, my friend,
> Take, for well it is due,
> This tribute of my rhymes
> With mind unswerved from you
> In these enormous times;
> Not that I wish to intrude
> To mix with mine your leaf,
> But that I would entwine
> In your magnificent sheaf,
> After sad interlude,
> A spray cut from that fine
> And rare plant, Gratitude,

For anything I owe
In the art of making songs
Largely to you is due,
To you the credit belongs
Who never stinted or spared
Yourself in the difficult feat
Of getting a man prepared
To sing in his own conceit.
None may carry a stone
To your high tower of thought
But surely I can own
Whose was the influence caught
Me in wild wear disguised
And undistinguished found me,
Encouraged, authorised
And with the laurel crowned me;
And make it lovingly clear
While memory is fresh
What manner of man you were
While here clothed on with flesh.
The world knows well your rhymes,
But I would depict you to please
The men in coming times
By a picture of you in these
And make them as grateful to me
As I would be could I find,
Searching past history,
Troubled Euripides
Or unvexed Sophocles,
By some contemporary mind.

II

The noble head held high,
The nose with an eagle's gaze,
The sharp appraising eye,
The brown unageing face,
The beautiful elegant hands
As white as the breasts of the love

Of Ossian in faerylands:
Among us but ever aloof,
He never hurried or ran,
With eyes on a lordly track
A tall upstanding man
You dared not slap on the back.
He moved in a diffident way
As if a new-comer to earth
Wrapped in a magical day
Older than death or than birth:
A man come down from the men
Who walked in the morning dew
Of dark Ferdia's strain
With lips like berries of yew:
A race that hosts in the hills,
A race few eyes can see,
A race that our day fills
With perverse, mischievous glee:
A head never turned by fame,
An eerie spirit that takes
Its preternatural calm
From sloe-black mountain lakes.
You heard the sound of his soul
Through words in their equipoise;
The sound of his soul was beautiful:
He had a most beautiful voice.

III

O brain that never lacked full power,
O spirit always of the tower
That never stooped to earthly lure
But at your height were self-secure:
With wistful child's benignity,
With Man's most noble dignity
You never compromised with Fear
You brought the Brave among us here,
And high above the tinsel scene
Strode with the old heroic mien,

And equalled to your intellect
The grandeur of your self-respect.

The diversity of Gogarty's life spirit is apparent from his close friendship with Lord
Dunsany. Lord Dunsany was every bit as much a countryman as Yeats was a metropolitan. Both were poets. Gogarty moved between them with a total ease.

TO EDWARD MORETON DRAX
18 BARON DUNSANY

To ward off Time's abuses
The name is set above,
By one who loves the Muses,
Of one the Muses love.

DUNSANY CASTLE

The twin dunes rise before it, and beneath
Their tree-dark summits the Skene river flows,
An old divine earth exaltation glows
About it, though no longer battles breathe.
For Time puts all men's swords in his red sheath,
And softlier now the air from Tara glows;
Thus in the royalest ground that Ireland knows
Stands your sheer house in immemorial Meath.

It stands for actions done and days endured;
Old causes God, in guiding Time, espoused,
Who never brooks the undeserving long.
I found there pleasant chambers filled with song,
(And never were the Muses better housed)
Repose and dignity and Fame assured.

Dunsany Castle

CATHERINE FLANAGAN

SEVEN

RENAISSANCE MAN

I F FRANCIS LEDWIDGE WAS LESS THAN LUCKY in the extent of his contacts among the good and the great of the Celtic twilight, he was many times blessed in the interest and friendship bestowed upon him by his great benefactor, Lord Dunsany. Lord Dunsany was soldier, poet, playwright, novelist, essayist, scholar, traveller, countryman, sportsman, and gamesplayer. He had a galaxy of talents. He was infinitely generous in the patronage which he gave Francis Ledwidge.

Both were Meathmen. Lord Dunsany was an aristocrat; educated, Eton and Sandhurst. Francis Ledwidge's origins were humble. His circumstances were stringent. When they met Francis Ledwidge was working as a ganger on the roads.

Francis Ledwidge was sociable. In particular he enjoyed the social life offered by the Conygham Arms in Slane. One night in the Conygham Arms he met John Cassidy. John Cassidy was a sculptor of distinction who lived and worked in Manchester. He was a native of Slane. His origins were modest. His early career was difficult. But he had received extensive encouragement from a Mr Davis of Drogheda. When John Cassidy returned from Manchester he gave the benefit of his attentions to social life in the Conygham Arms. He and Francis Ledwidge met. Cassidy's advice to Francis Ledwidge was that he should find a Davis in the world of letters to help him. He suggested Lord Dunsany.

In 1912 Francis Ledwidge sent Lord Dunsany his copybook of poems inviting his opinion as to whether they had any merit. Lord Dunsany travelled extensively. He was away. But when he returned he read Francis Ledwidge's poems and wrote an encouraging letter.

By 1912 Lord Dunsany was an established writer. A number of his books had been published; his play *'The Glittering Gate'* had been produced by the Abbey Theatre in 1909. In 1911 his play *'The Gods Of The Mountain'* was running at the Haymarket in London. In 1912 AE wrote to a friend 'The most prolific of Irish writers is now Lord Dunsany. Do you know his *Queer Tales, The Sword of Welleran, A Dreamer's Tales,* and *Time and the Gods.* He is improving and has a great splash of genius in him.' AE had been assisted, if not launched, into literary pursuits by Lord Dunsany's uncle Sir Horace Plunkett, prominent in agricultural reform and by 1899 Vice-President of the Irish Department of Agriculture. He met AE in a drapery shop. He established him as editor of an agricultural magazine. He wrote to Lady Betty Balfour of Lord Dunsany's development as a poet and of a publication in the Pall Mall magazine and 'some lines of a nephew of mine aetat eighteen. They are a happiness to me. If you knew the boy and his parents you would marvel at the product of his brain. He has a talent for chess and for upsetting things. He can draw a nightmare, but that he can write simple and rather musical English is a revelation that gladdens the avuncular heart.'

Uncle Horace introduced Lord Dunsany to some of the figures in the Celtic Renaissance including AE and WB Yeats.

Lord Dunsany had been born in 1878. He was thirty-four when he and Francis Ledwidge first met. Although by 1912 Lord Dunsany had arrived at the happy status of an established writer his journey had been hard and often disappointing. He did not use or seek to use his social pre-eminence in any way to advance his career as a writer. So Francis Ledwidge had the good luck to find a friend and patron who himself had had a hard struggle up the ladder.

Lord Dunsany invited Francis Ledwidge to Dunsany Castle. He opened the library to him for work or reading or to borrow books. He introduced him to the Editor of the Saturday Review; which unlike some of the Meath papers which had published Ledwidge's poetry, paid for it. The Saturday Review published among other of Ledwidge's poems *Behind The Closed Eye.* He was paid eight guineas for it.

He read his poems to Lord Dunsany who passed on to him his own expertise on how to write. He suggested improvements. He wrote letters of introduction to periodicals which he thought might be interested in Francis Ledwidge's work. He was in all senses his patron from when they met until Ledwidge's death in 1917.

Francis Ledwidge isolated the inspiration given to him by Lord Dunsany in a letter which he wrote to him in later years. 'I often think on the beautiful afternoons we used to spend at Dunsany Castle, I listening enraptured to your latest or wondering whether a comma or a semi-colon was the proper stop at some of my lines which you were soon to see. Then the long ride home with beautiful memories of your appreciation, reciting my latest all the miles until the pedals of my bicycle turned to the rhythm of the piece, delaying me often, for you know how I love slow rhythm and short words.'

In October 1912 Lord Dunsany introduced Francis Ledwidge to the National Library Society, 6 St Stephen's Green. His paper was called *A New Poet*. He said of Ledwidge 'He knows nothing about technique and far less about grammar, but he has great ideas and conceptions of the poet and sees the vaste figures, the giant forces, and the elemental powers striving amongst the hills.' He read a number of Ledwidge's poems. At the gathering was Padraic Colum whose connection with Francis Ledwidge we will explore in due course.

Padraic Colum wrote an appreciation. 'Can aught good come out of County Meath one of the speakers asked one of the speakers at this lecture. They thought that this land of ranches and bullocks did not favour the production of poetry. But Lord Dunsany insisted that Meath was the part of Ireland most favourable to the production of high-spirited things. Did not the Meath people live under the shadow of Tara? And since they had fought for the good lands, was not the dust of the best of Ireland's kings under their feet?

The unique knowledge which Mr Ledwidge possesses is of the fields of Meath, and this knowledge makes him one of the company of old Irish poets who sang of the deer on the hillside, the badger coming out of his holes, the crane crying over a lake, the blackbird singing in a bush. When he writes of Finn's men, I think he gets the atmosphere that is in the old Fenian poetry.

Francis Ledwidge is lucky in his birthplace, and lucky in his discoverer. Lord Dunsany has made a magnificent attempt to break the decree that a poet may not be famous till all the tale of the years is told.'

Lord Dunsany shared his love of poetry, his knowledge, his literary expertise with Francis Ledwidge. But as important as any of these he gave him confidence. He told Padraic Colum shortly after meeting him in 1912 that thanks to Lord Dunsany, his prospects of making a living out of writing poetry were bright.

The local press were aware of Lord Dunsany's interest in Francis Ledwidge's poetry. The Drogheda Independent wrote 'Our young friend, Mr FE Ledwidge has been getting on. His poetry has won for him a place among the sons of genius and last week Lord Dunsany, and some other literary celebrities feted the young Meathman in the Capital. His latest contribution to the Saturday Review was then read, and the congratulations of his new found friends was extended to the promising young Poet. The poem in question styled *All-Hallows Eve* is full of beautiful imagery and praising and quaint and rather creepy concepts.'

ALL-HALLOWS EVE

The dreadful hour is sighing for a moon
To light old lovers to a place of tryst,
And old footsteps from blessed acres soon
On old known pathways will be lightly prest;
And winds that went to eavesdrop since the noon,
Kinking at some old tale told sweetly brief,
Will give a cowslick to the yarrow leaf,
And sling the round nut from the hazel down.

And there will be old yarn-balls, and old spells
In broken lime-kilns, and old eyes will peer
For constant lovers in old spidery wells,
And old embraces will grow newly dear.
And some may meet old lovers in old dells.
And some in doors ajar in towns light-lorn –
But two will meet beneath a gnarly thorn
Deep in the bosom of the windy fells.

Then when the night slopes home and white-faced day
Yawns in the east there will be sad farewells;
And many feet will tap a lonely way
Back to the comfort of their chilly cells,
And eyes will backward turn and long to stay
Where love first found them in the clover bloom –
But one will never seek the lonely tomb,
And two will linger at the tryst alway.

There is no doubt that in this poem the concepts are more subtle, the language more taut, and the lines more disciplined than in earlier poetry. Francis Ledwidge would have been the first to acknowledge that improvement in the style of his poetry owed something to the guidance of Lord Dunsany.

It was through Lord Dunsany that Francis Ledwidge met Oliver St John Gogarty, Thomas McDonagh and Katherine Tynan. Lord Dunsany believed that it would help him to meet contemporary writers. He introduced him whenever possible. Thomas McDonagh was shot for his part in the 1916 East Rising. His death inspired one of Francis Ledwidge's greatest poems *Thomas McDonagh*. The executions following the Easter Rising affected Francis Ledwidge's attitudes more significantly than any other single event after he joined the army. We will consider it in the context of Francis Ledwidge and the Easter Rising.

Katherine Tynan was Ledwidge's most important contact in the literary world of Ireland after Lord Dunsany. She was particularly important to him after he went to war. It is apparent that Lord Dunsany treated Francis Ledwidge as a friend; and what a friend for someone starting out to become a poet.

Lord Dunsany was fanatically loyal to the art of poetry. He said speaking in London 'For what is it to be a poet. It is to see at a glance the glory of the world, to see beauty in all its forms and manifestations, to feel ugliness like a pain, to resent the wrongs of others as bitterly as one's own, to know mankind as others know single men, to know nature as botanists know a flower, to be thought a fool, to hear at moments the clear voice of God.' Is this Ireland's answer to Shelley's Defence of Poetry?

Lord Dunsany's support of Francis Ledwidge and his encouragement of his writing were unstinted. He wrote in 1913 on return from big game hunting in Africa 'I wrote little that summer but I had the interest and pleasure of collecting another man's poems to make a book. For a memorable event had occurred the year before when I got a letter from a young Irishman enclosing a copybook full of verses and asking if they were any good. He was Francis Ledwidge. I was astonished by the brilliance of that eye that looked at the fields of Meath and seen there all the simple birds and flowers, with a vividness that made those pages like a magnifying glass, through which one looked at familiar things seen thus for the first time. I wrote to him greeting him as a true poet, which indeed he was, and his gratitude for that was intense, though quite undeserved; for as I have said elsewhere, the lark owes nothing to us for knowing that he is a lark. From that time he poured out poems, and was still doing so, and I have made a selection of them for his book. These poems were so unexpected and were sent or brought to me so frequently that they gave me the impression that this Irish villager had found some offer, stored in a golden age, brimful of lyrics and lost long ago.'

Francis Ledwidge, when opportunity offered, detailed the pains and pleasures of his writing to Lord Dunsany. He wrote in 1914 before going to war 'I have been a few days without writing a line, and feeling very miserable when I recollected that the cure for that was a perusal of all your Lordship's letters to me, so now I have written the best things of my life in a poem *Ulysses With Calypso*. I scored inner after inner. I am as far as 100 lines but not near finished yet. So here are a few of my best Ulysses; weary wandering the seas, and thinking of his queen and son away in far Ithaca was now marooned on the island of Oxygia.

'In the ears
Of shadowy hollows and twisted crags
Bird song and water song made sweet alloy of sounds'
And speaking of whins (furz):
'So full of God
He thought he entered his beloved land
Under wide flags that whipped the coloured air'

'Beloved land' is bad. But 'wide flags' and 'whipped'
particularly the latter gave me such delight that I smoked an hour after getting them.'

It seems that this poem cannot have been finished. It does not feature in the
Complete Poems of Francis Ledwidge edited by Lord Dunsany or in the *Complete
Poems* edited by Alice Curtayne and published in 1974. It is not included as a poem
in Liam O'Meara's Complete Poems but is mentioned in a list said to be a list of all
poems together with all fragments and juvenilia.

Lord Dunsany included Francis Ledwidge in areas of his life other than poetry.
He was an enthusiastic cricketer. He had a cricket pitch at Dunsany Castle. He invited gentlemen and players of distinction to play. He devoted summer Sundays to village cricket. Francis Ledwidge wrote to him on 1 August 1914, three days before
England and Germany were at war 'You must be tired of the way I change my tune
so often. The enclosed may lightly be termed a serenade because I wrote it in the
middle of the night, not at another's window, but at my own. I meant to send your
lordship a better copy, but I am tired and couldn't face to type it over again until I
know if it is any good. Aren't you playing cricket next week? I would very much like
to see another game.'

This letter, as many other letters from Francis Ledwidge to Lord Dunsany, is interesting as a study of the Irish class structure before the First World War. Ledwidge's
letters are respectful but in no way deferential. They suggest that then, as now, in
Irish society everyone is included. They are in a sense, letters between equals; if not
equals in the nominal social sense; equals in the pursuit of perfection in the writing
of poetry.

Lord Dunsany was sociable rather than social. He enjoyed entertaining at
Dunsany Castle. His method of summoning the butler to the dining room was to
fire a bullet from his revolver at the bell which summoned the butler. On one particular occasion his eye was out. He continually missed the bell but surrounded its
immediate area with seven or eight shots. Eventually the butler entered no doubt
concerned with the firing from the dining room. Lord Dunsany said simply, 'I

didn't ring.' He hadn't hit the bell with a single shot.

On 6 August 1914 Francis Ledwidge wrote to Lord Dunsany 'I've sprained my ankle jumping at a sports here, and have been very bad all the week. Your Lordship knows the sickening sensation of a sprained ankle. I was in bad humour for poetry. There will be nobody to read us now at all on account of the war; but it will be easy for posterity to remember the dates of our writings, if we live.

PS I will probably be called to defend the coasts of Ireland from our common enemy. God send.'

... It was a PS which was fulfilled all too soon.

Lady Dunsany liked Francis Ledwidge and described him as 'A nice youth with a fine straightforward face and that combination of naturally perfect manners with a village education and accent that is found in Irish peasants, though by no means universally there, and certainly nowhere else. He seems a real poet, no imitations or affections.'

Lord Dunsany joined the army immediately on the declaration of war. He was posted to the Royal Inniskilling Fusiliers.

He settled an allowance on Francis Ledwidge to be paid during his absence at the war; an arrangement not in any way requested by Francis Ledwidge and which he was reluctant to accept. Lord Dunsany insisted. He wished him to be able to continue to write whatever financial turmoil might follow the outbreak of war.

We will see that the friendship and support which Lord Dunsany had given Francis Ledwidge from 1912 continued after he joined the army in 1914. It is scarcely surprising that Francis Ledwidge felt an intense gratitude for the years of support from 1912 apparent in his poem *To Lord Dunsany.*

> For you I knit these lines, and on their ends
> Hang little tossing bells to ring you home.
> The music is all cracked, and Poesy tends
> To richer blooms than mine; but you who roam
> Thro' coloured gardens of the highest muse,
> And leave the door ajar sometimes that we
> May steal small breathing things of reds and blues
> And things of white sucked empty by the bee,
> Will listen to this bunch of bells from me.
>
> My cowslips ring you welcome to the land
> Your muse brings honour to in many a tongue,

Not only that I long to clasp your hand,
But that you're missed by poets who have sung
And viewed with doubt the music of their verse
All the long winter, for you love to bring
The true note in and say the wise thing terse,
And show what birds go lame upon a wing,
And where the weeds among the flowers do spring.

This poem of welcome and admiration suggests at least some of the scope of Lord Dunsany's life and experience.

He was a traveller to obscure parts of Africa and the Sahara desert when travel was distinctly less comfortable than at present.

In the autumn of 1913 he wrote to Lady Dunsany at the end of a big game visit to Africa 'This is my bag. 3 Jackals, 4 Congoni, 4 Wart-berg, 3 Stainbuck, 6 Zebras, 1 Waterbuck, 1 Rhineoceros, 8 Impala, 5 Thompson Gazelles, 4 Hyena, 1 Lion, 1 Dik, 4 Oryx, 1 Gernock, 2 Queen Strats, 1 Hare, 1 Snake, 2 Great Bustard, 2 Lesser Bustard, 5 Guinea Fowl, 9 Spear Fowl, 2 Partridges, 10 Quail, 1 Snipe, 4 Pigeons, 9 Red-legged Plover, 1 Grey legged Plover and two various birds. Total 55 beasts and 47 birds. Total 102.'

He was a playwright. By 1910 he had published two books of plays; and by 1914 his plays had been produced at the Abbey Theatre in Dublin. *Gods Of The Mountain* was produced at the Haymarket in London. His plays have not survived the century as have the plays of Sean O'Casey. But to write plays at all which were produced at the same time in London and Dublin indicates a degree of expertise.

Lord Dunsany wrote at enormous speed. He did not revise. He was an inspirational writer. He wrote in 1916 to Stuart Walker 'I try sometimes to explain genius to people who mistrust or hate it by telling them it is doing anything as a fish swims or a swallow flies, perfectly, simply and with an absolute ease. Genius is in fact an infinite capacity for not taking pains.' Further, he wrote in an article in 1934 'Am I a high-brow'? 'My theory of the arts is that they are products of human emotions, that human feelings are their raw material and that intellect should not be brought in except when absolutely necessary, to put the material together. The more the intellect is used, the less in my opinion is the man an artist and the more he becomes a mathematician, a scientist or a trickster.'

He was a storyteller and novelist. He was a poet. His experiences of war stimulated his deepest poetic sensitivity.

A DIRGE OF VICTORY

Lift not thy trumpet, Victory, to the sky
Nor through battalions nor by batteries blow
But our hollows full of old wire go,
Where among dregs of war the long-dead lie,
With wasted iron that the guns passed by
When they went eastwards like a tide at flow;
Then blow they trumpet that the dead may know,
Who waited for thy coming, Victory,
It is not we that have deserved thy wreath
They waited then among the towering weeds:
The deep mud burned under the reservist's breath,
And winter cracked the bones that no man heeds
Hundreds of nights flamed by: the seasons passed
And thou hast come to them at last.

He wrote while in the trenches in 1917.

SONGS OF AN EVIL WOOD

There is no wrath in the stars,
They do not rage in the sky;
I look from the evil wood
And find myself wondering why.

Why do they not scream out
And grapple star against star,
Seeking for blood in the wood
As all things round me are?

But they do not glare like the sky
On flash like the deeps of the wood;
But they shine softly on
In their sacred solitude.

To their high happy haunts
Silence from us has flown

She whom we loved of old
And know it now she is gone.

When will she come again
Though for one second only?
She whom we loved is gone
And the whole world is lonely.

Lord Dunsany was an essayist. *Unhappy Far Off Things* is a supremely sensitive series of essays of the state of France in war; from *The Homes Of Arras*. 'Ruin today is destruction and sorrow and debt and loss, come down untidily upon modern homes and cutting off ordinary generations, smashing the implements of familiar trades and making common avocations obsolete. It is no longer the guardian and chronicle of ages that we should otherwise forget: Ruin today is an age heaped upon rubble around us before it has ceased to be still green in our memory. Quite ordinary wardrobes in unseemly attitudes gape out from bedrooms whose front walls are gone, in houses whose most inner design shows unconcealed to the cold gaze of the street. The rooms have neither mystery nor adornment. Burst mattresses loll down from bedraggled beds. No one has come to tidy them up for years. And roofs have slanted down as low as the first floor.'

Tales Of War is a series of stories and essays based on Lord Dunsany's experiences in the war in France. They illustrate his extraordinary power of creating something original and beautiful out of a horror situation. The quality of his writing has a liquid lucidity.

From *Spring In England And Flanders* in *Tales Of War*. 'To turn from Kent to Flanders is to turn to a time of mourning through all seasons alike. Spring there brings out no leaf on myriad oaks, nor the haze of green that floats like a halo over the heads of the birch trees, that stand with their fairy-like trunks haunting the deeps of the woods. For miles and miles and miles summer ripens no crops, leads out no maidens laughing in the moonlight, and brings no harvest home. When autumn looks on orchards in all that region of mourning he looks upon barren trees that will never blossom again. Winter draws in no sturdy farmers at evening to sit before cheerful fires, families meet not at Christmas, and the bells are dumb in Belfries; for all by which a man might remember home has been utterly swept away: has been swept away to make a maniacal dancing ground on which a murderous people dance to their deaths led by a shallow, clever, callous, imperial clown.

Then they dance to their doom till their feet shall find the precipice that was prepared for them on the day that they planned the evil things they have done.'

Tales Of War showed how Lord Dunsany merged his wide experiences of life when writing about war; before the war big game hunting had been a prominent interest. In the essay *Shells* he writes 'Another of the voices of the night is the whine the shell makes in coming; it is not unlike the cry the haena utters as soon as it is dark in Africa. 'How nice traveller would taste' the haena seems to say 'I want dead white man.' It is the rising note of the shell as it comes nearer, and its dying away when it has gone over, that makes it reminiscent of the haena's method of diction ... and then there is the gas shell, which goes over gurgling gluttonously probably in big herds, putting down a barrage. It is the liquid inside that gurgles before it is turned to gas by the wild explosion; that is the explanation of it yet does not prevent one picturing a tribe of cannibals who have wounded some nice juicy man and smacking their chops and dribbling in anticipation.'

Lord Dunsany's sense of climax, even in a short story is evident in *Herr Schhhhrilzchaun* from *Tales Of War*. It is a story of an old German couple, whose four sons are at the war, who are being slowly reduced to starvation. They have a pig. They are not allowed to kill it. The Kaiser is on manoeuvres nearby. When Herr Schnitzchaazer returned there was blood on his knife. 'What have you done' the old woman asked him calmly. 'I have killed our pig' he said 'We are lost, we are lost,' she cried 'We may not kill our pig. Hunger has made you mad. You have ruined us' 'I will not bear it any longer' he said 'I have killed our pig' 'But they will never let us eat it' she cried. 'Oh you have ruined us' 'If you do not dare to kill our pig' he said 'why did you not stop me when you saw me go? You saw me go with the knife' 'I thought' she said 'You were going to kill the Kaiser.'

He was a novelist. His most renowned novel being *The Curse Of The Wise Woman* written late in his life in 1933 and being autobiographical in tone. This was followed in 1936 by *Talks With Dean Stanley* and in 1939 by *The Story Of Mona Keen*.

Lord Dunsany was acquainted with the leaders of the Celtic Renaissance. He was not a part of it. His relationship with WB Yeats became more distant over time. In the course of a letter to his wife he wrote:

Kildare Street Club
Dublin M 24

My Darling Mink,

I forgot to tell you that when I suggested assisting Irish poets AE was for a paper that should give them an outlet. My offer of about £50 of course holds good if he wants a paper.

It will also bring them together to talk which stimulates the literary feeling. It is true that though Ireland is full of poets they don't trouble to write. I used to say so and now AE says it. But the paper will compel them to. Yesterday Miss Hamilton at my request invited Yeats to share my hospitality at the Arts Club. (I was talking rather well there, Mink).

Yeats mentioned an old idea of mine that he must have got hold of through Miss Hamilton. I had forgotten, so have you, but I recall it clearly now.

Yeats said I should write a little one-act play on it, it was such a good idea. I said I knew utterly nothing of the stage, or how to write a play. He also said that if I didn't write it he thought he should have to get someone to steal it from me! Then I thought I'd try. After lunch I came here, then I motored to Kilteragh by four and saw Baby for a moment and had tea and wrote the play by 7.30 said goodnight to Baby and dined here. After dinner I descended on the poet and read him the play and when all the good passages have been deleted by him and Lady Gregory it is going to be acted at the Abbey Theatre on April 29 and 30 and May 1. Plays never run more than three days there I think.

Lord and Lady Dunsany were very fond of Yeats referring to him as 'the Great Irish poet.' They were friendly but never close and grew more distant as the years went on.

Lord Dunsany gave Yeats £300 for the Abbey. Yeats wrote to his father 'Dunsany is a man of genius with a very fine style I think. I want to get him into the movement.' He described him as a handsome young man with a beautiful house full of pictures. He described his work to Lady Gregory as very nearly very good.

Yeats later described Lord Dunsany's talent. 'He is a man in whose genius I believe, though I am very doubtful if it will ever come to anything. He is one of the few English speaking men of today who has a gift for style like Baudelaire in the Prose poems. I am trying to make a dramatist of him. But he doesn't know how to revisit his work and he has little patience. He is splendid for a scene and then all goes to pieces. But what is good in his work is nearly as good as it can be. It is all worked out of time and out of space. Impossible cities and impossible wildernesses, and people with wonderful names, invented by himself, but alas! it is a great misfortune to be born in the Peerage. Life is too pleasant for him. Fifty pounds a year and a drunken mistress would be the making of him.'

His next letter was from the Kildare Street Club to his wife.

My Darling Mink,

I wrote a little more dialogue for my play yesterday as Yeats told me that I had left one of the characters silent for too long. So I'll probably send it to you tomorrow.

By the way I didn't have to speak on the Drama at the Arts club after all.

There died yesterday morning Synge, and Yeats came down to the Arts Club and spoke of him, I in the chair. He was quite young and a great gain to Ireland and a great loss. He was engaged to be married.

I admire Yeats more and more. AE should stand in huge metropolitan ways and prophesy downfalls and the ruin of Kings till the dusty grey winds wept; and Yeats should sing into being fantastic towns with Apollonian song.

I can see them both doing it, AE chanting with the wind in the ends of his beard and Yeats waving his right hand and singing more softly, his jet hair drooped to his left eyebrow …

He wrote in his diary dated 28 March 1910:

I think I will begin a diary again after five years interval. Lady Gregory and Mr WB Yeats have been staying here and left today. He is the most charming and wisest of people – very entertaining full of learning and with the most courteous manners. He is also handsome with a very nice voice.

In February 1911 Yeats wrote to Lord Dunsany asking permission for his sister to publish selections from his writing. 'You will be there with Lady Gregory and JM Synge, and Douglas Hyde and AE and the rest of us. It is my way of claiming you for Ireland.'

Lord Dunsany used his connection with the Earl of Iveagh, Chancellor of Trinity College, Dublin to attempt to get Yeats appointed to the Chair of English Literature at Trinity. The incumbent Professor was Dowden and he was against Yeats describing him as no scholar.

Lord Dunsany was significantly more friendly with Oliver St John Gogarty than with Yeats. Gogarty left his first impression of Lord Dunsany at a Hunt Ball at Dunsany. 'While it was in full swing I wandered through the passages searching for some place where I might sit in quiet and get, if necessary, the spirit of the thing, without the action; for I am strangely averse to group enjoyments of any kind. At last I found a settee in a corridor at one end of which a tall youth was seated biting a fingernail. His hair was fair, his forehead extraordinary high, noble and unfurrowed. His mouth which a light moustache left unconcealed, was imperious with a clear chin line under a cold beauty of eyes and brow. He looked as if he belonged to a race aloof, exempt from the pathos of the common concerns of mankind. I took a seat beside him for there was none other to be had.'

They remained close personal friends for the rest of their lives.

Gogarty wrote in an unpublished Essay on Dunsany 'It would be a mistake to think that the rivalry between Dunsany and Yeats was a literary one. Far from it. Yeats had no rival to fear among contemporary poets. It was not so much rivalry on

Yeats' part (shocking to say it before it can be explained) as it was envy. Yeats, though his descent was from parsons, dearly loved a lord. He was at heart an aristocrat, and it must always have been a disappointment to him that he was not born one. Not by taking thought could he trace his descent from the year 1181 ... This then was at the bottom the cause of the failure of friendship between Dunsany and Yeats. Dunsany sensed some sort of opposition, real and imaginary for some of the forms it was reputed to have taken were probably part of over sensitive suspicion.'

The Dunsanys were less well acquainted with Lady Gregory than with Yeats and referred to her as 'The Bad Old Woman in Black' from the title of one of his own stories.

He wrote in his diary in March 1910 'Lady Gregory is a wonderful old lady but she is obviously aware of the fact – it is doubtless very clever to begin writing books and plays (very very good ones too) quite late in life and to talk well too – but she has not Yeats's gift of helping her listener out and I am afraid is touched with the snobbishness which consists in gibing at Royalty while making it very clear that those are the circles she could move in if she wasn't so far above them.'

The poet Padraic Colum stayed at Dunsany. Lady Dunsany wrote 'I believe he started life as a cattle drover. He has a fine head and is a very nice little man. We had a heated argument at dinner ... Eddie, brilliant talker though he is, is so medieval in his views that it is difficult for him and an advanced nationalist to argue ... I think my parents' hair would stand on end if they knew we had guests of that kind for dinner.'

Lord Dunsany and Padraic Colum combined to write *Alexander*. Lord Dunsany's interest in the Celtic Renaissance and its characters declined after the war. He saw little of Yeats, more dominant than ever in Irish letters. Yeats founded his Irish Academy of Letters in 1932. He invited Lord Dunsany to be an associate member only. This offended Lord Dunsany significantly and they never became friendly again.

Yeats was however never hostile to the charms of the great country houses of Ireland.

ANCESTRAL HOUSES

> Surely among a rich man's flowering lawns,
> Amid the rustle of his planted hills,
> Life overflows without ambitious pains;
> And rains down life until the basin spills,
> And mounts more dizzy high the more it rains
> As though to choose whatever shape it wills

And never stoop to a mechanical
Or servile shape, at others' beck and call.

Mere dreams, mere dreams! Yet Homer had not sung
Had he not found it certain beyond dreams
That out of life's own self-delight had sprung
The abounding glittering jet; though now it seems
As if some marvellous empty sea-shell flung
Out of the obscure dark of the rich streams,
And not a fountain, were the symbol which
Shadows the inherited glory of the rich.

Some violent bitter man, some powerful man
Called architect and artist in, that they,
Bitter and violent men, might rear in stone
The sweetness that all longed for night and day,
The gentleness none there had ever known;
But when the master's buried mice can play,
And maybe the great-grandson of that house,
For all its bronze and marble, 's but a mouse.

O what if gardens where the peacock strays
With delicate feet upon old terraces,
Or else all Juno from an urn displays
Before the indifferent garden deities;
O what if levelled lawns and gravelled ways
Where slippered Contemplation finds his ease
And Childhood a delight for every sense,
But take our greatness with our violence?

What if the glory of escutcheoned doors,
And buildings that a haughtier age designed,
The pacing to and fro on polished floors
Amid great chambers and long galleries, lined
With famous portraits of our ancestors;
What if those things the greatest of mankind
Consider most to magnify, or to bless,
But take our greatness with our bitterness.

The closing lines of *A Prayer For My Daughter*:

> And may her bridegroom bring her to a house
> Where all's accustomed, ceremonious;
> For arrogance and hatred are the wares
> Peddled in the thoroughfares.
> How but in custom and in ceremony
> Are innocence and beauty born?
> Ceremony's a name for the rich horn,
> And custom for the spreading laurel tree.

Perhaps the explanation of the absence of any close literary contact between Yeats and Lord Dunsany was simply the chemistry of human nature. Yeats was essentially an intellectual, a city dweller preoccupied with his own art and with his dreams for an Irish National theatre. He was surrounded by a comparatively small group of friends, in particular Lady Gregory and Synge in his lifetime. Lord Dunsany was essentially a countryman, a sportsman, a traveller who was also a writer of mighty talent. But whatever the cause the loss was Francis Ledwidge's. If Lord Dunsany had been in close friendship with Yeats he would have insisted upon introducing Francis Ledwidge; and whatever Francis Ledwidge's reservation about Yeats's poetry contact with the dominant poet of Ireland would have been exciting for him.

The diversity of Lord Dunsany's life and achievements is most evident in his best book *My Ireland*. In addition to his accomplishments as a playwright, poet, novelist, essayist and soldier *My Ireland* shows in the clearest terms that he was a man of letters in the widest sense. It covers his close association with and admiration for the poetry, painting and imagination of AE; his fascination with Irish legend, particularly as centred in Tara, so near his own home; his enthusiasm for the inspiration of St Patrick: 'So St Patrick went from Tara, unhindered by the High King, although he had not converted him, and went westwards preaching and spreading the Christian faith. So that, as we stand on Tara, we look over land that knew Christianity when in most other lands there were still being worshipped gods against whom I do not wish to say anything critical, but who certainly had a liking for human sacrifice (if their priests understood their wishes), a custom with which since the teaching of Patrick no Irishmen have had anything to do, for any Cause except politics.'

It discloses his fascination with ruins, particularly ruins on or near the Boyne.

The book is also testament to Lord Dunsany's life as a sportsman. It gives a gorgeous picture of the life of sport, particularly shooting and hunting, available in

Ireland for those who could get it. He was a superb shot and devoted many happy hours to shooting woodcock, golden plovers, duck, pigeon, geese and teal.

He wrote extensively of woodcock: 'The woodcock is a bird far worthier of a sportsman, for his coming depends not on temporal things, like a cheque to a poulterer, but on powers that can grip man as well as the woodcock: the north wind and the cold. You do not depend for the woodcock on anything you can control, but on some fierce favourable wind and the full moon and the winter …'

'Possibly, if we could meet as disembodied spirits, far from our present prejudices and preferences, and could discuss the matter, we might admit that the woodcock's way of keeping warm, with a big trunk to the north of him and his feathers puffed out, and the storm rushing angrily by him a few inches away, was more exciting than ours. Possibly the spirit of the woodcock would not change, even if the change is allowed, his shelter of timber and branches or couch of moss, for our fires and our easy chairs and our bell to ring for more coal. And perhaps if we offered those comforts of ours in exchange, we might see the contempt of a spirit that had known the north wind close, for those who had heard it rarely and as a stranger. This seems to me likely enough, though some may find it too fanciful. But those who do not care for fanciful things have no reason to read about Ireland.'

'Though I have certainly never shown any gratitude to the woodcock, I am grateful to him for the romance of his great journeys, which add a thrill to sport. It is the same with the wild geese, and all these wanderers: they seem to bring the ends of the earth nearer; or rather, though leaving them infinitely remote, they bring their mystery nearer, till the splendour of Arctic mountains and Northern Lights are things at which our imaginations can peer, as they might otherwise never do, were they not awoken from sleep by the call in the sky that the geese make high in a wind going triumphing southwards; or the sudden notes, that a magical shepherd might draw from a hidden flute, which teach that the golden plover are moving inland from storms. Once by a camp-fire in Africa a man told me how, near where we then were, he had been called from his tent by his gun-bearer and saw a herd of elephants going by in the moonlight, quite silently, and evidently making some great journey. I felt, as I heard that story, as I do when I learn that the woodcock are in, or I hear the geese going over; it is as though for a moment we had a surreptitious glimpse of the affairs of Nature, great enterprises closely in touch with winds and seasons and moonlight, beside which our undertakings appear narrow and local.'

He writes of golden plovers, gray lags, duck, pigeons, geese, woodcock, snipe, teal with such enthusiasm and knowledge that it is difficult to imagine that his achievements extended far and wide in the realms of literature, poetry and writing.

Lord Dunsany's love of hunting was a close second to his love of shooting. He wrote extensively of the great sport of fox hunting in *My Ireland*. 'There was a time when I had come in from a very good day with my harriers, for I had a pack of my own in those days. It was a day in March, and I was having a cup of tea, after three good runs with my hounds: the first was twenty minutes, my hunting diary tells me, the next twenty-five and the last one thirty-five, and I felt I had had a good day. It was almost five o'clock and there was still plenty of light, when, looking out of the window, I saw battle running near a wood. And it turned out that the Ward Hounds were in the wood, and coming in my direction. I had a fresh horse saddled and got on to him as soon as I could, and galloped off to overtake the Ward. I came up with them before I had gone two miles; and there was I with a fresh horse, among men who had already done three miles when they came to my wood, and it was their second hunt that day. It was a piece of luck such as might come one's way once in a lifetime; and here it had come to me.

And when it came, it came abundantly. For not only was I there on a fresh horse with the Ward, but I was in one of the finest hunts they were ever to have. I do not say that they have not had many as good, but it was one of their great hunts and it was the first time that they had enlarged that wonderful hind that became an outlier, living most in my woods and being hunted off and on for several years, giving a memorable hunt every time. Of course with my fresh horse, once I had caught them up, I had the advantage that a man with a joker in his hand would have at a game of bridge, or a bowler at cricket enjoying the use of a Mills bomb.

We were going westwards and a tired field were dropping away, until there was only one other man beside myself with the hounds, a Mr Davis, as my hunting diary records. A house that I knew flashed by us, and I knew we had come eight miles from my own door, going straight. And then for a very brief time I remember being alone with the Ward Hounds, which I never had been before and was never to be again. Brindley, the huntsman, soon came up again and one of the whips and, I think, Mr Davis, although the *Irish Times* of March 15, 1904, only records Brindley and one whip and me as reaching the end of the run. And the end of the run was simply the end of the day; with the Boyne before us and night coming up from behind, Brindley called his hounds off and we turned homewards. Then night came down in earnest and even the white patches on the hounds' backs disappeared, and the only light we saw was from sparks from the horses' hooves. It had been a run of two hours, the first twenty minutes of which I had not seen, and I had nothing to boast of in getting to the end of it, when luck played so large a part; but the time when I was alone with them in the sunlight, and Brindley in the twilight at the back of the Boyne, and the dark road, riding home, live clearly yet in my memories.'

In the summer it was cricket. 'One field of mine, in between two woods, has always a lonely look to me, especially at evening; most of all on a fine summer's evening with the sun still in the sky; for it is a cricket-field, and the late light of warm days always reminds me of old cricket-matches, when the excitement was increasing with every over and umpires would soon draw stumps. Here, since the later years of the last century, we used to play cricket through most of August and into September, against the cricket teams of cavalry regiments from the Curragh and battalions quartered in Dublin, as well as the Free Foresters, the MCC and other English teams, and the Shulers, the Irish equivalent of the Zingari, and many other Irish teams. With the exception of the war we played cricket there right up to the time when Parliament passed what they called the Treaty, and the resultant troubles made the roads too difficult and uncertain for me to be able to collect a team.

During those years all the principal cricketers of Ireland played cricket on that ground, and it looks lonely without them ... Bowling on the damper Irish wicket, some of those who played cricket for me were able to get work on the ball that sometimes surprised more experienced English cricketers. One often played all the week, including Sundays; but on Sundays it was village cricket, cricket played by workmen who had no other day on which to play it. There was a school of thought in those days that held that cricket was a form of slavery inflicted on free men by a bloody tyrant, but this view was not so widely held as to prevent one easily finding twenty-two men to play on Sundays, and a much greater number to watch and have tea in the tent. And they played it well and enjoyed it.'

EIGHT

THE BLAST
OF WAR

*God, who at this time didst teach the hearts of thy faithful people, by
the sending to them the light of thy Holy Spirit; Grant us by the same
Spirit to have a right judgment in all things.*

[From the Collect for Whit Sunday]

ON 24 OCTOBER 1914 Francis Ledwidge joined the British Army; in particular the Royal Inniskilling Fusiliers then at Richmond Barracks, Dublin.
Why?

He was nationalist in sympathy; socialist in politics; Roman Catholic by way of
faith. So what was a nationalist, a socialist, a Roman Catholic up to in joining the
British Army in October 1914?

This matter has given rise to some speculation by those interested in the life and
times of Francis Ledwidge; in particular it is considered in some depth by Alice
Curtayne in her biography of Francis Ledwidge. Explanations vary. It has been suggested that frustration in love, based upon the last poem in *Songs Of The Fields* was
significant.

~~Morning in January~~

~~(~~Seen from the door of the Guard room, Richmond Barracks.)

----- ------

I would I had a little field somewhere
Beyond the cares of State to watch this bloom
Kindling ~~Kindling~~ in the distant east so fair
And lighting with *a* red dusk this sleepy room.
Surely 'tis Janus at the gate of Spring
Smiling with both his faces at the death
Of winter, ~~and~~ the near eves blackbirds sing
Along the country miles 'til out of breath.

The *starry pageant of the night* ~~night's torch-light procession now~~ has passed,
And where I stand in spirit other lights
Are on the waters' broken spaces massed,
Tumbling upon the wind-blown waves delights.
But here I must not linger lest my ear
Should hear the calling of the milk-white fall,
For I'm the slave of calls,now there,now here,
Where Life has strewn its gains,but to miss all.

Francis.E.Ledwidge.

Jan.'15.

A hitherto unpublished poem by Francis Ledwidge
from a private collection

AFTER MY LAST SONG

Where I shall rest when my last song is over
The air is smelling like a feast of wine;
And purple breakers of the windy clover
Shall roll to cool this burning brow of mine;
And there shall come to me when day is told
The peace of sleep when I am grey and old.

I'm wild for wandering to the far-off places
Since one forsook me whom I held most dear.
I want to see new wonders and new faces
Beyond East seas; but I will win back here
When my last song is sung, and veins are cold
As thawing snow, and I am grey and old.

Oh paining eyes, but not with salty weeping,
My heart is like a sod in winter rain;
Ere you will see those baying waters leaping
Like hungry hounds once more, how many a pain
Shall heal; but when my last short song is trolled
You'll sleep here on wan cheeks grown thin and old.

So a broken heart and an interest, perhaps a passion, in seeing far-off places were undoubtedly a part of Francis Ledwidge's psychological luggage in the months before he signed on at Richmond barracks.

He joined the regiment which Lord Dunsany had joined some weeks earlier. There is no evidence of any kind to suggest that he joined at Lord Dunsany's persuasion. Quite the reverse. Lord Dunsany advised him to continue his writing at home and arranged an allowance for him while, he, Lord Dunsany, was at war.

Francis Ledwidge was ill at ease having been elected to the Navan Rural District Council and Board of Guardians. It was an elected body which considered issues of local concern. Francis Ledwidge first attended on 1 July 1914. In August, September and October its meetings were embittered by discussions of the pro- or anti-Redmond position. Redmond's speech at Woodbridge, County Wicklow had excited deep division among the politically conscious:

> The interests of Ireland, of the whole of Ireland are at stake in this war
> undertaken in defence of the highest interests of religion and morality and

right. It would be a disgrace for ever to our country, a reproach to her manhood, and a denial of the lessons of her history if young Ireland confined their efforts to remaining at home to defend the shores of Ireland from an unlikely invasion, and shrinking from the duty of proving on the field of battle that gallantry and courage which have distinguished their race all through its history. I say to you therefore, your duty is two-fold. I am glad to see such magnificent material for soldiers around me, and I say to you, go on drilling and make yourselves efficient for the work, and then account yourselves as men not only in Ireland itself, but where ever the firing line extends in defence of right, of freedom and religion in this war.

The Navan Rural Council was strongly in favour of Redmond. Francis Ledwidge was less confident and more critical of the Redmond position. In one debate on a vote of congratulations to Mr Redmond and the Irish Parliamentary Party on their success in placing Home Rule on the Statute Book he expressed the view that 'so far as real Home Rule was concerned, they were as far off it today as ever.' In one debate when Councillor Bowens said, 'What was England's difficulty was now Ireland's difficulty, and what was England's downfall would also be Ireland's. What was England's uprise would be also Ireland's uprise.' *(Applause)*

He wondered at Mr Ledwidge or any other man calling himself an Irishman to stand up in that room and give expression to what he had said. Francis Ledwidge replied 'England's uprise has always been Ireland's downfall': Mr Bowens 'No, the days are gone when we had to complain of England. I tell you that these Irish soldiers who today are fighting in Belgium and France and elsewhere are the men who will raise Ireland here after.' *(Applause)* It is not the men who are talking in this boardroom, will they go out – these three or four little Sinn Feiners.' Mr Ledwidge 'In the North of Ireland the recruiting sergeants have been saying to the men "Go out and fight with anti-papal France". In the south of Ireland they will say "Go out and fight for Catholic Belgium". The people around Liege and Namur are the greatest Wallons and anti-clerics in the world and they have shown their brutality by their treatment of German prisoners'.

Mr Bowens: 'Does anyone believe in the sincerity of the Kaiser when he says that his heart bleeds for these people and the next day he goes and causes even more damage'? What was he (Mr Ledwidge)? Was he an Irishman or a pro-German? Mr Ledwidge 'I am anti-German and an Irishman.' Mr Bowens 'You are a pro-German.' Mr Bowens: 'It was on the fields of France that the young men of Ireland should be found if they wished to defeat the Germans because if the Germans ever landed in Ireland, our lands and property and possessions would be confiscated by the Germans. The Irish people were too few to be divided, and the whole trouble arose from publications in the Irish Volunteer.' Mr Kelly: Objected to Mr Ledwidge's remark that the Board was getting a name for being inconsistent. He thought he should withdraw that. He did not think that the Council was ever inconsistent. It was not he who proposed or seconded that the Irish Volunteer get the contract. Mr Ledwidge: 'I went even further and told the Council that it was becoming a name for inconsistency.' Chairman: 'What reason have you for saying that? I think you should withdraw that.' Mr Carty: 'Yes he should.' Mr Ledwidge: 'Every time I attend here something passed at the previous meeting is rescinded.' Mr Bowens: 'At the time the advertisement was given there was no division in the Volunteers.'

It is clear that Francis Ledwidge's days on the Navan District Council were less than fulfilled. Dissatisfaction with his first entry into public life was an element of his experiences at the outbreak of war.

In a letter dated 6 August 1914, two days after the declaration of war on 4 August, to Lord Dunsany, Francis Ledwidge added a post-script:

> P.S.: I will probably be called to defend the coasts of Ireland from our common enemy. God send.

Thoughts of service were in his mind from the earliest stage. This letter was written over two months before he was called a pro-German at a Navan Rural District Council meeting in October 1914.

Francis Ledwidge later said to Professor Lewis Chase 'Some of the people who knew me least imagine that I joined the army because I knew men were struggling for higher ideals and great enterprises, and I could not sit idle to watch them make for me a more beautiful world. They are mistaken. I joined the British army because she stood between Ireland and an enemy common to our civilization, and I would not have to say that she defended us while we did nothing at home but pass resolutions.'

Accordingly while in the summer and early autumn of 1914 when Europe shook with the blast of war it is correct that Francis Ledwidge's life was in the disarray of disappointment in love and disappointment in local politics; while it is correct that he cared for the idea of travel and that Lord Dunsany had already joined the British army in August 1914. It is not correct that he joined the British army for any of these reasons. He joined the British army because in the particular circumstances of the time he believed it to be the right thing to do; and because he had a right judgment in all things.

On 24 October 1914 Francis Ledwidge joined the Royal Inniskilling Fusiliers. His training was at Richmond Barracks, Dublin. According to early correspondence he enjoyed army life. He wrote in an early letter 'You can see I am not so badly off after all. I see Lord Dunsany every day, and in the evening we meet in his quarters and discuss poetry, the thing that matters.' It was a happy chance that he was in the same regiment and in the same place as Lord Dunsany. It was not every writer's experience to be able to carry on with their literary interests during their basic training. The letter continues 'At the recreation rooms on Saturday night next I am giving a reading from some of my embryo books. We will soon be leaving here for the North of Ireland to a shooting range there, and from thence to the seat of war. I look forward to poetry and fame after the war and feel that by joining I am helping to bring about peace and the old sublimity of which the world has been robbed.'

As soon as Francis Ledwidge was in the army he insisted that his allowance from Lord Dunsany ceased. He gave his mother's name as his dependent; in consequence she received half his pay. His pay was approximately 30 pence a week plus keep.

While in training he was advanced to the rank of Lance corporal. He became extremely friendly with an Ulsterman, Robert Christie, in the same regiment. Robert Christie's play '*The Dark Hour*' had been produced by the Abbey Theatre. He was in barracks in Omagh at the time and was unable to see his own play being produced.

Francis Ledwidge was given Christmas leave in December 1914. He spent it with his mother and brother Joe in Slane. Over Christmas 1914 he met up again with Lizzie Healey. She was a comfort after the heart-breaking loss of Ellie Vaughey whose marriage had taken place on 25 November while Francis Ledwidge was training at Richmond Barracks. He returned to Richmond Barracks after Christmas and wrote to Lizzie Healey on 6 January 1915 'I hope you are back in Wilkinstown again. Since I was home I was watching the days to pass when I could write to you as I promised. I did not like to write to you while you were in Slane: you know why. Of my life in the army since I was speaking to you there is nothing to write. In fact of my life anywhere it is not worth saying anything. I walk the bye-ways of the world like one pursued by a monstrous fear. Sometimes I think I am wandering towards a life full of sunshine and full of song and love, but it appears far away yet lures like the distances of my natural fields.'

He wrote again on 27 January 'I was home a fortnight ago and thought I might see you. When I came back we went away on a long march to the Curragh and are just back. I seize the very first opportunity of writing to you. Dear Lizzie, God bless you for the photograph. You can't ever know how much I prize it. I will always carry it with me until I bring it home again, and then I will work hard for one day to ask if I will be worthy of loving you. This is a terrible lot to hope for but I was ever strong in hope and why not one more effort at the greatest hope of all. My dear Lizzie, I am just after hearing that I am not for the war. I am sorry in a way as I would like to enter Berlin with the boys I trained with. It seems that they are going to keep me for clerical work and training recruits and as a reward will make an officer of me. Of course it is as an officer I entered the army and am on the waiting list for my commission. But I will try to get to the front as it would be a great experience.'

His army life and career were to develop differently from this optimistic forecast. In February 1915 he wrote to Lizzie Healey 'When I come home I will do great things, there is very little chance here, and besides I am so lonesome I can think of nothing but Slane and the great peace of the homeways, and you.

The enclosed verses are from my heart and if you discover faults in the lines pass them over on that account. I must close as it is growing late and I have a roll to call. Write when you can. Remember me to the bog and all the trees around Wilkinstown.'

Francis Ledwidge's enthusiasms for Lizzie Healey suggest that, however bitter his disappointment over his failure in love with Ellie Vaughey, he was one of those men who believed that there were as good fish in the sea as came out of it.

In March 1915 he wrote to Lizzie Healey 'When you have a minute to spare, drop me a few lines as I watch and watch for something from the old place everyday. I hope the little lad is very well. I saw Larry on duty yesterday. We were sending the Lord Lieutenant away and Larry was just opposite me. I winked at him and he winked back and I made a gesture which he must have understood. I was thinking of Fleming's gramophone and the 'Little Grey home in the West.' Larry was Lizzie Healey's brother. He was in the Dublin Metropolitan Police. These two letters of February and March 1915 are an indication that Slane and home were to remain an abiding source of strength throughout the war. They were to continue to be the principal fountains of inspiration of his poetry written at war as they had been before he joined the army.

He wrote again to Lizzie Healey from Richmond Barracks 'It is spring now and it must be lovely down in Wilkinstown. Are the birds singing yet? When you hear a blackbird think of me. A very nice lady journalist came to look for information from me yesterday. It seems my poem in 'The Times' (did you see it?) caused a little splash. She was about 20, tall, fair and passing for handsome. She asked me to tea on Sunday, but I am not going. You are very busy I am sure, but whenever you can won't you write me a few lines? I will remember you always.'

In the course of a letter written on 9 March 1915 to his great friend Matty McGoona he said 'I am glad we are going to the war, it will cheer me up, it will dispel those thoughts which are at war with me so long. Ellie Vaughey got married. That was a great blow, perhaps the greatest of all. I am going to try for a day home for St Patrick's Day. If I manage it, could you come to Slane. I want to see you so badly. How is your Pegasus? And how is the violin. Do you ever play sweet music now? Every time you play 'The Blackbird' think on me. I love that tune and snatches of it sing in my memory an odd time like ghosts haunting an old garden. My memory is no more than an old garden now full of the withered flowers of a dead summer.'

This letter makes clear that friends were as crucial to Francis Ledwidge as ever. Barrack life had done nothing to blunt the importance of friendship to him. Friends were to remain a sustaining strength and a continuing source of inspiration for his poetry.

Shortly afterwards he wrote to Lizzie, 'I must see you before I go to France. I have determined to go. We will not be longer than a few weeks now, and I must see you before I go. I feel sure that I will return again safely and then and then! Yes, when the war is over, if I am not shot I am coming back to Slane. I love it very much because from nowhere else have I ever had such calls to my heart. I love Stanley Hill and all the distances so blue around it. I love the Boyne and the fields through which it sings. I love the peace of it above all.'

This is the clearest testament in all his writing that Francis Ledwidge's treasure was in Slane, the blue distances of the Boyne and the fields through which it sings 'For where your treasure is, there will your heart be also' St Matthew, ch 5, v21.

He wrote a few days later to tell her about a dream, 'I thought I was out of the army and home again. It was a beautiful day, flowers everywhere, and birds. I could see all the old landmarks so loved by me as I crossed the fields down to the Boyne to meet you. We met at the Mill House. The meeting was by arrangement. You were sitting on the old paling there and singing a song I wrote many years ago. When you saw me coming you raced to meet me, and when we had greeted each other, we walked slowly down by the river, and you were telling me that you missed me when I was away. You said there was a void in your life, a sort of feeling making you hope no more for old aspirations. All our talk was of the past. I wonder why. It was a beautiful dream and when I wakened I was lonesome. I was lonesome all day thinking about it. I wrote this in a hurry to know if you had any unusual experience. I believe in dreams, and hope my pleasant one was not news of some misfortune having befallen you. You will let me know.'

Did wishful thinking have an input into this dream? Whatever the inspiration for this dream, it was not well received by Lizzie Healey. Thereafter Francis Ledwidge backed off dreams in his pursuit of Lizzie Healey. He wrote, 'I am very sorry that I surprised you so much with the hasty letter I wrote about my dream. I promise not to do so anymore. Looking at it now, it was very foolish of me, but God knows I am always doing things like that and never know how absurd it is until afterwards. It is the hurry to get things off my mind, and this hurry has often made me make mistakes in my life that I will lament forever. I will be home for St Patrick's Day. Of course I would love to cycle from Slane to Wilkinstown to see you. I won't see you anymore until after the war. We leave about the 29. I go home Tuesday evening and return Thursday morning.' Then a note 'This in a hurry to let you know I am on my way home. I will see you tomorrow (DV) about 3 o'clock. I wrote another note like this in barracks but can't find it. Perhaps someone would post it also.'

His leave for St Patrick's Day was cancelled and for the following weekend. He wrote:

> I am extremely sorry to let you know that I will hardly have the pleasure of seeing you this weekend no more than on St Patrick's Day. It is a terrible thing to think of but I'm afraid it must be. You see there are only two of us in the Orderly Room who can use a typewriter and while I was away at Dollmount last week firing, the other man went away on leave. Dear Lizzie, I must tell you about the violets. You don't understand. The mistake must have been mine. I will tell you all about it when I see you.

He did see her shortly afterwards on a Sunday visit to Wilkinstown where she was then living. On return to barracks he wrote:

> I am back again in the tents of Mars. I can hardly yet realise that I am really back, but it must be true as I see from my office window three or four hundred men at drill. I am back again indeed or at least my body is, but my soul is on a little road looking across a gate at a girl standing in a doorway. The road is in the village of Wilkinstown and you are the girl at the door.
>
> I am a thousand times the better of my visit to Wilkinstown. I had the happy realisation of hearing you say you would wait for me until I came back and of taking you in my arms. But although I am so much the better for this I am a lot the worse of it, as now, more than ever I know how much I want you and how much I love you. My love for you is as high as the stars.
>
> We enjoyed the evening immensely, the sport and the company. You must have been pretty sick of us by the time you got us away and I am sure you haven't recovered from the fatigue of the occasion yet. I forgot my stick, the little block which I meant to bring back. If you haven't burned it ere this, hang it upon a nail at the gable of the house until the war is over. It will be an excuse for me to go down again.

There is no doubt that Francis Ledwidge had moved into top romantic gear in pursuit of Lizzie Healey. On 31 March he wrote to her:

There is not a day in the calendar since I came here that I have not thought of everybody in our circle. I am sure it is lovely in the bog now. I would very much like to be walking to Carlonstown via Fletcherstown chapel, you with me of course. The people will be planting potatoes down there now and I am certain there is a scent in the air like a feast of wine. From the desk where I am writing this I see through a window across the soldiers' recreation ground spire on spire of Dublin, and hear the bells of trams and the shout of all its worry and woe, but my thoughts are in Wilkinstown in the little kitchen where I first took you in my arms. I see by a Liverpool paper today that I am at the war for the past fortnight and according to the Evening Mail, I sailed early in March.

I suppose you will spend Easter in Slane. I won't see poor old Slane any more until after the war. I can't rightly say when we leave here. I should say about the 15.

Most young men, particularly most young Irishmen, called to the army in war would carry with them thoughts of home and friends. Francis Ledwidge's letters to Lizzie Healey in his early days in the army are important as indicative of friends and the country of home as a living spiritual force inside him.

On 13 April he wrote to Lizzie Healey 'I can't tell you know I feel as post after post comes in and no letter from my dear Lizzie. I met Larry yesterday evening, he was going to the train en route for Slane. I wished that I was going along with him. He told me he had joined King Edward's Horse. I will see him again on Friday evening. We are on top-toe ready to depart at a moment's notice but something for which we are waiting will not come. The suspense is dreadful. In any case I am sure we will be away this month.'

His next letter was concerned about her hair being put up 'Who made you do that. I bet it was Mr Farrelly. I suppose he was jibbing you. You are no longer a young girl now, you are a young woman. We can't be much longer than a week here now, and am working like a Trojan, noon and night on documents which will be required at the Front.'

Francis Ledwidge's expressed suspense at the prospect of departure is a barometer of his apparent enthusiasm for military service. There is not a hint of depression in any of his Richmond barracks' letters to Lizzie Healey except the sadness of being separated from her, from family, friends, and the fields and bogs, and birds of the Boyne.

He wrote again on 21 April 'We are off to the war at the end of this week. Our king and country need us at last. We leave here about Saturday, or Sunday morning, for Reading, England. The Tenth Division mobilises there, thence we proceed to some part of the great battlefield. It is for you I will fight as you are all I have or ever will have, worth fighting for. When I come back I will claim you. I may not be long away as immediately the war is over I will be free again.'

In this letter Francis Ledwidge clearly allowed himself some romantic license. In fact his mother and brother Joe were still living in Slane; Matty McGoona and other close friends were alive and well. In fact he had family, friends, and home whom he believed were worth fighting for. In these letters he was putting his emotional case to Lizzie Healey in the strongest terms. Lizzie Healey was living in Wilkinstown, sometimes visiting Slane on a Sunday. Francis Ledwidge was given an unannounced day's leave on the Sunday before departure. Lizzie Healey was not in Slane. They never met again.

The Royal Inniskilling Fusiliers had a rousing send-off from the Dublin crowds when they marched from Richmond Barracks to Dublin Bay on 27 April 1915. Ireland was still firmly behind the war effort.

Francis Ledwidge had not abandoned writing poetry over his months of training from 24 October 1914 to 27 April 1915 when he sailed from Ireland for war.

The poems which he wrote over those months show in the clearest way that barrack life and military training had in no way pierced the citadels of his inner spiritual being.

His finest poem of that period, and one of the finest he ever wrote, was, inspired by home and friends. A neighbour's son had died while Francis Ledwidge was training at Richmond Barracks. He wrote *A Little Boy in the Morning* (see page 25).

Also included in *Songs Of Peace – At Home* and *A Dream Of Artemis.* Lord Dunsany, in his introduction, says that it was being written in the summer of 1914. If so, it predates Ledwidge's entry into the army. Lord Dunsany: 'I read the Dream of Artemis as an expression of things that the poet has seen and dreamed in Meath, including a most beautiful description of a fox-hunt in the north of the county, in which he has probably taken part on foot.'

It is clear that Francis Ledwidge's interest in classical mythology was alive and well as he went to war:

> ... And then the flowers came back behind the heel
> Of hunted Io: she, poor maid, had fear
> Wide in her eyes looking half back to steal
> A glimpse of the loud gadfly fiercely near.
> In her right hand she held a slanting light,
> And in her left her train. Artemis here
> Raised herself on her palms, and took a white

Horn from her side and blew a silver peal
'Til three hounds from the coppice did appear.

The white nine left the spaces of flowers, and now
Went calling thro' the wood the hunter's call.
Young echoes sleeping in the hollow bough
Took up the shouts and handed them to all
Their sisters of the crags, 'til all the day
Was filled with voices loud and musical.
I followed them across a tangled way
'Till the red deer broke out and took the brow
Of a wide hill in bounces like a ball.
Beside swift Artemis I joined the chase;
We roused up kine and scattered fleecy flocks;
Crossed at a mill a swift and bubbly race;
Sealed in a wood of pine the knotty rocks;
Past a grey vision of a valley town;
Past swains at labour in their coloured frocks;
Once saw a boar upon a windy down;
Once heard a cradle in a lonely place,
And saw the red flash of a frightened fox. [...]

And when the white procession of the stars
Crosses the night, and on their tattered wings,
Above the forest, cry the loud night-jars,
We'll hunt the stag upon the mountain-side,
Slipping like light between the shadow bars
'Til burst of dawn makes every distance wide.
Oh, Artemis – what grief the silence brings!
I hear the rolling chariot of Mars!'

If, as Lord Dunsany asserts, this poem contains a description of a fox-hunt in the north of the county, it is the only evidence that Francis Ledwidge was in any way interested in the sport of fox-hunting.

So at this period of his life just before joining the army Francis Ledwidge was sufficiently into the classics to write convincingly on a classical subject. Primary education in Slane may have been of higher quality to those prepared to take advantage of it than its humble position in the social ladder might suggest. If not, Francis

Ledwidge must have read deeply and widely in the classics.

His poetry under the title *In Barracks* was written over the period of his training in Richmond Barracks. It is the writing of a man just beginning to experience the flavour of military life.

THE PLACE

Blossoms as old as May I scatter here,
And a blue wave I lifted from the stream.
It shall not know when winter days are drear
Or March is hoarse with blowing. But a-dream
The laurel boughs shall hold a canopy
Peacefully over it the winter long,
Till all the birds are back from oversea,
And April rainbows win a blackbird's song.

And when the war is over I shall take
My lute a-down to it and sing again
Songs of the whispering things amongst the brake,
And those I love shall know them by their strain,
Their airs shall be the blackbird's twilight song,
Their words shall be all flowers with fresh dews hoar. –
But it is lonely now in winter long,
And, God! to hear the blackbird sing once more.

It was one of the tragic misconceptions of many young men joining the army in 1914 that the war would be shortly over; that Great Britain would achieve a knock-out victory in early days. It was not to be. In fact Francis Ledwidge was continuing to sing. The blackbird was ever a source of inspiration to him.

His romantic instincts were also highly tuned while at Richmond Barracks. *To A Distant One*, whose lines have a haunting sadness rising to an ultimate optimism, was sent from Richmond Barracks to Lizzie Healey in early 1915.

When Francis Ledwidge came to write the last poem *In Barracks* the object of his romantic attachments had clarified. He declared firmly for Lizzie Healey.

TO LIZZIE
(EILISH OF THE FAIR HAIR)

I'd make my heart a harp to play for you
Love songs within the too dim dusk of day,
Were it not dumb with ache and with mildew
Of sorrow withered like a flower away.
It hears so many calls from homeland places,
So many sighs from all it will remember,
From the pale roads and woodlands where your face is
Like laughing sunlight running thro' December.

But this it whispers still for all its pain,
To bring the greater ache: what may befall
The love that oft-times woke the sweeter strain
Shall turn to you always. And should you call
To pity it some day in those old places
Angels will covet the loud joy that fills it –
But thinking of the bye-ways where your face is
Sunlight on other hearts, Ah! how it kills it.

Barracks, particularly for a trainee soldier, are not conducive to creative or any writing. Most recruits are hard pressed to find time and energy to write home. But the quality of Francis Ledwidge's writing as detailed in these love poems improved while he was training in Richmond Barracks and as Francis Ledwidge's military career moved from barracks to camp the light of his creative imagination was burning brightly.

The Tenth Division, to be slaughtered later, took up camp in Hampshire in the spring of 1915. Francis Ledwidge was with them. He wrote 'I like being under canvas in a beautiful country like this, but my thoughts are in Slane and Wilkinstown and in the little roads about Crocknaharna.'

His period in camp from the end of April 1915 to 10 July 1915 was blighted by emotional problems. Shortly after arrival in camp he wrote to Lizzie Healey 'The country around is beautiful. The fields are very nice and green and full of chalk where the banks are broken. The birds sing here too, but my thoughts are in Slane and on the road to the bog. Write to me when you get this and let me know how all are. I hear so little from my home friends.' On 31 May 1915 he wrote 'It is too bad that I have been so long in answering your welcome letter, but since we came here we have been in a state of great unrest, one day here and three somewhere else, as Paddy can tell you. Basingstoke is a beautiful place in the middle of Hampshire. It is a town not as big as Drogheda but better populated. The country around is beautiful. I have even come across a bog of several acres, on which turf never was cut, full of heather and little pools, white at the bottom with shells. We had dinner there on Whit Monday and Lizzie, as true as God I left my dinner and with a couple of bars of chocolate went out to a little copse to dream of the bog far away. You are beautiful Lizzie, and I must win you for I am lonely without you and always thinking of you in the land of good hearts. God bless you and keep you until I return. I will never forget the night myself and Paddy spent in Wilkinstown. I thought then I would be home by now but I seem to be as far away from returning as when I first joined the colours. We expect to be going away soon and are glad as we are tired of the monotony of camp. The weather is frightfully warm here for a month now. Remember me to all. I am sure the bog is lovely now, how I wish I were there! There's the bugle.'

Lizzie Healey could be excused if she read that letter as a strong expression of Francis Ledwidge's enthusiasm for her.

In June 1915 he received the shattering news that Ellie Vaughey, his first and greatest love, married to John O'Neill on 25 November 1914 had died. It was a blow which struck him hard. He was given leave and went to Manchester where the O'Neills had been living, for the funeral. In fact she was buried on the Hill of Slane. The unhappiness of her life in Manchester, of which Ledwidge heard after her death, added to his grief. She died in childbirth, but she was still alive in his heart. Ellie Vaughey's death inspired some of his best poetry as she had when she was alive, unmarried and by his side.

TO ONE DEAD

A blackbird singing
On a moss-upholstered stone,
Bluebells swinging,
Shadows wildly blown,
A song in the wood,
A ship on the sea.
The song was for you
And the ship was for me.

A blackbird singing
I hear in my troubled mind,

Bluebells swinging
I see in a distant wind.
But sorrow and silence
Are the wood's threnody,
The silence for you
And the sorrow for me.

This poem was undoubtedly written at Basingstoke while the anguish of Ellie O'Neill's death was upon him. It appears in Lord Dunsany's arrangement of his war poems *Songs Of Peace* significantly later in Ledwidge's war experiences.

Life in camp at Basingstoke was happy days so far as Francis Ledwidge's friendship with Lord Dunsany was concerned. Lord Dunsany had rented a house in Basingstoke. Lady Dunsany came to live with him there. He was openly friendly to Ledwidge in camp within the austere limits of an officer/non-commissioned soldier contact. A non-commissioned soldier had to salute an officer, on however many different occasions they met each day, even if they were brothers.

Lord Dunsany offered Francis Ledwidge a room in his house in Basingstoke. The quiet of that room was important in contributing to one of the most creative periods in Ledwidge's career. The wonderful quality of his poetry written while he was in Basingstoke can scarcely have been inspired by route marches across Hampshire.

In June 1915 Lord Dunsany was able to tell Francis Ledwidge that Herbert Jenkins had decided to publish *Songs Of The Fields*. Lord Dunsany and Ledwidge worked together on a final check of every word, line and comma when the proofs arrived. Lord Dunsany added to the introduction:

Lord Dunsany, *c.* 1915

I wrote this preface in such a different June, that if I sent it out with no addition it would make the book appear to have dropped a long while since out of another world, a world that none of us remembers now, in which there used to be leisure.'

Ledwidge came last October into the Fifth Battalion of the Royal Inniskilling Fusiliers, which is one of the divisions of Kitchener's first army, and soon earned a lance corporal's stripe.

All his future books lie on the knees of the gods. May They not be the only readers. Any well-informed spy can probably tell you our movements, so of such things I say nothing.

June 1915 Dunsany, Captain
5 R'Inniskilling Fusiliers

These lines tell us Lord Dunsany had lost none of his literary imagery. The knees of the gods' is an expression in themes of Lord Dunsany's writing. The well-informed spy is indicative of Lord Dunsany's sceptical slant on army life.

Whatever his lack of enthusiasm for some of the pomposity of military hierarchy, Lord Dunsany was a good officer. He was respected and well liked by the men. In June 1915 he was ordered to Londonderry to train recruits. His departure left a lonely gap in Francis Ledwidge's life. It was one more break with Ireland, County Meath and a shared love of poetry.

It is extraordinary that amid the rigours of route marches and bayonet practise Ledwidge summoned up the creative energy to write poetry at all at Basingstoke. His lovely nature poem *May* written in this period indicates a sharpening style and a deep attachment, evident in his earlier writing, to nature as a living person. Lord Dunsany places this under the heading *In Barracks* but it seems from the title that it was more likely written in Basingstoke. But whenever written it is one of Ledwidge's finest poems.

MAY

She leans across an orchard gate somewhere,
Bending from out the shadows to the light,
A dappled spray of blossom in her hair
Studded with dew-drops lovely from the night
She smiles to think how many hearts she'll smite
With beauty ere her robes fade from the lawn.
She hears the robin's cymbals with delight,
The skylark in the rosebush of the dawn.

For her the cowslip rings its yellow bell,
For her the violets watch with wide blue eyes.
The wandering cuckoo doth its clear name tell
Thro' the white mist of blossoms where she lies
Painting a sunset for the western skies.
You'd know her by her smile and by her tear
And by the way the swift and martin flies,
Where she is south of these wild days and drear.

So in Francis Ledwidge's imagination as he marched across Hampshire *May* was a living lady. The poem imports Ledwidge's prevailing mood of romanticism into its incidents, 'She smiles to think how many hearts she'll smite.' The lyricism is delicate and forceful, 'A dappled spray of blossom in her hair, studded with dew-drops love-ly from the night.'

A dream inspired *Caoin* written in June 1915. The poet imagined himself in the West of Ireland. It was shortly after writing this poem that Francis Ledwidge heard of Ellie O'Neill's (Vaughey's) death.

CAOIN

Over the border of the dawn
Far as the blue Atlantic sky,
The white birds of the sea go on
In breezefuls, wailing as they fly.
What lure of light calls them afar
From sheltered niche and sandy dune
Built in the changes of the moon
And yet where all their nestlings are?

'Tis star-set now where Una lies,
And on the little holy road
Morn breaks the windows of the ice
That all night round her dwelling glowed.
No barking fox, or banshee tale
With terror filled me in that dream,
But white birds, wither with your scream?
And cloudy winds, wherefore your wail?

Francis Ledwidge's mood at Basingstoke had its serious downswings, perhaps occasioned by the death of Ellie O'Neill. A deep sadness is evident in *Crewbawn*.

CREWBAWN

White clouds that change and pass,
And stars that shine awhile,
Dew water on the grass,
A fox upon a stile.

A river broad and deep,
A slow boat on the waves,
My sad thoughts on the sleep
That hollows out the graves.

But also the broader horizons of England and life in camp found their way into
Francis Ledwidge's writing in this period.

EVENING IN ENGLAND

From its blue vase the rose of evening drops.
Upon the streams its petals float away.
The hills all blue with distance hide their tops
In the dim silence falling on the grey.
A little wind said 'Hush!' and shook a spray
Heavy with May's white crop of opening bloom,
A silent bat went dipping up the gloom.

Night tells her rosary of stars full soon.
They drop from out her dark hand to her knees.
Upon a silhouette of woods the moon
Leans on one horn as if beseeching ease
From all her changes which have stirred the seas.
Across the ears of Toil Rest throws her veil,
I and a marsh bird only make a wail.

While the Meath country remained an abiding inspiration this poem is interesting as telling that Ledwidge's creative spirit was by no means limited to it.

He expected the war to be over quickly. When he thought of the front he thought
of France where the British and German armies faced each other in murderous stale-
mate. But fate had other battlefields in mind for Francis Ledwidge. Turkey had
joined the war on the German side. One of the results of this unhappy decision was
that the British military command decided to attack Turkey through the
Dardenelles. It was an attack which was expensive in lives and strictly limited in
achievement. Francis Ledwidge became part of that attack. A foothold in Turkey was
gained at a cost of twenty thousand British and Commonwealth casualties. It was
decided to commit further troops including the Tenth Division and Francis
Ledwidge.

The prospect of service in the East appealed to his romantic temperament. The classical nuance of the Dardenelles with the Hellespont and Troy in their antecedents heightened his interest. The campaign was particularly alive with poignancy for poets since Rupert Brooke's untimely death from blood poisoning on the way to the Dardenelles.

He sailed for the Dardenelles on 10 July 1915. It was to be a campaign wholly devoid of romanticism or any chance to explore the classical sites in and about the Dardenelles.

Difficult circumstances could not stop Francis Ledwidge from writing poetry. While at sea from England to Gallipoli he wrote three poems notwithstanding seriously overcrowded conditions for the troops, stinking smells and a serious lack of air below deck. *Crocknaharna* suggests a deep sadness prompted by moving away from Ireland. It emphasises the strength of country, home and family to his spirit as he sailed closer to war.

CROCKNAHARNA

On the heights of Crocknaharna,
(Oh, the lure of Crocknaharna)
On a morning fair and early
Of a dear remembered May,
There I heard a colleen singing
In the brown rocks and the grey.
She, the pearl of Crocknaharna,
Crocknaharna, Crocknaharna,
Wild with gulls is Crocknaharna
Twenty hundred miles away.

On the heights of Crocknaharna,
(Oh, thy sorrow Crocknaharna)
On an evening dim and misty
Of a cold November day,
There I heard a woman weeping
In the brown rocks and the grey.
Oh, the pearl of Crocknaharna
(Crocknaharna, Crocknaharna),
Black with grief is Crochnaharna
Twenty hundred miles away.

On the understanding that the colleen in verse one is his mother and a woman weeping in verse two is his mother then it expresses his thoughts in respect of her sadness, no doubt because he has left for war.

His second poem at sea shows that strength can be inspired by new stimulus.

IN THE MEDITERRANEAN —
GOING TO THE WAR

Lovely wings of gold and green
Flit about the sounds I hear,
On my window when I lean
To the shadows cool and clear.

Roaming, I am listening still,
Bending, listening overlong,
In my soul a steadier will,
In my heart a newer song.

The only other poem which he wrote on the high seas was *The Gardener*. It is difficult to calculate the inspiration for this poem if not his mother, even distantly. If his mother was the inspiration it is yet another instance of the abiding strength of family in his spirit.

THE GARDENER

Among the flowers, like flowers, her slow hands move
Easing a muffled bell or stooping low
To help sweet roses climb the stakes above,
Where pansies stare and seem to whisper 'Lo!'
Like gaudy butterflies her sweet peas blow
Filling the garden with dim rustlings. Clear
On the sweet Book she reads how long ago
There was a garden to a woman dear.

She makes her life one grand beatitude
Of Love and Peace, and with contented eyes
She sees not in the whole world mean or rude,
And her small lot she trebly multiplies.

And when the darkness muffles up the skies
Still to be happy is her sole desire,
She sings sweet songs about a great emprise,
And sees a garden blowing in the fire.

The regiment started landing into Salva Bay in Gallipoli on 6 August 1915. The Turks did everything to make them unwelcome. Their guns bombarded the British troops in their ships, in their landing craft, on the beaches. It was a stern introduction to war for Francis Ledwidge. Twenty thousand British troops were penned on the beaches by one thousand five hundred Turks in command of the surrounding hills. Drinking water was in hideously short supply. Many dead men were not buried. The place swarmed with flies. Dysentary was rife.

On 15 August D Company in which Ledwidge was serving and A Company were ordered to attack a hill position. The attack was in due course called off at a cost of six officers killed, two hundred and thirty men wounded and seventy-eight men missing. In fact there were so many wounded in this attack that Ledwidge was detailed to act as a stretcher bearer. He helped to carry in his best friend Robert Christie.

Robert Christie came from Belfast. They had met at Richmond Barracks. They became the closest of friends from Dublin to Gallipoli. Christie had been hit on the leg; he was transported by ship out of Gallipoli to England. He was fourteen months in hospital. He was then invalided out. He never recovered the use of his left ankle. At least he survived.

> The battle raged on. On 16 August Ledwidge's Company captured the hill detailed for them. There was a slaughter of officers and men. Only two officers survived. Ledwidge finished a letter to Paddy Healey with the words 'Tell them all in the hotel I am well and glad to be here for it is great to be here after all. I saw half the world. I was in Egypt and Greece, saw Italy, Spain and all my dream countries and now I am in Turkey, wanting to be back in Slane again.

A further assault was planned for 22 August; British and Commonwealth forces suffered five thousand three hundred casualties for a tiny advance. They were at a hopeless disadvantage to the Turks on higher ground and knowing the country well. The slaughter was particularly grievous among officers.

The order to abandon the ill-fated campaign was given to D Company on 26 September; on 30 September Francis Ledwidge and other survivors were ferried out at night into the S.S. Sarnia. He was glad to be alive. Nineteen thousand men of the

Tenth Division had been killed in Gallipoli. There were many more casualties before the scheme was finally abandoned in November 1915 and the evacuation complete in January 1916.

It is scarcely surprising that under the barrage of Turkish fire Francis Ledwidge wrote no poetry. He shot a Turkish sniper sneaking into the British lines when on night duty.

He did find time to write to Lord Dunsany of the 15 August engagement:

> It is surprising what silly things one thinks of in a big fight. I was lying one side of a low bush on 15 August, pouring lead across a little ridge into the Turks and for hours my mind was on the silliest things of home. Once I found myself wondering if a cow that I knew to have a disease called 'timber-tongue' had really died. Again a man on my right who was mortally hit said 'It can't be far off now' and I began to wonder what it was could not be far off. Then I knew it was death and I kept repeating the dying man's words 'It can't be far off now'.
>
> But when the Turks began to retreat I realised my position and, standing up, I shouted out the range to the men near me and they fell like grass before a scythe, the enemy. It was Hell! Hell! No man thought he would ever return. By Heavens, you should know the bravery of these men: Cassidy standing on a hill with his cap on top of his rifle shouting at the Turks to come out; stretcher-bearers taking in friend and enemy alike. It was a horrible and a great day. I would not have missed it for worlds.

The long days of training were well and truly over. Francis Ledwidge was blooded.

The lines in his poem *In The Mediterranean-Going To The War* 'In my soul a steadier will. In my heart a newer song' were hardened into reality on the shores of Gallipoli.

Francis Ledwidge and the remains of the Tenth Division were ordered to Serbia via a short stay in the Greek island of Lemnos. Bulgaria had joined the war on Germany's side. He landed in Salonika on 15 October 1915.

By November The Royal Inniskilling Fusiliers were in the mountains. The weather was freezing. Rations were at near starvation level. Bulgarians in the area substantially outnumbered British and French forces. The retreat from the mountains began on 8 December. Ledwidge later described the horrors of it in a letter to Paddy Healey, Lizzie Healey's brother. 'It poured rain on us all the long ninety miles we had to march, and what with sleeping in wet clothes, sweating and cooling down, I got an attack of Barny Fitzsimmons back. You have read of our retreat. Shall I ever forget it. We should have left the previous evening but just as we mustered to go we received word that a French brigade was almost surrounded higher up and we were called to do a flank attack. We did, and extricated the French, but got into a similar condition ourselves by morning. The Bulgars came on like flies and though we mowed down line after line, they persisted with aweful doggedness and finally gave us a bayonet charge which secured their victory. We only just had about 200 yards to escape by and we had to hold this until next evening and then dribble out as best we could.'

It was a horrific march in cold and hunger. Francis Ledwidge collapsed with an inflamed back before he reached Salonika. He was taken by ambulance to Salonika; and then transferred to a hospital in Egypt.

Serbia was as painful militarily as Gallipoli. But it was a time of triumph for his poetry.

In October 1915 he received a copy of *Songs Of The Fields*; it had been published. He wrote to Lord Dunsany on 31 October:

> Thanks very much for your two letters received a couple of days ago. Yes I received your cigarettes alright. We had a busy day with the Turks when they came; but that didn't prevent us from smoking them. So *Songs Of The Fields* were out at last. I suppose the critics are blowing warm and cold over them with the same mouth, like the charcoal burner in Aesops fables. Jenkins sent me a copy. It is a lovely book and quite a decent size, but my best is not in it. That has to come yet. I feel something great struggling in my soul but it can't come until I return; if I don't return it will never come.
>
> I wish the damned war would end; we are all so sick for the old countries. Still our hearts are great and we are always ready for anything that may be required of us.
>
> I am writing a poem which I will send you when finished; meanwhile I hope my book sells by thousands. I won't try to thank you for all you have done for me and are doing. You know how grateful I am.

It was fame. *The Times, Truth, Bookman,* the *Tatler, Pall Mall Gazette,* the *Standard, Sphere, Globe, Daily Telegraph* and the *Manchester Guardian* were all in their different ways strongly supportive. The first issue was sold. *Songs Of The Fields* went rapidly into a second impression.

Lord Dunsany sent the admiring press reviews to Francis Ledwidge, who replied on 15 November:

> Thank you very much for your two letters and press cuttings. These were the first I had seen and I am delighted beyond words. I cannot tell you how grateful to you I am for all you have done for me and when you congratulate me on the success of my book, you forget that but for you it could never be,

and you leave me with all the glory. The reviews are better because each critic appreciated different poems, this shows a worthiness from cover to cover, a worthiness I had only hoped for in two or three pieces. None of them have selected the verses Mr March took, this makes the whole book more valuable still. I wish I were back again, but there seems no hope yet of our returning. The weather is getting bad, the nights in particular. Being in a mountainy country we suffer much from rain and cold. A goodly few of us have rheumatism badly, but the work is still here and the driver is still inexorable. The enclosed poem is the one I wrote in a thunder shower in Salonika. There are still great things to come from me and I am full up but have no time. I will not accept any post, if I return, but what you approve of. I would rather sweep the roads for the people who are so free, and write pure poetry than deceive people for £100 a year in the city. I am called. Thanks very much again and best wishes to you.

His back was about to collapse. But his confidence was high. Mr March referred to in letter of 15 November was an important patron of poetry. He founded with others the Poetry Bookshop in London. In the second volume of his *Georgian Poetry* he published three Ledwidge poems. *A Rainy Day In April*, The Lost Ones and *Wife Of Llew*. Francis Ledwidge's foot was firmly on the literary ladder even while he was plodding through the Balkans far removed from County Meath.

Lord Dunsany was still his guiding star. He communicated with him on subjects of poetry throughout the Balkins' campaign. In November he wrote again to Lord Dunsany.

I am too short of paper to send you copies of some poems I have written, but I will be careful of them until an issue takes place, if one ever does in this aweful place. I wish I could get back for a rest and go to France in the spring. I will never hold out here as I suffer terribly from rheumatism. The nights when not raining are freezing and one wonders which is the worse for the pains.

Of course you understand that we are quite different from what we have been in your day. We are all weak and sick, but we suffered much.

Would there be a chance of getting home for a month? The doctor will only give me a day's rest, that is no cure for rheumatism when the same day miles of a march have to be done and that night a 'listening post' in some outlandish hollow.

When I get paper I will send you copies of my latest work, meanwhile if you could get a holiday for me I would be so grateful and so would my mother.

Unhappily, holidays to give or to withhold were not at Lord Dunsany's command.

The period of the Balkan campaign up until he collapsed outside Salonika was one of the most creative in his writing life.

WHEN LOVE AND BEAUTY WANDER AWAY

When Love and Beauty wander away,
And there's no more hearts to be sought and won,
When the old earth limps thro' the dreary day,
And the work of the Seasons cry undone:
Ah! what shall we do for a song to sing,
Who have known Beauty, and Love, and Spring?

When Love and Beauty wander away,
And a pale fear lies on the cheeks of youth,
When there's no more goal to strive for and pray,
And we live at the end of the world's untruth:
Ah! what shall we do for a heart to prove,
Who have known Beauty, and Spring, and Love?

NOCTURNE

The rim of the moon
Is over the corn.
The beetle's drone
Is above the thorn.
Grey days come soon
And I am alone;
Can you hear my moan
Where you rest, Aroon?

When the wild tree bore
The deep blue cherry,
In night's deep hall
Our love kissed merry.
But you come no more
Where its woodlands call,
And the grey days fall
On my grief, Astore!

Francis Ledwidge sent these two poems to Lord Dunsany with these comments 'Remember in reading the enclosed the circumstances under which they were written. *When Love And Beauty Wander Away* was written by Lake Dorian one awful night of thunder and rain I was thinking of the end of the world as the Bible predicts it and tried to imagine Love and Beauty leaving the world hand in hand, and we who could not yet die standing on the edge of a great precipice with no song, no love, no memory. At the same place, thinking of another thing I wrote *Nocturne*. *Nocturne* was written, Ledwidge later said, of Ellie. 'I have no rest of Ellie even yet.'

THE COBLER OF SARI GUEUL

A cobbler lives in Sari Gueul
Who has a wise mind, people say.
He sits in his door on a three-legged stool,
Hammering leather all the day.
He laughs with the boys who make such noise
And loves to watch how the children play.
Gladly I'd shuffle my lot in a pool
With that of the cobbler in Sari Gueul.

Sorrow to him is a ball of wax
That melts in the sun of a cheerful smile
And all his needs are, a box of tacks,
Thread and leather, old boots in a pile.
I would give my art for half of his heart.
Who wants the world with all its guile?
And which of us two is the greater fool,
Me, or the cobbler of Sari Gueul?

At evening an old cow climbs the street,
So lean and bony you'd wonder how.
He hears the old cracked bell from his seat
And the wrinkles move on his yellow brow,
And he says as he strikes, 'To me or my likes
You are coming faster, old brown cow.
Slow steps come fast to the knife and rule!
Says the wise old cobbler of Sari Gueul.

Often I hear him in my sleep,
Hammering still in the little town.
And I see the queer old shops on the steep,
And the queerer folk move up and down.
And the cobbler's sign creaks up in a vine,
When the wind slips over the housetops brown.
Waking, I pray to the Gods who rule
For the queer old cobbler of Sari Gueul.

Francis Ledwidge sent this to Lord Dunsany with the comment 'Sara Jul (Sari-Gueul) is a village in Serbian Macedonia about half-way between Lake Dorian and Salonika. Like all the Greek villages Sara Jul is quaint and very beautiful, seen even in the worst conditions of weather as I have seen it. We stood there two days on our retreat, waiting for a train which never came. Sara Jul is one hilly street with the houses built very much out of line. Bread (Oh dear me! Bread! What wouldn't we give for a mouthful of bread) tins langthornes, clothes of all colours are displayed in the windows. Quaint signs creak in the wind and where you see a vine climbing up a housefront, underneath you hear my cobbler's hammer. I wonder if people will understand the line 'Slow steps come fast to the knife and rule.' Of course an old cow walks very slowly and as it grows older it goes slower and therefore faster to the tan yard.'

The syntax in verse two of this poem is a little rough. But it tells us how vital and alive Francis Ledwidge's poetic impulses were in conditions of dreadful physical endurance. This poem is indicative of a new aspect of his writing; it is one of the first poems written on active service in which his fascination with the small details of life in a foreign land is apparent. It shows that his sensitivity to the atmosphere and nuances of places is in no way limited to County Meath.

Other poems which Francis Ledwidge wrote while fighting in the Serbian campaign show that the inspirations of nature were still at the heart of his creative writing.

AUTUMN EVENING IN SERBIA

All the thin shadows
Have closed on the grass,
With the drone on their dark wings
The night beetles pass.
Folded her eyelids,

A maiden asleep,
Day sees in her chamber
The pallid moon peep.

From the bend of the briar
The roses are torn,
And the folds of the wood tops
Are faded and worn.
A strange bird is singing
Sweet notes of the sun,
Tho' song time is over
And Autumn begun.

SPRING AND AUTUMN

Green ripples singing down the corn,
With blossoms dumb the path I tread,
And in the music of the morn
One with wild roses on her head.

Now the green ripples turn to gold
And all the paths are loud with rain,
I with desire am growing old
And full of winter pain.

The finest poem of his Balkan campaign and one of the loveliest he ever wrote was *The Home-Coming Of The Sheep*. It is entirely clear that the guns of Serbia had done nothing to blunt the lyricism of his writing.

THE HOME-COMING OF THE SHEEP

The sheep are coming home in Greece,
Hark the bells on every hill!
Flock by flock, and fleece by fleece,
Wandering wide a little piece
Thro' the evening red and still,
Stopping where the pathways cease,
Cropping with a hurried will.

Thro' the cotton-bushes low
Merry boys with shouldered crooks
Close them in a single row,
Shout among them as they go
With one bell-ring o'er the brooks.
Such delight you never know
Reading it from gilded books.

Before the early stars are bright
Cormorants and sea-gulls call,
And the moon comes large and white
Filling with a lovely light
The ferny curtained waterfall.
Then sleep wraps every bell up tight
And the climbing moon grows small.

It can only be assumed that Francis Ledwidge was very observant of all the sights of the Balkans as he trudged through the winter of 1915.

Mythology as an inspiration and source of material had assumed an increasing importance in Francis Ledwidge's work before the war. It returned to inspire his writing in the Balkan campaign.

THE DEPARTURE OF PROSERPINE

Old mother Earth for me already grieves,
Her morns wake weeping and her noons are dim,
Silence has left her woods, and all the leaves
Dance in the windy shadows on the rim
Of the dull lake thro' which I soon shall pass
     To my dark bridal bed
Down in the hollow chambers of the dead.
Will not the thunder hide me if I call,
Wrapt in the corner of some distant star
The gods have never known?
     Alas! alas!
My voice has left with the last wing, my fall
Shall crush the flowery fields with gloom, as far
     As swallows fly.

Would I might die
And in a solitude of roses lie
As the last bud's outblown.
Then nevermore Demeter would be heard
Wail in the blowing rain, but every shower
Would come bound up with rainbows to the birds
Wrapt in a dusty wing, and the dry flower
                    Hanging a shrivelled lip.
This weary change from light to darkness fills
My heart with twilight, and my brightest day
Dawns over thunder and in thunder spills
                    Its urn of gladness
                    With a sadness
Through which the slow dews drip
And the bat goes over on a thorny wing.
Is it a dream that once I used to sing
From Aegean shores across her rocky isles,
Making the bells of Babylon to ring
                    Over the wiles
That lifted me from darkness to the Spring?
                    And the King
Seeing his wine in blossom on the tree
Danced with the queen a merry roundelay,
And all the blue circumference of the day
Was loud with flying song –
– But let me pass along:
What brooks it the unfree to thus delay?
No secret turning leads from the god's way.

The lugubrious concepts expressed in parts of this poem reflected his own gloom with the horrors and discomforts of war. But *The Home-coming Of The Sheep*, written in the same period shows that his appreciation of the beautiful was still burning bright.

If interest in travel had any part in prompting Francis Ledwidge's decision to join the British Army he was getting travel in full measure. He was transported to a hospital in Egypt. In the course of a letter to Paddy Healey he wrote 'You see I am in hospital. I am not wounded, though only God knows how I escaped the fields of the Bulgars. I saw horrors there must have made the soul of Dante envious. What really drove me in here was the bad weather we experienced in our retreat.' This is one of a number of letters from Francis Ledwidge which show that self-pity never entered his spirit. He ends the letter with the lines 'Thanks for congratulations on my book. It is a great success financially and I think, from the reviews a great literary success too.'

Enthusiastic notices of *Songs Of The Fields* continued to find their way to his hospital bed in Egypt. The superb reception of his first book of poetry was one of the spurs which drove him to write some of his finest poetry in the Balkan/Egyptian period of his war.

He was moved to a hospital at Helwar, near Cairo; he was then moved again. Fortunately his doctor was interested in poetry. He borrowed *Songs Of The Fields*. He was familiar with Lord Dunsany's books. He started making preparations for Francis Ledwidge's transfer to a hospital in England. On 19 January 1916 he wrote to Lord Dunsany: 'Many thanks for your book of writing paper. You will have received my other letter ere this letting you know I was admitted to hospital. I am getting on first class except for my back which is still painful and very weak. The doctors in Giza hospital recommended me to be sent home but I have heard nothing of it here so far. I write an occasional little thing yet which you will read some day, but I lost a lot of manuscripts in the long retreat from the Balkan front.

Will such evenings as we knew at Dunsany ever be again? I hope so, although for me a lot of the old glamour has passed and my poetry is written for other reasons than at first. When I stand on the balcony here and look down at the city, with all its pinnacles and mosques, as if the gods were disturbed at a game of chess aeons ago, it seems to me that I have left this world and live along the Yann with the inhabitants of Mandaroon, still wanting to return but unable to find the back door of that little shop, which to me is our doctor's heart.

Lord Clare one time invited Goldsmith to dinner and introduced him to Lord Calmot, who paid little heed to the great man before him. Next night, the poet, relating his experiences to Johnson, Reynolds and the rest, said in an earnest joke: 'Lord Calmont treated me as if I were an ordinary man.' I repeat this jokingly: 'The doctor treats me as an ordinary man.'

Did you ever hear the natives here sing down the streets in the evenings? A friend of mine who knows Arabic very well gave me a translation one evening as we listened and I set it ringing thus:

> What time is it, Mr Mahommed?
> Its just a little bit after seven,
> Where are you going to, Mr Mahommed?

I'm going the long white way to heaven.
And will you come back again, Mr Mahommed?
I'll be back at a little bit after eleven,
If the world doesn't end before.

P.S. Your new seals are charming, particularly the one about the flower of fame. 'Mortal soil' is a wonderful conception 'F.E.L.'

This is a reference to Milton's line 'Fame is no plant that grows on mortal soil.' Lord Dunsany had inscribed the line on a seal and sealed his letter to Francis Ledwidge with it.

This letter shows how much war had matured him. It shows that memories of County Meath are still fully alive. It shows that self-pity had taken no hold upon him. It is the first indication of his interest in eighteenth century Irish literary and social history.

Francis Ledwidge wrote to Lord Dunsany on 5 February, 14 February, 8 March, 12 March and 21 March. He wrote on 5 February: 'Thanks for *Georgian Poetry* to hand a few days ago, also for other parcel just received. Mr Marsh is to be congratulated on his selection of verse, but somehow I think he could have got better from *Songs Of The Fields*. I am glad to be there all the same. I enclose three small things of many I have written in Greece and Serbia, some of them indeed under shrapnel.

I'm afraid I'm not getting better. My back is very painful and weak and I have a terrific headache. There are Navvy imps in my head. I am going somewhere for sulphur baths, perhaps these will do me good. My dreams are awful things and I hate going asleep because of them. Sometimes I am lying in a coffin in a terrific dream. I will be alright again some time.

I wonder if I might trouble you for a small book of poetry. There is nothing to read here but prose and I have read the few books worth while. Charles Garvice and Nat Gould I have strongly denounced, and many others whose very names are anathema to me.

A 'C. of E.' chaplain who lives here called to see me one day because he had heard of my book. He seemed to be taking a great interest in me and promised me a book of poetry, but suddenly he saw on my chart that I was an R.C. and hurried from me as if I were possessed.

He never came over to me since although he has been in the ward many times. I wonder if God asked our poor chaps were they R.Cs or C. of Es when they went to Him on 15 August. Thanks again for your thoughtfulness.'

He wrote again on 14 February, having been moved from the Citadel Hospital to a hospital at Helwan, near Cairo 'I enclose a few short poems which I ask you to read while I do a better one that is haunting me. You see I have come further south for more heat and sulphur baths as the doctors in the Citadel think these things are what I want mostly. Helwan is close to the lesser pyramids known as the Sakarrah group. There is another Sakarrah thousands of miles away where I wish to be. There are greater wonders at the Sakarrah of Slane now; for all across the field of that name the half daisies are waiting and watching for the further advance of Spring ere they open fully and hold up cymbals to the music of the rain. 'Oh, to be in Ireland now that Spring is there!' Is there any place like Ireland? Why even the fields have their names and traditions.

Somehow I don't seem to get better of these pains at all. My back is very painful and weak still, but this place may improve it. It is my last chance anyway. I used to think if I had a book published it wouldn't matter how soon I died but now that I have one before the public I want to live to do better. I suppose such aspirations are really the striving of the soul for the greater things beyond its prison walls of the body.

You are so good and obliging that I venture to ask you another favour. Will you send the best of the enclosed somewhere and in advance send my brother £2. I have no means of sending him any money from here and he wants £2 for some particular spring work. He is a student severe on himself and I like him to be able to pursue his studies so I subsidise all his necessities. Jenkins would do this but I thought it better ask you. But you must ask the reviewer to make the cheque payable to you. His name is Joseph, old address.

I will let you know how I am getting along with the new poem. It will run to some length.

Who would think James Stephens could write such a poem as *The Goat Paths?*'

On 8 March he wrote again 'I haven't heard from you for a long time. I hope you haven't left Ireland anyway. I am still in bed. The doctors don't seem to do me much good. I had jaundice and divers other complaints. The jaundice left me with a pain in my side which annoys me greatly. Also my back is bad and my right ankle.

It is spring in Ireland. If you love the gods who govern the seasons don't be anxious to leave Ireland now. I know how eager you are for the field, but it will soon be all over. The Turks are beaten, and the struggle at Verdun is Germany's last great effort. By the way I have great respect for the Turks. They fought us a clean fight, and we must admit they are brave soldiers. In my admiration for them I have read 'The Koran'. Mahommed nearly equals you in finding a simile for the moon. You have said: 'When she is old she hobbles away from the hills.' Mahommed says: 'She is twisted and broken like an old palm branch.' I am not able to transcribe some few poems from an old book. This letter is causing me some trouble to write.'

Optimism about the impending end of the war was a recurring feature of Francis Ledwidge's thoughts. His admiration for the Turks and his reading of the Koran tell a great deal about his capacity for capturing the best in every experience.

He wrote again to Lord Dunsany on 12 March 'Your letter of 20 February did me more good than all the dirty medicine I have been drinking for the past three months. So you liked the poem about the sheep? So do I, very much. Did you get the Arab poems? I like these also and the ones I now send, particularly *The Cobbler*.

I didn't get your books yet. I am eagerly watching them. I like Matthew Arnold's *The Forsaken Merman* and *The Scholar Gipsy*. But I love Keats. I think poor Keats reaches the top of beauty in *Odes to a Grecian Urn, To a Nightingale* and *Autumn*, as well as in several of his beautiful apostrophes in the poem *Endymion*. I like Keats best of all. I remember years ago praying to Keats for aid.

I am still a-bed. The doctor says he thinks there is an abscess coming on my liver. I will not undergo any operation no matter how I fare. Just now I am told I am to be sent to the 27 General Hospital, Abyssia. If you write again, that will be my address.

They send me to doctors who are murdering me. Damn them! If they only knew all I want to do. They don't care. Why won't they send me home where I would get well?'

Keats had long been the poetic inspiration of Francis Ledwidge's spirit. He was at a low ebb physically in Egypt. But his heart was bright as we shall see from his pro-lific output of poetry while lying on a bed of pain. He wrote again to Lord Dunsany on 21 March by which date he had been moved to another hospital by a doctor familiar with Lord Dunsany's books and enthusiastic about *Songs Of The Fields* which he borrowed from his patient Ledwidge.

> As I anticipated they have sent me here from Helwan. I am now much better and hope to be allowed up in a couple of days. The doctor who is attending me is a fine man. He knows all your books and even heard of mine. He has spoken to me about Sime's work and believes as I do that your books have immortalised the fame of Sime.
>
> I send you a copy of a small thing recently written. You will know all about it when you read it, and who it is about, for you will remember my telling you at Basingstoke about someone who died. That was the time I went home and was six days absent. Was it much wonder?
>
> If you listen very carefully by the time you get this letter you will hear that 'wandering voice' as Wordsworth calls the cuckoo. I would like to hear him and will too, in dreams.
>
> I wonder when you were in Africa was it the little things of home which

annoyed you? An old broken gate I thought of and a plough in a ditch and other similar neglected things are always in my mind. Did you receive the last poems I sent, the one about the *Cobbler*, etc I have many more old ones in my haversack and some day soon will transcribe them and send you copies. They are all faded with Balkans rains, but I will remember the lines that are obliterated.

I hope you are enjoying good health, that is worth many castles; still I would sooner write a great poem and die than live out the century unknown.'

His period of convalescence in Egypt was one of the most creative in his writing career. The stimuli were, no doubt, the recent publication of *Songs Of The Fields* and the extensive correspondence with Lord Dunsany. The prevailing theme was the remembrance of people past. The reference in letter of 21 March to the small thing which he sent was a reference to the poem *The Resurrection* inspired by the memory of Ellie Vaughey (O'Neill) who had died in Manchester. She was his first great love and her memory was still fully alive. It is apparent from the last letter to Lord Dunsany that his ambition was still burning bright.

THE RESURRECTION

My true love still is all that's fair,
She is flower and blossom blowing free,
For all her silence lying there
She sings a spirit song to me.

New lovers seek her in her bower,
The rain, the dew, the flying wind,
And tempt her out to be a flower,
Which throws a shadow on my mind

All the poems of the Egyptian convalescence period show that Francis Ledwidge is still being sustained and inspired by memory of the people of home, County Meath and Ireland.

TO ONE DEAD

A blackbird singing
On a moss-upholstered stone,
Bluebells swinging,

Shadows wildly blown,
A song in the wood,
A ship on the sea.
The song was for you
And the ship was for me.

A blackbird singing
I hear in my troubled mind,
Bluebells swinging
I see in a distant wind.
But sorrow and silence
Are the wood's threnody,
The silence for you
And the sorrow for me.

Alice Curtayne in her *Francis Ledwidge Complete Poems* says that this poem was written in camp in Basingstoke, shortly after Ellie's death. This view is supported by Liam O'Meara. In Lord Dunsany's edition of *Songs Of Peace* it is placed in the section headed In Hospital In Egypt. Whenever it was written there can be little doubt that Ellie's death was the inspiration. The blackbird is incorporated in the scheme of sadness.

The Shadow People tells that the images and inspiration of the Boyne were fully alive for Francis Ledwidge in Egypt.

THE SHADOW PEOPLE

Old lame Bridget doesn't hear
Fairy music in the grass
When the gloaming's on the mere
And the shadow people pass:
Never hears their slow grey feet
Coming from the village street
Just beyond the parson's wall,
Where the clover globes are sweet
And the mushroom's parasol
Opens in the moonlit rain.
Every night I hear them call
From their long and merry train.

Old lame Bridget says to me,
'It is just your fancy, child'
She cannot believe I see
Laughing faces in the wild,
Hands that twinkle in the sedge
Bowing at the water's edge
Where the finny minnows quiver,
Shaping on a blue wave's ledge
Buddle foam to sail the river.
And the sunny hands to me
Beckon ever, beckon ever
Oh! I would be wild and free
And with the shadow people be.

In early April 1916 Francis Ledwidge, still unwell, was ordered back to England. This was consequent to the efforts of the friendly doctor who had borrowed *Songs Of The Fields* and was familiar with Lord Dunsany's writing. The ship called in Naples. On 20 April he wrote to Lord Dunsany from hospital in Manchester.

> I arrived In England late last night. I cannot tell you how glad I was to return to western civilisation once again. Coming from Southampton in the train, looking on England's beautiful valleys all white with Spring, I thought indeed its freedom was worth all the blood I have seen flow. No wonder England has so many ardent patriots. I would be one of them myself did I not presume to be an Irish patriot. I am not yet very well, indeed I am far from it; nevertheless I am asking to be sent to Ireland soon. I remember you once said of Manchester that God only sends fogs to it. You are quite right, but even the English fog is dear to me now and prized by me above Turkish sunshine, or Serbia's beautiful autumn.
>
> I expect to be home in the course of a week, if I succeed in pretending that my back is strong again. I am so accustomed to asking you to do me favours that I venture this one with no reluctance. I request you to find me clerical work in the Orderly Room for a while, as I am not fit for parades and can't carry anything on my back. The doctors call my disease 'cholecystitis', that is the insane name the medical profession give a bad liver.'

This is a fascinating letter, not least because it shows that for Francis Ledwidge his Irish patriotism did not involve an ounce of animosity towards England. This combination of love for Ireland and at least admiration for England was characteristic of many thousands of Irishmen fighting in the British Army.

But terrible events were about to break in Ireland in April 1916. The Easter Rising shook the foundations of Francis Ledwidge's life. Its consequences are with us still.

The Nomad Girl.

Hark! in the golden lemon fields I hear the
                    voice of On!
And will you stay with me, my love, or will
                You too, begone?
What is there in a camel-bell, or in a
                    nomad's song,
That you must leave the tethered kids where you
                were happy long?

You will go with the white wanderers & they shall
                        give you gold
To wear upon your ankles, and silver wands
                        to hold,
Purple for your raiment & perfume for your
                        hair,
The wonder of strange queens to be, the marvel
                    of the fair.

In the distance of some morning when
      Damascus, dome by dome,
Bulges up like Beauty bursting on a sea of
      gold and chrome,
And you turn awhile to Allah with your brow
      upon the sands,
Shall there be a wish for Smyrna & the
      mingling of our hands?

On, at night, when dusky winds are blowing round
      The starry wells
And your dreamy sleep is broken by the
      stopping of the bells.
Shall you think the flocks are waiting in the
      hollow of the hill?
That the walls are left unmended & the corn
      waits in the mill?

We are nothing, we who love you, we are nothing
                    in our place.
The spirit fires are quenched in us, our
                    hearts have no wild grace.
But the starry wilds are calling, &, I bless
you, love, who hear
With the blessing of my sorrow and the
          blessing of a tear.

Frank Ledwidge.

Feb. 12 — 17

hitherto unpublished poem by Francis Ledwidge
om a private collection

NINE

A TERRIBLE BEAUTY
IS BORN

The Easter Rising had been planned by a number of Irish Volunteers for Easter Sunday 1916. Unhappily those planning the Rising had not observed the formality of informing Eoin MacNeill, leader of the Irish Volunteers that an insurrection was contemplated. He countermanded the revolt. In consequence very many fewer Irish Volunteers supported the Rising than if all in the Irish Volunteer movement had been *Ad Idem*. Much of the inspiration for the Rising had come from the words and speeches of the poet and mystic Padraic Pearse. In particular, speaking at the funeral of a Fenian Revolutionary in 1915 he had said 'Life springs from death, and from the graves of patriotic men and women spring living nations. The defenders of this realm have worked well in secret and in the open. They think that they have pacified Ireland. They think that they have purchased half of us and intimidated the other half. They think that they have foreseen everything, think that they have provided against everything, – but the fools, the fools, the fools. They have left us our Fenian dead, and while Ireland holds these graves, Ireland unfree shall never be at rest.'

Pearse's fatalistic acceptance of sacrifice was one of the main driving inspirations of the Easter Rising. He believed that bloodshed was sanctifying. He was fully prepared and totally willing to die for what he believed to be in Ireland's interests.

In consequence of Eoin MacNeill's countermanding order very many Irish Volunteers did not turn out. James Connelly, the leader of the Rising on the ground, had only 700 men at his command. The Irish Volunteers had a membership of

10,000, many of whom were outside Dublin where the Rising was launched. Pearse had drafted a Proclamation

THE PROVISIONAL GOVERNMENT OF
THE IRISH REPUBLIC –
TO THE PEOPLE OF IRELAND

Irishmen and Irishwomen. In the name of God and of the dead generations from which she receives her old tradition of nationhood, Ireland, through us, summons her children to her flag and strikes for her freedom.

Having organised and trained her manhood through her secret revolutionary organisation, the Irish Republican Brotherhood, and through her open military organisations, the Irish Volunteers and the Irish Citizen Army, having patiently perfected her discipline, having resolutely waited for the right moment to reveal itself, she now seizes that moment, and, supported by her exiled children in America and by gallant allies in Europe, but relying first on her own strength, she strikes in the first confidence of victory.

We declare the right of the people of Ireland to the ownership of Ireland, and to the unfettered control of Irish destinies, to be sovereign and indefeasible. The long usurpation of that right by a foreign people and government has not extinguished the right, nor can it ever be extinguished except by the destruction of the Irish people. In every generation the Irish people have asserted their right to national freedom and sovereignty; six times during the past three hundred years they have asserted it in arms. Standing on that fundamental right and again asserting it in arms in the face of the world, we hereby proclaim the Irish Republic as a Sovereign Independent State, and we pledge the lives of our comrades-in-arms to the cause of its freedom, of its welfare, and of its exaltation among the nations.

The Irish Republic is entitled to, and hereby claims, the allegiance of every Irishman and Irishwoman. The Republic guarantees religious and civil liberty, equal rights and equal opportunities to all its citizens and declares its resolve to pursue the happiness and prosperity of the whole nation and of all its parts, cherishing all the children of the nation equally, and oblivious of the differences carefully fostered by an alien government, which have divided a minority from the majority in the past.

Until our arms have brought the opportune moment for the establishment of a permanent National Government, representative of the whole people of Ireland and elected by the suffrages of all her men and women, the Provisional Government, hereby constituted, will administer the civil and military affairs of the Republic in trust for the people.

We place the cause of the Irish Republic under the protection of the Most High God, Whose blessing we invoke upon our arms, and we pray that no one who serves that cause will dishonour it by cowardice, inhumanity or rapine. In this supreme hour the Irish nation must, by its valour and discipline and by the readiness of its children to sacrifice themselves for the common good, prove itself worthy of the August destiny to which it is called.

THOMAS J CLARKE
SEAN MacDIARMADA
THOMAS MacDONAGH
PH PEARSE
EAMONN CEANNT
JAMES CONNOLLY
JOSEPH PLUNKETT

Among the leaders of the Easter Rising were James Connolly, a militant and successful labour leader of extreme left wing views; Joseph Mary Plunkett, son of Count Plunkett and a poet of distinction. He was chronically ill with tuberculosis by April 1916. He was engaged to Grace Clifford. Padraic Pearse who had a diversity of gifts. He was a playwright, a teacher and a founder of two schools; a lawyer and an orator. In particular he was the leading mystic of the Easter Rising. He was a very fine poet. Thomas MacDonagh was probably the finest poet of the Rising. Others among the leaders were Thomas Clarke and Sean MacDiarmada. There is no doubt that among the leaders of the Easter Rising were men of high idealism, in particular the poets, Pearse, Plunkett and MacDonagh. Their military expertise did not match their political idealism.

The Easter Rising was launched on Easter Monday, 24 April 1916. A platoon of about 40 men marched to the General Post Office in O'Connell Street. Guns and ammunition followed them in two trucks, a cab and a touring car.

Connolly ordered the attack on the General Post Office. Customers were dispersed. Shots were fired at the roof. Staff fled. The Easter Rising was under way. A British lieutenant attempting to use the telegraphic services offered by the Post Office was taken prisoner; one of his captors was Michael Collins.

Other strongholds were besieged, among which the most important were Boland's bakery, St Stephen's Green, the Four Courts, Jacob's biscuit factory, the Mendicity Institution and Gilbey's distillery. No attack was launched on Guinness's premises.

Pearse read the Proclamation of the Provisional Government of the Irish Republic from a first floor balcony of the General Post Office to the crowd below. It was not enthusiastically received. Pearse was disappointed. Connolly was full of confidence.

The Proclamation was posted on walls surrounding the building.

Reaction from the British military presence was swift. A mounted squadron of Lancers was the first to arrive. The insurgents fired on them as they passed Nelson's pillar. Three were killed instantly. The squadron retreated.

The General Post Office was the nerve centre of the Rising to which messages from other parts of the City were sent on motorcycles. Among reports coming through was one that a detachment commanded by the Countess Markiewicz had taken St Stephen's Green. The Countess Markiewicz as Constance Gore-Booth of Lissadel had inspired some of Yeats's loveliest lines. There were reports that at the Four Courts two more Lancers had been killed; that Jacob's factory had been successfully seized; that the Mendicity Institute and the South Dublin Union were under the control of the insurgents. Eamon De Valera, who was to survive the Rising and many other battles including the Irish Civil war to become a prominent politician and leader of the Irish Free State and Republic of Ireland, was in command at Boland's Mill.

A large collection of ladies of humble origin started to congregate near the post office. They received what was termed 'separation money' in respect of sons and husbands serving in the British Army; by 1916 there were 150,000 Irishmen in the British Army. The ladies were not at all keen on the idea of insurrection against Great Britain or separation money. They subjected the insurgents in and around the General Post Office to the most violent abuse.

Monday came to a close; but before the end of the day the most serious looting of the expensive shops in and around O'Connell Street was in full swing. Connolly, Pearse, Plunkett and other leaders of the Rising were completely aghast at this. It was no part of the plan for a Rising that it should be characterised by unbridled theft from honest shopkeepers. But as so often when the forces of revolt are unleashed the leaders are quite powerless to stop them. The leaders were in command of the General Post Office but not of the surrounding streets, the subject of rioting and looting. Pearse in particular was wholly appalled. The scenes of riot and looting before his eyes struck at his imaginary ideal of revolutionary sacrifice for Ireland.

The British Government reacted to the Rising with a Proclamation:

> Whereas an attempt designed by the foreign enemies of our King and country to incite a rebellion in Ireland, and thus endanger the safety of the United Kingdom, has been made by a reckless, though small body of men, who have been guilty of insurrectionary acts in the city of Dublin: Now we, Ivor Churchill, Baron Wimborne, Lord-Lieutenant-General and Governor-General of Ireland, do hereby warn all His Majesty's subjects that the sternest measures are being taken and will be taken for the prompt suppression of the

existing disturbances and the restoration of order: And we do hereby enjoin all loyal and law-abiding citizens to abstain from any acts or conduct which might interfere with the action of the Executive Government, and, in particular, we warn all citizens of the danger of unnecessarily frequenting the streets or public places or of assembling in crowds.

Given under our Seal, on the 24 day of April 1916.

Wimborne.

The battle lines were being drawn. Pearse was concerned for the spiritual welfare of his followers who might face death. He sent for a priest to hear confessions of those who had not attended confession recently. Father Flanagan attended and heard confessions in the General Post Office until late into Monday night. By the end of Monday night the Rising was in place, if far from victorious.

On Tuesday the leaders of the Rising at the General Post Office were awaiting news that the Rising had spread throughout Ireland and that Volunteers would mobilise. It is far from clear how much planning had gone into organising a Rising on a national basis; such an extension of the Rising would have greatly extended British forces. If limited to Dublin, the Rising's chance of success was significantly more slender. Pearse was optimistic that Ireland would answer his mystical call to sacrifice. However the war had increased the material prosperity of Ireland, not least from the separation money coming to the women of Ireland in respect of the 150,000 Irishmen serving in British forces. Rebellion and sacrifice for Ireland as advocated by Pearse was a hard cause to promote as the Rising entered its second day.

Publicity attaching to the Rising did not present it as a major event. The Irish Times published Lord Wimborne's proclamation. Otherwise its report of the Rising was limited to five lines: 'Yesterday morning an insurrectionary Rising took place in the city of Dublin. The authorities have taken active and energetic measures to cope with the situation. The measures are proceeding favourably. In accordance with this official statement early and prompt action is anticipated.' As a forecast of the terrible consequences of the Rising for the peace of Ireland this review was woefully inadequate.

Tuesday wore on. Looting was rampant, stimulated by excessive alcoholic refreshment seized from plundered public houses. The insurgents stood firm in the General Post Office, shocked by the wholesale looting which surrounded them but quite unable to do anything about it. Pearse, among the leaders in the General Post Office was the most distressed by the surrounding lawlessness. It struck at his ideal of an Ireland triumphing through sacrifice to independence. On Tuesday night Pearse read to a substantial gathering at Nelson's Pillar a further Proclamation.

It was a proud and confident Proclamation expressed in the high moral tones of Pearse's devotion to the Rising. The looting of the last twenty-four hours was totally alien to his concept of revolution. The forecast of a national Rising and victory was far from the reality of the situation however much Pearse believed in it.

On Wednesday 26 April British forces shelled Liberty Hall, the headquarters of Connolly's Irish Citizen Army. In fact it had been abandoned and was not manned by the insurgents. But the sound of artillery was not good for confidence at the General Post Office, still the nerve centre of the Rising. British formations were closing in around it. Rifle and machine gun fire were beginning to strike the actual building, anyone walking in O'Connell Street was liable to catch bullets from the British moving closer or the insurgents attempting to return fire. Pearse believed in blood sacrifice. He was fully prepared to give his own life for the freedom of Ireland. By Wednesday 26 April he saw that sacrifice coming closer. He contemplated with apparent equanimity the death of his fellow leaders in the General Post Office. Joseph Plunkett, in dire physical condition from tuberculosis in any event, was equally resigned to die for Ireland. The drama of his impending sacrifice was heightened by his passionate love for Grace Gifford whom he was to marry shortly, if he survived.

The men in the General Post Office continued to hold out although most of the positions seized on Monday had been recaptured by British forces or totally surrendered. Thomas MacDonagh, the poet and Eamon De Valera with their men were still holding out in Jacob's Biscuit Factory and Boland's Mill respectively.

The tenacity of Pearse, Plunkett and Connolly is quite staggering; by Wednesday they realised that there was no national Rising throughout Dublin or the country to support them; that the majority of Irishmen were quite out of sympathy with the Rising; indeed that the bulk of the Irish Volunteers stood firm by MacNeill in his repudiation of the Rising.

On Thursday 27 April British forces were drawing closer to the General Post Office. Pearse issued another Proclamation but this time only to those inside the General Post Office. He assembled his troops and said: 'The forces of the Irish Republic, which we proclaimed in Dublin on Easter Monday, have been in possession of the central part of the capital since twelve noon on that day. Up to yesterday afternoon, headquarters was in touch with all the main outlying positions, and despite furious and almost continuous assaults by the British forces all those positions were then still being held, and the commanders in charge were confident of their ability to hold them for a long time.

During the course of yesterday afternoon and evening, the enemy succeeded in cutting our communication with other positions in the city, and headquarters is being isolated. The enemy has burnt down whole blocks of houses, apparently with the object of giving themselves a clear field for the play of artillery and field guns against us. We have been bombarded during the night with shrapnel and machine gun fire, but without material damage to our position, which is of great strength. We are busy completing arrangements for the final defence of headquarters, and are determined to hold it while the buildings last. I desire now, lest I may not have the opportunity later, to pay homage to the gallantry of the soldiers of Irish freedom who have during the last four days been writing with fire and still the most glorious chapter in the later history of Ireland. Justice can never be done to their heroism, to their discipline, to their gay and unconquerable spirit in the midst of terror and death.

Let me, who have led them into this, speak in my own name and in my fellow commanders' name, and in the name of Ireland present and to come, their praise, and to ask those who come after them to remember them. For four days they have fought and toiled, almost without cessation, almost without sleep, and in the intervals of fighting they have sung songs of the freedom of Ireland. No man has complained, no man has asked 'why'. Each individual has spent himself, happy to pour out his strength for Ireland and for freedom. If they do not win this fight, they will at least deserve to win it. But win it they will, although they may win it in death. Already they have done a great thing. They have redeemed Dublin from many shames, and made her name splendid among the names of cities. They have held out for four days against the might of the British Empire. They have established Ireland's right to be called a Republic and they have established this government's right to sit at the peace table at the end of the European war.'

Nothing written or spoken in the course of the Easter Rising establishes more clearly than this speech delivered in the General Post Office by Pearse on the Thursday of the Rising, the high and fatalistic idealism with which Pearse regarded the Rising and the actual hopelessness of any kind of military victory. In reality Pearse and Connolly knew from the start of the Rising that it had no chance of actual military victory. It was the victory of sacrifice for Ireland which inspired Pearse.

On Friday 28 April the rallying Proclamation to the men in the General Post Office, signed by Connolly was made by another of the leaders, O'Rahilly, Army of the Irish Republic, Headquarters (Dublin Command).

To Soldiers,

This is the fifth day of the establishment of the Irish Republic, and the flag of our country still floats from the most important buildings in Dublin, and is gallantly protected by the officers and Irish soldiers in arms throughout the country. Not a day passes without seeing fresh postings of Irish soldiers eager to do battle for the old cause. Despite the utmost vigilance of the enemy, we have been able to get information telling us how the manhood of Ireland, inspired by our splendid action, are gathering to offer up their lives, if necessary, in the same holy cause. We are hemmed in, because the enemy feels that in this building is to be found the heart and inspiration of our great movement. For the first time in seven hundred years the flag of a free Ireland floats triumphantly in Dublin city. The British Army whose exploits we are forever having dinned into our ears, which boasts of having stormed the Dardenelles and the German lines on the Marne, behind their artillery and machine guns, are afraid to advance to the attack or storm any positions, held by our forces. The slaughter they suffered in the first few days has totally unnerved them, and they dare not attempt again an infantry attack on our positions. Our commandants around us are holding their own.

The Proclamation then set out the details of other positions being held which included:

Commandant MacDonagh is established in an impregnable position, reaching from the walls of Dublin Castle to Redmond's Hill and from Bishop Street to Stephen's Green. As you know, I was wounded twice yesterday, and am unable to move about, but have got my bed moved into the firing line and, with the assistance of your officers, will be as useful to them as ever. Courage, boys, we are winning, and in the hour of our victory let us not forget the splendid women who have everywhere stood by us and cheered us on. Never had a man or woman a grander cause; never was a cause more grandly served.

James Connolly
COMMANDANT-GENERAL
DUBLIN DIVISION.

These were brave words. Connolly knew that the situation was growing more hopeless by the hour. He was as resigned to death as Pearse. He clearly felt it right to exhort his men even though he must have known that at least some of them were sure to die.

Pearse had not slept since Monday. It is surprising that his Friday message was as coherent as it was. It was truthful, generous, and resigned to death.

If we accomplish no more than we have accomplished, I am satisfied. I am satisfied that we have saved Ireland's honour. I am satisfied that we should have accomplished more, that we should have accomplished the task of enthroning as well as proclaiming the Irish Republic as a Sovereign State, had our arrangements for a simultaneous Rising of the whole country, with a combined plan as sound as the Dublin plan has proved to be, been allowed to go through on Easter Sunday. Of the fatal commanding order which prevented these plans being carried out, I shall not speak further. Both Eoin MacNeill and we have acted in the best interests of Ireland.

For my part, as to anything I have done in this, I am not afraid to face the judgement of God or the judgement of posterity.

Signed P.H. Pearse
COMMANDMENT GENERAL OF THE IRISH REPUBLIC
AND PRESIDENT OF THE IRISH REPUBLIC
COMMANDER-IN-CHIEF, THE ARMY
AND PRESIDENT OF THE PROVISIONAL GOVERNMENT.

The situation grew more hopeless on Friday as British forces continued to surround the General Post Office. It was thought advisable by Connolly and Pearse that as many women as possible should leave. Pearse addressed twenty girls detailed to leave:

> When the history of this week is written, the highest honours will be afforded to all of you, whose bravery, heroism and devotion in the face of danger have surpassed even that of the women of Limerick in the days of Sarsfield. You have taken part in the greatest armed attempt at liberation by Ireland since 1798. You have obeyed the order to come here. Now I ask you to obey a more difficult order – the order to leave. Remember it is equally binding upon you. It may not be easy for you to escape from here safely. There is a possibility that some of you may be shot after you leave this building. But you showed your readiness for that when you came here. Now go and God be with you.

The girls were reluctant to leave while the men stayed. Pearse and Desmond Fitzgerald prevailed upon them. They left and were, within a few hundred yards, taken into custody by British soldiers.

Incendiary shells were landing in the General Post Office. Fires were breaking out. They were extinguished by available hoses. By Friday night evacuation plans were under consideration by Pearse, Plunkett, Connolly and the other leaders in the Post Office, MacDermott, Clarke and the O'Rahilly. One idea was to use the sewers; but a brief reconnoitre disclosed the dirt to be impenetrable.

On Friday night Plunkett sent what he believed to be his last note to his beloved fiancée, Grace Clifford; he also enclosed his will leaving her all his worldly goods which were not negligible. The courier was to be a lady still in the General Post Office. Plunkett believed she would escape execution. His own health was so ravaged by tuberculosis that apart from the perils of the Rising he was unlikely to survive.

Connolly, although on a stretcher, refused to leave in the proposed evacuation of the wounded.

Father Flanagan was engaged in giving the Last Absolution to those who felt that the end was approaching fast.

The few prisoners who had been taken during the week were released to make it back to the British lines, drawing ever closer to the General Post Office, if they could.

Fires were still burning in the General Post Office. Very few of the insurgents remained inside. Pearse was in command of the evacuation. He was with the final party to leave. Pearse, Connolly and others found temporary refuge in the home of a Mr and Mrs McKane in Moore Street. When the battered remnants of the Rising arrived at the McKane home a soldier fired a shot at McKane's locked door. It wounded Mr McKane and killed their sixteen year old daughter Bridget.

Patrick Pearse arrived after this incident. He was distraught at Bridget McKane's death. On that Friday night seventeen wounded men lodged in the McKane household including one British soldier rescued from the street having been seriously wounded.

Saturday's problem was how to get out of Moore Street where the leaders of the Rising were trapped in the small McKane house with many wounded: one wounded British soldier, nine McKane children and one dead McKane daughter.

Pearse decided that further resistance could only lead to pointless bloodshed of many innocent people. He sent a Miss O'Farrell, who had served as a nurse all week, under cover of a white flag to seek out the nearest officer in command. British barricades were at the end of Moore Street. Moore Street was close to destruction. Many civilians lived in it. The message sent back to Pearse was a demand for unconditional surrender.

From Commander of Dublin Forces
To P.H. Pearse
29 April 1916
1.40pm

A woman has come in and tells me you wish to negotiate with me. I am prepared to meet you in Brittain Street (Parnell Street) at the north end of Moore Street provided you surrender unconditionally. You will proceed up

Moore Street accompanied only by the woman who brings this note – under a white flag.

W.H.M. Lowe

B.Genl.

Brigadier-General Lowe's message via Miss O'Farrell demanded unconditional surrender; and that when Pearse surrendered Connolly must follow on a stretcher.

Pearse, Connolly, Plunkett, MacDermott and Clarke decided that there was no alternative but to surrender. Each knew that they would face a firing squad. A continuation of the Rising would involve a bloodbath of innocents. At 2.30pm Pearse surrendered himself to Brigadier-General Lowe. He handed over his sword. Connolly was carried slowly afterwards on a stretcher. Each signed a surrender order to be carried by Miss O'Farrell to the remaining outposts of the Rising.

> In order to prevent the further slaughter of Dublin citizens, and in the hope of saving the lives of our followers now surrounded and hopelessly outnumbered, the members of the Provisional Government present at headquarters have agreed to an unconditional surrender, and the Commandants of the various districts in the City and country will order their commands to lay down arms.
>
> P.H. Pearse
>
> 29 April 1916
>
> 3.45 pm.

> I agree to these conditions for the men only under my own command in the Moore Street District and for the men in the Stephen's Green command.
>
> James Connolly
>
> 29 April 1916

Clarke, McDermott and Joseph Plunkett were still in Moore Street; also in Moore Street was Michael Collins. All four supported the Pearse/Connolly call to surrender. Some of the men wanted to fight on. McDermott eventually persuaded them all to agree to follow the Pearse/Connolly orders. The Parnell Monument was the designated place for the surrender of men and arms; before long four hundred men had arrived from different areas of the city to surrender and were marched away for the night in a nearby yard. On Sunday morning, 30 April most men who had surrendered were marched to Richmond Barracks. Such spectators as were in the streets were far from friendly to them. Abuse was poured upon the prisoners including some rotten fruit as they were marched through the streets. The mob was against them.

McDermott, Plunkett and Pearse were taken to Killmainham jail. Fourteen of the leaders of the Easter Rising were court-martialled. They were executed by firing squad within twelve days. They included Patrick Pearse, Joseph Plunkett, Thomas McDonagh and James Connolly. Joseph Plunkett was shot four hours after he was married in his cell to Grace Gifford.

The unhappy consequences of the Easter Rising and particularly the execution of the leaders including three poets Patrick Pearse, Joseph Plunkett and Thomas McDonagh are with us still in Ireland. No doubt they will be for many years to come. Irish public opinion had been at best indifferent and at worst hostile to the Easter Rising. The leader in the Drogheda Independent on 29 April reflected the opinion of many 'Since Monday last the people of Ireland have been hearing of strange doings in Dublin – a Rising of Sein Fein Volunteers, street disturbances, and such like. It would appear that an armed conjunction of Liberty Hall heroes, with some of the Sinn Fein Volunteers has made an attempt at some kind of miserable Rising. The King's troops and the police force have now got Larkinites and the Sein Feiners well in hand, and the ridiculous Rising has been crushed and broken.' These are sentiments far removed from the heady proclamations of Pearse throughout the Rising. However the Meath Chronicle was significantly more sympathetic. Under the heading of 'A Tragic Blunder' it asserted 'No one, we feel sure, can refuse a tribute to these gallant young fellows who harkened to the call of duty to fight against desperate odds for the liberation of their country.'

After the executions public opinion swung to an increasingly nationalist and republican position. By 1919 England and the Republic of Ireland were at war. The Treaty which brought that war to an end in 1921 was followed by a bitter Civil War in Ireland between the pro and anti Treaty factions.

Four poems by Yeats tell all of the tragic consequences of the Rising and more particularly the executions following its suppression.

EASTER 1916

I have met them at close of day
Coming with vivid faces
From counter or desk among grey
Eighteenth–century houses.
I have passed with a nod of the head
Or polite meaningless words,

Or have lingered awhile and said
Polite meaningless words,
And thought before I had done
Of a mocking tale or a gibe
To please a companion
Around the fire at the club,
Being certain that they and I
But lived where motley is worn:
All changed, changed utterly:
A terrible beauty is born.

That woman's days were spent
In ignorant good-will,
Her nights in argument
Until her voice grew shrill.
What voice more sweet than hers
When, young and beautiful,
She rode to harriers?
This man had kept a school
And rode our wingéd horse;
This other his helper and friend
Was coming into his force;
He might have won fame in the end,
So sensitive his nature seemed,
So daring and sweet his thought,
This other man I had dreamed
A drunken, vainglorious lout.
He had done most bitter wrong
To some who are near my heart,
Yet I number him in the song;
He, too, has resigned his part
In the casual comedy;
He, too, has been changed in his turn,
Transformed utterly:
A terrible beauty is born.

Hearts with one purpose alone
Through summer and winter seem

Enchanted to a stone
To trouble the living stream.
The horse that comes from the road,
The rider, the birds that range
From cloud to tumbling cloud,
Minute by minute they change;
A shadow of cloud on the stream
Changes minute by minute;
A horse-hoof slides on the brim,
And a horse plashes within it;
The long-legged moor-hens dive,
And hens to moor-cocks call;
Minute by minute they live:
The stone's in the midst of all.

Too long a sacrifice
Can make a stone of the heart.
O when may it suffice?
That is Heaven's part, our part
To murmur name upon name,
As a mother names her child
When sleep at last has come
On limbs that had run wild.
What is it but nightfall?
No, no, not night but death;
Was it needless death after all?
For England may keep faith
For all that is done and said.
We know their dream; enough
To know they dreamed and are dead;
And what if excess of love
Bewildered them till they died?
I write it out in a verse –
MacDonagh and MacBride
And Connolly and Pearse
Now and in time to be,
Wherever green is worn,
Are changed, changed utterly:
A terrible beauty is born.

SIXTEEN DEAD MEN

O but we talked at large before
The sixteen men were shot,
But who can talk of give and take,
What should be and what not
While those dead mean are loitering there
To stir the boiling pot?

You say that we should still the land
Till Germany's overcome;
But who is there to argue that
Now Pearse is deaf and dumb?
And is their logic to outweigh
MacDonagh's bony thumb?

How could you dream they'd listen
That have an ear alone
For those new comrades they have found,
Lord Edward and Wolfe Tone,
Or meddle with our give and take
That converse bone to bone?

THE ROSE TREE

'O words are lightly spoken',
Said Pearse to Connolly,
'Maybe a breath of politic words
Has withered our Rose Tree;
Or maybe but a wind that blows
Across the bitter sea.'

'It needs to be but watered,'
James Connolly replied,
'To make the green come out again
And spread on every side,
And shake the blossom from the bud
To be the garden's pride.'

> 'But where can we draw water',
> Said Pearse to Connolly,
> 'When all the wells are parched away?
> O plain as plain can be
> There's nothing but our own red blood
> Can make a right Rose Tree.'

This poem expresses exactly the sentiments of Patrick Pearse.

If the reference in *Easter 1916* to the girl who rode to harriers growing shrill is a reference to Constance Markiewicz, formerly Constance Gore-Booth of Lissadel, Yeats returns to her in his poem *On A Political Prisoner*. She was the most overtly passionate of the insurgents in her hatred of England and her support for a Republican Ireland, coining the expression 'Burn everything British except their coal.' She was imprisoned rather than executed, no doubt because she was a woman. Yeats recalls her former loveliness (*On A Political Prisoner*, see p. 65).

The news of the executions struck Francis Ledwidge to the centre. He was in hospital in Manchester. The Rising, its failure and the executions touched different and important areas of his life and experience. He had been an Irish Volunteer. They were defeated in the Rising. He had been an enthusiastic supporter of the Trade Unions and workers' rights. Connolly and the Citizen Army had been to the forefront of the Rising. Connolly was executed. The poets, Patrick Pearse, Joseph Plunkett and Thomas MacDonagh were brothers of Ledwidge in the same great calling of literature. He wrote to his friend Bob Christie from Manchester:

> Poor MacDonagh and Pearse were two of my best friends, and now they are dead, shot by England; MacDonagh had a beautiful mind. Don't you know his poetry:
>
> > 'Sweeter than violin and lute
> > Is my love – and she left me behind.
> > I wish that all music were mute
> > And I to all beauty were blind.'
>
> That is a verse from one of his Irish love songs.
>
> My recollections of poor MacDonagh are forever more full of sorrow. I have no rest because of Ellie, even yet. I wrote many keens for her. The poem in the *Saturday Review* is of her. The Saturday has another of mine, one written in Greece. I hope to get home in a few days, but you must write again. I will

run to see you when I go to Derry. I hear often from Lord Dunsany. He wrote
to welcome me home. I didn't know his mother was dead.

I must write condoling with him.

Francis Ledwidge's return was heralded by the *Meath Chronicle* on 13 May 'Meath
Poet – Soldier among the Serbians' 'Francis Ledwidge, the gifted Meath poet, who
joined the Inniskilling Fusiliers, and who has been on active service for the past year,
and at present home on leave, speaking to our representative remarked: 'The
Serbians impressed me very much. I consider Serbia, poetically, like Ireland – a poor
old woman wandering the roads of the world.' In the course of further conversation
he stated that they found strips of cloth in some of the Serbian houses bearing in
faded letters the word WELCOME. Those clothes had been hung across the streets.
'While in the Dardanelles' he said with a smile 'We were not short of eggs. The Turks
exchanged eggs with us for beef and biscuits. If I give you more information I'll have
nothing left for the book I am going to write on my experiences out there.'

He was deeply shaken by the Rising and more particularly by the executions. He
visited Dublin and contemplated the rubble and ruin occasioned by the fighting. In
Slane he met up again with old friends. His mood was down. He told his brother 'If
I heard the Germans were coming in over our back wall, I wouldn't go out now to
stop them. They could come.'

He went to Richmond Barracks, where he was training in connection with his
return to active service. Pearse and MacDonagh had been sentenced at Richmond
Barracks; a fact which deepened Francis Ledwidge's gloom at this time. He was
ordered to return to Londonderry. He travelled via Belfast where he stayed some
days with his friend Christie with whom he had served in Gallipoli and the Balkans.

Christie had been invalided out consequent to severe injuries sustained in the
Balkan's campaign. Christie advised Francis Ledwidge to seek a medical discharge in
respect of his own injuries. Ledwidge, although wholly disillusioned with the army
and the war and wholly sympathetic with the men of the Easter Rising, would not
pretend that his condition was worse than it was.

By early June 1916 he was back in Ebrington Barracks, Londonderry.

The anguish in his soul consequent to the Rising and its aftermath inspired
Ledwidge's finest poetry.

He had known Thomas MacDonagh. Ledwidge's poem *Thomas MacDonagh* tells
all his sadness expressed in his own particular lyricism.

> He shall not hear the bittern cry
> In the wild sky, where he is lain,

Nor voices of the sweeter birds
Above the wailing of the rain.

Nor shall he know when loud March blows
Thro' slanting snows her fanfare shrill,
Blowing to flame the golden cup
Of many an upset daffodil.

But when the Dark Cow leaves the moor,
And pastures poor with greedy weeds,
Perhaps he'll hear her low at morn
Lifting her horn in pleasant meads.

The harrowing circumstances of Joseph Plunkett's last hours, executed four hours after his marriage to Grace Gifford, prompted two poems.

THRO' BOGAC BAN

I met the Silent Wandering Man,
Thro' Bogac Ban he made his way,
Humming a slow old Irish tune,
On Joseph Plunkett's wedding day.

And all the little whispering things
That love the springs of Bogac Ban,
Spread some new rumour round the dark
And turned their faces from the dawn.

My hand upon my harp I lay,
I cannot say what things I know;
To meet the Silent Wandering Man
Of Bogac Ban once more I go.

DREAMS

The little black cow with the golden horn
Lows in my sleep and saddens my dreams,
Her eyes are like shades on an upland croft,
Rich and soft 'mid its lovely streams.

The Big Black Crow leaves its rookery
Behind the sea, when I close my eyes,
His shadow blighting the golden crops
That wave to the top of the Spring's emprise.

I see Grace Gifford with pallet red,
When I lay my head in the poppy dawn,
And I would greet her as poets might
But I wake from the night with my dreaming gone.

In *The Blackbirds* Francis Ledwidge laments all three poets executed for their part in the Rising (see p. 10). It was written in July 1916, when Ledwidge was still at Ebrington Barracks, Londonderry. County Londonderry is full of little hills. It is clear that the pain of the events of Easter 1916 is still very much alive in July.

The memory of Plunkett and Pearse haunts *At Currabwee.*

Every night at Currabwee
Little men with leather hats
Mend the boots of Faery
From the tough wings of the bats.
So my mother told to me,
And she is wise you will agree.

Louder than a cricket's wing
All night long their hammer's glee
Times the merry songs they sing
Of Ireland glorious and free.
So I heard Joseph Plunkett say,
You know he heard them but last May.

And when the night is very cold
They warm their hands against the light
Of stars that make the waters gold

Where they are labouring all the night.
So Pearse said, and he knew the truth,
Among the stars he spent his youth.

And I, myself, have often heard
Their singing as the stars went by,
For am I not of those who reared
The banner of old Ireland high,
From Dublin town to Turkey's shores,
And where the Vardar loudly roars?

TO MRS JOSEPH PLUNKETT

You shall not lack our little praise
If such can win your fair renown.
The halcyon of your lost days
We shall replace with living crown.

We see you not as one of us
Who so lament each little thing,
You profit more by honest loss,
Who lost so much, than song can sing.

This you have lost, a heart which bore
An ideal love, an ideal shame,
And earned this thing, for evermore
A noble and a splendid name.

He wrote much later and shortly before his death of the actual Rising *O'Connell Street*.

A noble failure is not vain
But hath a victory its own.
A bright delectance from the slain

Is down the generations thrown.
And, more than Beauty understands,
Has made her lovelier here, it seems.
I see white ships that crowd her strands,
For mine are all the dead men's dreams.

Thoughts of the dead poets were with him to the end of his own life.

The only other poem directly related to the detail of the Rising as opposed to its tragic outcome was *Jeu d'esprit*.

What rumours filled the Atlantic sky,
And turned the wild geese back again;
When Plunkett lifted Balor's eye,
And broke Andromeda's strong chain?
or did they hear that Starkie, James,
Among the gallipots was seen,
And he who called her sweetest names,
Was talking to another queen?

Now all the wise in quicklime burn,
And all the strong have crossed the sea;
But down the pale roads of Ashbourne,
Are heard the voices of the free.
And Jemmy Quigley is the boy,
Could say how queenly was her walk,
When Sackville Street went down like Troy,
And peelers fell in far Dundalk.

There were many bizarre features about the Easter Rising; but perhaps the most extraordinary was that it was led by three very fine poets. If Pearse, Plunkett and MacDonagh had lived their work would have featured significantly in Irish twentieth century literature. The poetry which they did write in their lives has been extensively acclaimed. But if those lives had not been cut short by a hopeless, if idealistic Rising, and its cruel aftermath, their positions in Irish literature would have been dominant.

JOSEPH PLUNKETT

JOSEPH PLUNKETT was born in 1887. He was the son of Count and Countess Plunkett. In early life he met Thomas MacDonagh who was teaching at St Enda's School, Rathfarnham. Thomas MacDonagh taught him Irish. He lived principally in Donnybrook, Dublin sharing a house with his sister when he was not travelling abroad. He was particularly friendly with Pearse and MacDonagh. In 1913 he became editor of the Irish Review to which Roger Casement contributed. In 1914 he was a founder member of the Irish Theatre with Edward Martyn and Thomas MacDonagh. Its purpose was to produce Irish plays, plays in Irish and foreign masterpieces. He disagreed with Martyn and Thomas MacDonagh and gave up his interest in it.

He was chronically ill with tuberculosis at the start of and throughout the Easter Rising. He was the most overtly religious of the three poets executed after the Rising. His faith shone through his poetry.

I SEE HIS BLOOD UPON THE ROSE

I see his blood upon the rose
And in the stars the glory of his eyes,
His body gleams amid eternal snows,
His tears fall from the skies.

I see his face in every flower;
The thunder and the singing of the birds
Are but his voice – and carven by his power
Rocks are his written words.

All pathways by his feet are worn,
His strong heart stirs the ever-beating sea,
His crown of thorns is twined with every thorn,
His cross is every tree

THE STARS SANG IN GOD'S GARDEN

The stars sang in God's garden;
The stars are the birds of God;

The night-time is God's harvest,
Its fruits are the words of God.

God ploughed His fields at morning,
God sowed His seed at noon,
God reaped and gathered in His corn
With the rising of the moon.

The sun rose up at midnight,
The sun rose red as blood,
It showed the Reaper, the dead Christ,
Upon His cross of wood.

For many live that one may die,
And one must die that many live –
The stars are silent in the sky
Lest my poor songs be fugitive.

It is apparent that Joseph Plunkett's poetry had a deeply religious strain. Love and passion were also significant inspirations for his writing.

TO GRACE

On the morning of her Christening, April 7 1916

The powerful words that from my heart
Alive and throbbing leap and sing
Shall bind the dragon's jaws apart
Or bring you back a vanished spring;
They shall unseal and seal again
The fount of wisdom's awful flow,
So this one guerdon they shall gain
That your wild beauty still they show.

The joy of Spring leaps from your eyes,
The strength of dragons in your hair,
In your young soul we still surprise
The secret wisdom flowing there;

But never word shall speak or sing
Inadequate music where above
Your burning heart now spreads its wing
In the wild beauty of your Love.

He was shot four hours after marrying Grace Gifford, the object and inspiration of his finest love poems.

Joseph Plunkett, like most Irish poets, was not far removed from the joy of all things natural.

A WAVE OF THE SEA

I am a wave of the sea
And the foam of the wave
And the wind of the foam
And the wings of the wind.

My soul's in the salt of the sea
In the weight of the wave
In the bubbles of foam
In the ways of the wind.

My gift is the depth of the sea
The strength of the wave
The lightness of foam
The speed of the wind.

The concepts of sacrifice were very much part of Joseph Plunkett's spiritual equipment.

I SAW THE SUN AT MIDNIGHT

I saw the sun at midnight, rising red,
Deep-hued yet glowing, heavy with the stain
Of blood-compassion, and I saw It gain
Swiftly in size and growing till it spread
Over the stars; the heavens bowed their head
As from Its heart slow dripped a crimson rain,

Then a great tremor shook It, as of pain -
The night fell, moaning, as It hung there dead.

O Sun, O Christ, O bleeding Heart of flame!
Thou givest Thine agony as our life's worth,
And makest it infinite, lest we have dearth
Of rights wherewith to call upon Thy Name;
Thou pawnest Heaven as a pledge for Earth
And for our glory sufferest all shame.

In the end Joseph Plunkett sacrificed his own life for what he believed to be the cause of Ireland's salvation. Ireland was robbed of a fine and highly original poetic voice.

PATRICK PEARSE

PATRICK PEARSE was the most passionate Irishman of the century. His father was English. He was born in Dublin. He learnt Irish by living for long periods in Connaught which he loved. He learnt Irish so well that he could write, speak and think in Irish. He founded a school where the education was in Irish. Napoleon was one of his great heroes.

'At break of day I chanced to stray where Seine's fair waters glide
When to raise my heart young Bonaparte came forward for to ride;
On a field of green, with gallant men, he formed his men in square,
And down the line, with looks divine, he rode the oul' grey mare.'

He combined passion with extreme gentleness. He was playwright, storyteller, poet.

He was on the executive of the Gaelic League; he became editor of the Gaelic League weekly which he said he would make the organ of militant Gaeldom.

He founded St Enda's and St Ita's schools to provide a national Irish education. He caused a fresco to be painted on the wall of St Enda's school of the boy Cuchullan taking a run. The boy is warned by a Druid that he will make his name famous but will die an early death. Cuchullan's reply, in Irish, was on the walls 'I care not if my life has only the span of a day and a night if my deeds be spoken of by the men of Ireland.' He hoped that his review of St Enda's activities, which he occasionally published, would be a rallying point for the thought and aspirations of all those who

would bring back again in Ireland that Heroic Age which reserved its highest honour for the hero who had the most childlike heart, for the king who had the largest
pity, and for the poet who visioned the truest image of beauty.

In 1913 he published a series of articles on Wolfe Tone, John Mitchell, Thomas
Davis and Fenton Labour as the Evangelists of Irish Nationalism. He was a deeply
committed Christian.

The impulse towards and the necessity for a sacrifice of blood for Ireland perme-
ated his spirit. The theme of sacrifice is ever recurring in much of his writing. His
plays were inspired by concepts of struggle, agony, death. They are principally set in
the Gaelic West of Ireland. They set out to advance the dream of a triumphant
Gaelic revival.

In his play *The Singer*, Sighle says 'I shiver when I think of them all going out to
fight. They will go out laughing; I see them with their cheeks flushed and their red
lips apart. And then they will lie very still on the hillside, – so still and white, with
no red in their cheeks, but maybe a red wound in their white breasts, or on their
white foreheads. Colm's hair will be dabbled with blood – I am proud other times
to think of so many young men, young men with straight, strong limbs, and
smooth, white flesh, going out into great peril because a voice has called to them to
right the wrong of the people. Oh, I would like to see the man that has set their
hearts on fire with the breath of his voice! They say that he is very young. They say
that he is one of ourselves, – a mountainy man that speaks our speech, and has
known hunger and sorrow' *(The Singer – The Complete Works of P.H. Pearse, 9)*.

(At 31 The Complete Works of P H Pearse) MacDara. 'The true teacher must suffer
and do. He must break bread to the people: he must go into Gethsemane and toil
up the steep of Golgotha.'

In this play as elsewhere Patrick Pearse's concepts of sacrifice are expressed in language of higher romanticism. Did he foresee his own sacrifice in the last lines of his
play *The Singer* 'One man can free a people as one Man redeemed the world. I will
take no pike, I will go into battle with bare hands. I will stand up before the Gall as
Christ hung naked before men on the tree!'

He wrote a number of other plays *The King, The Master, Iosagen*. They exalt the
spiritual values in human affairs. In *The Master* Ciaran says 'I chose self-abnegation,
not out of humility, but out of pride: and God, that terrible hidden God, has punished me by withholding from me His most precious gift of faith. Faith comes to the
humble only … Nay, Lord, I believe: this is but a temptation. Thou, too, wast
tempted. Thou, too, wast forsaken. O valiant Christ, give me Thy strength! My need

is great. He also wrote stories: *The Mother, The Dearg-Daol, The Roads, Brigid Of The Songs, The Thief, The Keening Woman, Iosagan, The Priest, Barbara, Eoineen Of The Birds*, all speak in their different ways of those inspirations close to his heart.

He was a deeply religious man. From *The Mother (Complete Works of PH Pearse)* 'Doesn't the world know that the glorious Virgin goes round the townlands every Christmas Eve, herself and her child'? 'I heard the people saying she does': 'And don't you know if the door is left ajar and a candle lighting in the window, that the Virgin and her Child will come into the house, and that they will sit down to rest themselves'?

From *The Roads* 'She heard a noise, and the place was filled with armed men. She saw dark, devilish faces, and grey swords and edged weapons. The gentle Man was seized outrageously, and His share of clothes torn from Him, and He was scourged with scourges there till His body was in a bloody mass and in an everlasting wound from His head to the soles of His feet. A thorny crown was put on His gentle head, and a cross was laid on His shoulders, and He went before Him, heavy-footed, pitifully, the sorrowful way of His journey to Calvary. The chain that was tying Nora's tongue and limbs till that broke, and she cried aloud: 'Let me go with You, Jesus, and carry Your cross for You.' Irish nationalism was never far below the surface in his stories. In *The Keening Woman,* a story of beautiful simplicity, 'Her son died twenty years since, Coilin' says my mother. 'He didn't die at all', says my father, and a very black look on him. 'He was murdered.' 'Who murdered him'? It's seldom I saw my father angry, but it's awful his anger was when it would rise up in him. He took a start out of me when he spoke again, he was that angry. 'Who murdered your own grandfather? Who drew the red blood out of my grandmother's shoulders with a lash? Who would do it but the English. My curse on –' *(204/205 The Complete Works of PH Pearse).*

(The Keening Woman, 207 and 208 The Complete Works of PH Pearse) – 'Did ye hear, people', says he to us, and he drinking with us, 'that the lord is to come home tonight'? 'What business has the devil here'? says someone. 'Bad work he's up to, as usual', says the black man. 'He has settled to put seven families out of their holdings.' 'Who's to be put out'? says one of us. 'Old Thomas O'Drinan from the Glen, – I'm told the poor fellow's dying, but it's on the roadside he'll die, if God hasn't him already; a man of the O'Conaire's that lives in a cabin on this side of Loch Shindilla; Manning from Snamh Bo; two in Annaghmaan; a woman at the head of the Island; and Anthony O'Greelis from Lower Camus.' 'Anthony's wife is heavy in child', says Cuimin O'Niadh. 'That won't save her, the creature', says the black man. 'She's not the first woman out of this country that bore her child in a ditch-side of the road.'

Patrick Pearse was not, even in his short life a prolific poet. His only book of poems 'Suantraidhe agus Goltraidhe (*Songs Of Sleep And Sorrow*) was published in 1914. But in such poetry as he did write the theme of religious faith is powerfully present.

CHRISTMAS 1915

O King that was born
To set bondsmen free,
In the coming battle,
Help the Gael!

While Patrick Pearse was in no way necrophiliac he was deeply sensitive to life in death and death in life.

Patrick Pearse was a prominent leader of an insurgent Rising in which violence was contemplated. His poetry suggests that he had the gentlest of temperaments.

O LITTLE BIRD

(A sparrow which I found dead on my doorstep on a day in winter.)

O little bird!
Cold to me thy lying on the flag:
Bird, that never had an evil thought,
Pitiful the coming of death to thee!

He was passionate about his loved ones as he was about his country, and the wonder of all natural things inspired his poetry:

ON THE STRAND OF HOWTH

On the strand of Howth,
Breaks a sounding wave;
A lone sea-gull screams
Above the bay.

In the middle of the meadow
Beside Glasnevin
The corncrake speaks
All night long.

There is minstrelsy of birds
In Glenasmole,
The blackbird and thrush
Chanting music.

The poetry of Patrick Pearse tells of his coming sacrifice. The most famous fore-
sight of the sacrifice in the Rising is the terse and beautiful poem

RENUNCIATION

Naked I saw thee,
O beauty of beauty,
And I blinded my eyes
For fear I should fail.

I heard thy music,
O melody of melody,
And I closed my ears
For fear I should falter.

I tasted thy mouth,
O sweetness of sweetness,
And I hardened my heart
For fear of my slaying.

I blinded my eyes,
And I closed my ears,
I hardened my heart
And I smothered my desire.

I turned my back
On the vision I had shaped,
And to this road before me
I turned my face.

I have turned my face
To this road before me,

To the deed that I see
And the death I shall die.

Patrick Colum, *In Road Round Ireland*, compares this poem with the lovely poem of the blind Connaught poet Rafferty written many years before.

I am Rafferty the poet,
Full of hope and love,
With eyes that have no light,
With gentleness that has no misery.

Going west upon my pilgrimage
By the light of my heart,
Feeble and tired
To the end of my road.

Behold me now,
And my face to the wall,
A-playing music
Unto empty pockets.

Sacrifice was at the heart of Patrick Pearse's life and poetry:

THE MOTHER

I do not grudge them: Lord, I do not grudge
My two strong sons that I have seen go out
To break their strength and die, they and a few,
In bloody protest for a glorious thing,
They shall be spoken of among their people,
The generations shall remember them,
And call them blessed;
But I will speak their names to my own heart
In the long nights;
The little names that were familiar once
Round my dead hearth.
Lord, thou art hard on mothers:
We suffer in their coming and their going;

And tho' I grudge them not, I weary, weary
Of the long sorrow – And yet I have my joy:
My sons were faithful, and they fought.

The *Mother* and *Renunciation*, written before 1916, were an uncanny forecast of Patrick Pearse's own part in the Rising.

Patrick Pearse had a simplicity that was childlike; he was humble; he was an idealist; he was a mystic. He had none of the apparent qualities of a leader of a potentially violent uprising.

He was driven to a prominent participation in the Easter Rising by the certain conviction that sacrifice, blood and death were wholly necessary for a resurgent, independent Ireland. Was he right?

THOMAS MACDONAGH

He might have won fame in the end,
So sensitive his nature seemed
So daring and sweet his thought.

WB Yeats on Thomas McDonagh in Easter 1916

THOMAS MACDONAGH was undoubtedly the most sophisticated poet of the three. He wrote *Literature In Ireland*. This is an extremely erudite review of Irish poetry, ancient and modern, and Irish poetry written in Irish and English. It covers the writing of Callanan, Colum, Ferguson, Hyde, Mangan, Moore, Pearse, Petrie, Plunkett, Sigerson, Walsh and Yeats. It is not surprising that the poetry of someone so deeply knowledgeable in Irish literature should have a particular edge to it. In *Literature In Ireland* Thomas MacDonagh wrote 'Propaganda has rarely produced a great poem. A great poem, whether of religion or patriotism, is rarely other than the cry of a poet calling to his God or his country as if he alone experienced the emotion that he sings, though poignantly mindful that many felt it in a better day. The poet once again is his own first audience. If others afterwards come and share his joy, the gain is theirs.'

He was a close friend of Patrick Pearse. He taught in his school, St. Enda's. He was also a close friend of Joseph Plunkett. He supervised the publication of Plunkett's *The Circle* and *The Sword* when Plunkett was abroad for health reasons in 1911.

He was a stern critic of his own writing. He wished that only his *Songs Of Myself,* *Lyrical Poems, Miscellaneous Poems* and some translations should be preserved. He made a bonfire of some of his own writing in the playing fields of St. Enda's with the comment that no poet burns a poem unless he has a second copy. He preserved a few copies of the poems which he consigned to flames for future publication.

His *Literature In Ireland,* recently republished, is a masterly analysis of some of the great strands of Irish writing. He was vastly cultivated in every area of literature. He was knowledgeable in classic, European, English and Irish literature. It is scarcely surprising that his poetry has a supreme vitality and loveliness; that it has a rare combination of depth and scope.

He was a translator. His translation of *The Yellow Bittern (1916 Poets, 80)* from the Irish inspired the opening line of Francis Ledwidge's lament (see p. 203) for him 'He shall not hear the bittern cry.'

> The yellow bittern that never broke out
> > In a drinking bout, might as well have drunk;
> His bones are thrown on a naked stone
> > Where he lived alone like a hermit monk.

Thomas MacDonagh was a man of Munster. He loved the country and all things natural.

AT DAWN

> Lo! 'tis the lark
> Out in the sweet of the dawn!
> Springing up from the dew of the lawn,
> Singing over the gurth and the park! -
> O Dawn, red rose to change my life's grey story!
> O Song, mute lips burning to lyric glory!
> O Joy! Joy of the lark,
> Over the dewy lawn,
> Over the gurth and the park,
> In the sweet of the dawn!

Thomas MacDonagh was a man of variable moods as expressed in his poetry. There was a distinctly melancholic area of his personality which surfaced in his writing.

THE SUICIDE

Here when I have died,
    And when my body is found,
They will bury it by the roadside
    And in no blesséd ground.

And no one my story will tell,
    And no one will honour my name:
They will think that they bury well
    The damned in their grave of shame.

But alike shall be at last
    The shamed and the blesséd place,
The future and the past,
    Man's grace and man's disgrace.

Secure in their grave I shall be
    From it all, and quiet then,
With no thought and no memory
    Of the deeds and the dooms of men.

But his mood lifted and some of his poems have a real lightness of touch.

JOHN-JOHN

I dreamt last night of you, John-John,
    And thought you called to me;
And when I woke this morning, John,
    Yourself I hoped to see;
But I was all alone, John-John,
    Though still I heard your call:
I put my boots and bonnet on,
    And took my Sunday shawl,
And went, full sure to find you, John,
To Nenagh fair.

The fair was just the same as then,
Five years ago today,

When first you left the thimble men
And came with me away;

For there again were thimble men
        And shooting galleries,
And card-trick men and Maggie men
        Of all sorts and degrees, –
But not a sight of you, John-John,
        Was anywhere.

I turned my face to home again,
        And called myself a fool
To think you'd leave the thimble men
        And live again by rule,
And go to Mass and keep the fast
        And till the little patch:
My wish to have you home was past
        Before I raised the latch
And pushed the door and saw you John,
        Sitting down there.

How cool you came in here, begad,
        As if you owned the place!
But rest yourself there now, my lad,
        'Tis good to see your face;
My dream is out, and now by it
        I think I know my mind:
At six o'clock this house you'll quit,
        And leave no grief behind; –
But until six o'clock, John-John,
        My bit you'll share.

The neighbours' shame of me began
        When first I brought you in;
To wed and keep a tinker man
        They thought a kind of sin;
But now this three year since you're gone
        'Tis pity me they do,

And that I'd rather have, John-John,
 Than that they'd pity you.
Pity for me and you John-John,
 I could not bear.

Oh, you're my husband right enough,
 But what's the good of that?
You know you never were the stuff
 To be the cottage cat,
To watch the fire and hear me lock
 The door and put out Shep –
But there now, it is six o'clock
 And time for you to step.
God bless and keep you far, John-John!
 And that's my prayer.

It is in no way surprising that WB Yeats wrote of his sensitive nature and his sweetness of thought; sensitivity and sweetness are crystallised in his lovely poem. *Litany Of Beauty* is further justification for WB Yeats's view of his personality.

Joy, if the soul or aught immortal be,
How may this Beauty know mortality?

O Beauty, perfect child of Light,
Sempiternal spirit of delight!
White and set with gold like the gold of the night,
The gold of the stars in quiet weather, –
White and shapely and pure! –
O lily-flower from stain secure,
With life and virginity dying together!
One lily liveth so,
Liveth for ever unstained, immortal, a mystic flower:
Perfectly wrought its frame,
Gold inwrought and eternal white,
White more white than cold of the snow,
For never, never, near it came,
Never shall come till the end of all,
Hurtful thing in wind or shower,

Worm or stain or blight;
But ever, ever, gently fall
The dews elysian of years that flow
Where it doth live secure
In flawless comeliness mature,
Golden and white and pure,
In the fair far-shining glow
Of eternal and holy Light.

Beauty of earthly things
Wrought by God and with hands of men!
Beauty of Nature and Art,
Fashioned anew for each lift Time brings,
For each new soul and living heart!
Beauty of Beauty that fills the ken
Till the soul is swooning, faint with delight!
Beauty of human form and voice,
Of eyes and ears and lips! –
O golden hair and brow of white! –
Wine of Beauty that who so sips
Doth die to a spirit free, and rejoice,
Living with God and living with men,
Rapt rejoice in eternal bliss,
Raising his face to meet the kiss
Of the Beauty seraphic he sees above
In figure of his love.

O Beauty of Wisdom unsought
That in trance to poet is taught,
Uttered in secret lay,
Singing the heart from earth away,
Cunning the soul from care to lure, –
O mystic lily, from stain and death secure,
Till the end of all to stay!
O shapely flower that must for ever endure!
O voice of God that every heart must hear!
O hymn of purest souls that dost unsphere
The ravished soul that hears! O white, white gem!

O rose that dost the senses drown in bliss!
No thought shall stay the wing, or stem
The song or win the heart to miss
Thy love, thy joy, thy rapture divine!
O Beauty, Beauty, ever thine
The soul, the heart, the brain,
To own thee in a loud perpetual strain,
Shriller and sweeter than song of wine,
Than song of sorrow or love or war!

Beauty of heaven and sun and day,
Beauty of water and frost and star,
Beauty of dusk-tide, narrowing, grey!
Beauty of silver light,
Beauty of purple night,
Beauty of solemn breath,
Beauty of closed eye, and sleep and death!

Beauty of dawn and dew,
Beauty of morning peace,
Ever ancient and ever new,
Ever renewed till waking cease
Or sleep for ever, when loud the angel's word
Through all the world is heard!

Beauty of brute and bird,
Beauty of earthly creatures
Whose hearts by the hand of God are stirred!

Beauty of the soul,
Beauty informing forms and features,
Fairest of God's eye, –
Beauty that cannot fade or die
Though atoms to ruin roll!

Beauty of blinded Trust,
Led by the hand of God
To a heaven where Cherub hath never trod!

Austere Beauty of Truth
Lighting the way of the just!

Splendid Beauty of Youth,
Staying when Youth is sped,
Living when Life is dead,
Burning in funeral dust!

The glory of form doth pale and pall,
Beauty endures to the end of all.

What compelled this man of sensitive nature and sweetness of thought to join a
Rising which he must have known could, as it in fact did, cause his death. The concepts of blood and sacrifice for Ireland are significantly less evident in his poetry
than they are in the poetry of Patrick Pearse. It is not clear to what extent he was
influenced by Patrick Pearse in whose school, St Enda's he was a teacher. His son
was born on St Cecilia's Day 1912; by Easter 1916 he had everything and more to
live for.

WISHES FOR MY SON
BORN ON SAINT CECILIA'S DAY 1912

Now, my son, is life for you,
And I wish you joy of it, –
Joy of power in all you do,
Deeper passion, better wit
Than I had who had enough,
Quicker life and length thereof,
More of every gift but love.

Love I have beyond all men,
Love that now you share with me –
What have I to wish you then
But that you be good and free,
And that God to you may give
Grace in stronger days to live?
For I wish you more than I
Ever knew of glorious deed,

Though no rapture passed me by
That an eager heart could heed,
Though I followed heights and sought
Things the sequel never brought…

God to you may give the sight
And the clear undoubting strength
Wars to knit for single right,
Freedom's war to knit at length,
And to win, through wrath and strife,
To the sequel of my life.
But for you, so small and young,
Born on Saint Cecilia's Day,
I in more harmonious song
Now for nearer joys should pray -
Simpler joys: the natural growth
Of your childhood and your youth,
Courage, innocence, and truth:

These for you, so small and young,
In your hand and heart and tongue.

Did he foresee his own death in *Death In The Woods*?

When I am gone and you alone are living here still,
You'll think of me when splendid the storm is on the hill,
Trampling and militant here – what of their village street? -
For the baying of winds in the woods to me was music sweet.

Oh, for the storms again, and youth in my heart again!
My spirit to glory strained, wild in this wild wood then,
That now shall never strain – though I think if the tempest
    should roll
I could rise and strive with death, and smite him back from my soul.

But no wind stirs a leaf, and no cloud hurries the moon;
I know that our lake tonight with stars and shadows is strewn –
A night for a villager's death, who will shudder in his grave
To hear – alas, how long! – the winds above him rave.

How long! Ah, Death, what art thou, a thing of calm or of storms?
Or twain – their peace to them, to me thy valiant alarms?
Gladly I'd leave them this corpse in their churchyard to lay at rest,
If my wind-swept spirit could fare on the hurricane's kingly quest.

And sure 'tis the fools of knowledge who feign that the winds of the
  world
Are but troubles of little calms by he greater Calm enfurled:
I know them for symbols of glory, and echoes of one Voice dread,
Sounding where spacious tempests house the great-hearted Dead.

And what but a fool was I, crying defiance to Death,
Who shall lead my soul from this calm to mingle with God's very
  breath! –
Who shall lead me hither perhaps while you are waiting here still,
Sighing for thought of me when the winds are out on the hill.

TEN
FRIENDS
OLD AND NEW

Think where man's glory most begins and ends
Say my glory was I had such friends.

The Municipal Gallery Revisited, WB Yeats

FRANCIS LEDWIDGE'S NEXT POSTING was to Londonderry in May 1916. Pearse and MacDonagh had been sentenced in Richmond Barracks. His request for an extension of leave was refused. He travelled to Londonderry via Belfast where he stayed with his great friend Robert Christie with whom he had fought in Gallipoli. Christie had been invalided out of the army. Ledwidge was two weeks overdue in Londonderry. The company was good. Christie advised him to seek a discharge on medical grounds. He refused to consider it even though his sympathies were with the men who had risen in Dublin. He would leave the Army only with an honourable discharge. Duty and honour were high in his scale of values.

On 2 June 1916 he wrote from Ebrington Barracks, Londonderry, 'I should have been here fourteen days ago and yet expect to be called upon for an account of my absence. But my trust is in Dunsany when he comes on Monday.' Lord Dunsany did return. Francis Ledwidge was court-martialled. Lord Dunsany could do nothing for

Londonderry

him. He later wrote 'Ledwidge was not in my company and I was glad of that, for his movements had a little of the unpredictable nature of will-o-the wisps roaring bogs of the land that he loved; as you might expect of a poet in a lance corporal's uniform. One day he had a bit of a night out, and I was too much annoyed to feel very sympathetic about the trouble in which it landed him, for it looked as if he was deliberately harming his own prospects. Being a lance corporal, and not a private soldier, it landed him in a court-martial; and I said to Major Willock, who was president of the court-martial 'You will go down to posterity as an afflicter of poets.' Major Willock was quite distressed but found no way of avoiding sentencing Ledwidge to lose his lance corporal's stripe.'

As already mentioned, the experience, however unpleasant, inspired one of Ledwidge's finest poems.

AFTER COURT MARTIAL

My mind is not my mind, therefore
I take no heed of what men say,
I lived ten thousand years before
God cursed the town of Nineveh.

The Present is a dream I see
Of horror and loud sufferings
At dawn a bird will waken me
Unto my place among the kings.

And though men called me a vile name,
And all my dream companions gone,
'Tis I the soldier bears the shame,
Not I the king of Babylon.

There is an undercurrent of depression in this poem. It might be thought that war is horrific enough without adding the annoyance of a court-martial. Francis Ledwidge lost his lance corporal's stripe. However his friend Bob Christie with whom he had overstayed in Belfast sent his own poetry for Ledwidge's consideration. He guided Christie as Lord Dunsany had guided him in the elements of writing poetry. He wrote to Christie 'I think I told you before that poets should always wait until the gods say 'Write' and not to try to do things when their souls are not in rapport with the divinities who dictate in their own good time.'

The Anglican Church in Slane

SIMON MCKINSTRY

One of his fellow soldiers in the Royal Inniskilling Fusiliers wrote of Ledwidge at this time in Londonderry 'dark-featured, of medium height, very athletic in appearance; a good soldier in dress bearing and discipline; also a brave one because he had been invalided home from Gallipoli and Serbia before coming to Derry. There was a great deal of fuss made of him in the barracks because he was a poet. He was addicted to drink and lost his corporal's stripe for this reason. He often talked about the Easter Week Rising and said since it happened he regretted having joined the Army. He was really a great Irishman and his heart was with the men of 1916.'

It may be that Ledwidge enjoyed a good drink when out and about with friends. There is not a shred of evidence that he was addicted to drink in any habitual sense. However there is no doubt that he was most deeply affected by the terrible events of the Easter Rising. They cast a haunting shadow over the rest of his life.

Lord Dunsany had taken a house in Londonderry for his wife shortly after his arrival. When Francis Ledwidge arrived in June 1916 Lord Dunsany gave him a room for work. He revised the poems which he had written since his first volume went for publication; poems which he had written since 1914 at home, in Richmond Barracks, in Basingstoke camp, at sea, in Serbia, in Greece and in hospital in Egypt, at which we have looked in detail. Lord Dunsany advised; Francis Ledwidge added some poems under the heading Ebrington Barracks. The volume of poetry was sent for publication under the title *Songs Of Peace*.

The staggering feature of these poems, at which we have looked in detail, is the absence of the theme of the horrors of war. The poems cover the period of Ledwidge's participation in the Gallipoli and Balkans campaigns. Campaigns in which he lived daily among blood and death. The themes of suffering and death, which so engaged the imagination and writing of other soldier poets, is almost entirely lacking in Ledwidge's poetry in the years 1914–1916 in which he was a fully trained fighting soldier at the front line. The absence of the themes of suffering and death in Ledwidge's poetry in these years is no reflection in any way on any lack of sensitivity to the horrors of war which he experienced. The themes of his poetry in these years as set out in *Songs Of Peace* reflect the sustaining power of the basic inspirations of his life; nature, home, family and friends. Lord Dunsany wrote the Introduction to *Songs Of Peace*: it was detailed Ebrington Barracks, September 1916. He comments on a number of the poems; about *The Shadow People*, Lord Dunsany wrote: 'The Shadow People seems to me another perfect poem. Written in Serbia and Egypt it shows the poet still looking steadfastly at those fields, though so far distant from them, of which he was surely born to be the singer. And this devotion to the fields of Meath that, in nearly all his songs, from such far places brings his spirits home, like the instinct that has been given to the swallows, seems to be the

Meath Countryside

CATHERINE FLANAGAN

key-note of the book. For this reason I have named it *Songs Of Peace*, in spite of the circumstances under which it was written.

Once the swallow instinct appears again in a poem called *The Lure* and a longing for the South, and in a poem called *Song*, and then the Irish fields content him again, and we find him in the last page but one in the book making a poem for a little place called Faughan, because he finds that its hills and woods and streams are unsung. Surely for this, if there be, as many believed, Gods lesser than those whose business is with destiny, thunder and war, small Gods that haunt the groves, seen only at times by few, and there instinctively at evening, surely from gratitude they will give him peace.'

The last section of *Songs Of Peace* was written in Londonderry from June to September 1916. Accordingly it was a most creative period of his writing. Military life was fully into his blood and bones. But the inspiration for his writing was the same powerful forces of earth, nature, home, family, friends as before he went to war. His spirit was wholly undefeated by the horrors of war and the discomfort of barracks.

His years of travel away from Ireland had expanded his love of nature to beautiful places other than Meath. Poems from this period include:

EVENING CLOUDS

A little flock of clouds go down to rest
In some blue corner off the moon's highway,
With shepherd winds that shook them in the West
To borrowed shapes of earth, in bright array,
Perhaps to weave a rainbow's gay festoons
Around the lonesome isle which Brooke has made
A little England full of lonely noons,
Or dot it with his country's mountain shade.

Ah, little wanderers, when you reach that isle
Tell him, with dripping dew, they have not failed,
What he loved most; for late I roamed awhile
Thro' English fields and down her rivers sailed;
And they remember him with beauty caught
From old desires of Oriental Spring
Heard in his heart with singing overwrought;
And still on Purley Common gooseboys sing.

Also from the same period:

THE HERONS

As I was climbing Ardan Mor
From the shore of Sheelan lake,
I met the herons coming down
Before the waters wake.

And they were talking in their flight
Of dreamy ways the herons go
When all the hills are withered up
Nor any waters flow.

This poem, according to Alice Curtayne, commemorates a visit to Mountnugent on Lough Sheelan to Father Edward Smyth. He had been curate in Slane from

1907–1911. It is indicative of a massive advance in Ledwidge's technique towards the most lovely simplicity of writing.

BY FAUGHAN

For hills and woods and streams unsung
I pipe above a rippled cove.
And here the weaver autumn hung
Between the hills a wind she wove
From sounds the hills remember yet
Of purple days and violet.

The hills stand up to trip the sky,
Sea-misted, and along the tops
Wing after wing goes summer by,
And many a little roadway stops
And starts, and struggles to the sea,
Cutting them up in filigree.

Twixt wind and silence Faughan flows,
In music broken over rocks,
Like mingled bells the poet knows
Ring in the fields of Eastern flocks.
And here this song for you I find
Between the silence and the wind.

This lovely poem was written in Londonderry in 1916. Lord Dunsany in his introduction refers to Faughan as a little place. The poem is equally apposite for the River Faughan which runs through County Londonderry near where he served. The reference to mingled bells in the fields of Eastern flocks is clearly a reference to *The Home-coming Of The Sheep*.

The sheep are coming home in Greece
Hark the bells on every hill
Flock by flock, and fleece by fleece.

This section of *Songs Of Peace* is a supreme example of the very real advance in the quality of Ledwidge's writing over the period June to December 1916. The concepts are more subtle, the scope is wider, the language is purer; the overall creation is more magnificent than any phase of his earlier phase of his writing.

The memory of loves past suggest a loneliness in his spirit at this time.

AN OLD DESIRE

I searched thro' memory's lumber-room
And there I found an old desire,
I took it gently from the gloom
To cherish by my scanty fire.

And all the night – sweet-voiced one,
Sang of the place my loves abide,
'Til Earth leaned over from the dawn
And hid the last star in her side.

And often since, when most alone,
I ponder on my old desire,
But never hear the sweet-voiced one,
And there are ruins in my fire.

And in the after silences
Of flower-lit distances I'll be,
And who would find me travels far
In lands unsung of minstrelsy.
Strong winds shall cross my secret way,
And planet mountains hide my goal,
I shall go on from pass to pass,
By monstrous rocks, a lonely soul.

Days of loneliness and sadness while in Londonderry were interspersed with at least some romantic uplift; from this period we have *The Wedding Morning* and *The Lure*.

THE WEDDING MORNING

Spread the feast, and let there be
Such music heard as best beseems

A king's son coming from the sea
To wed a maiden of the streams.

Poets, pale for long ago,
Bring sweet sounds from rock and flood
You by echo's accent know
Where the water is and wood.

Harpers whom the moths of Time
Bent and wrinkled dusty brown,
Her chains are falling with a chime,
Sweet as bells in Heaven town.

But, harpers, leave your harps aside,
And, poets, leave awhile your dreams.
The storm has come upon the tide
And Cathleen weeps among her streams.

THE LURE

I saw night leave her halos down
On Mitylene's dark mountain isle,
The silhouette of one fair town
Like broken shadows in a pile.
And in the farther dawn I heard
The music of a foreign bird.

In fields of shady angles now
I stand and dream in the half dark:
The thrush is on the blossomed bough,
Above the echoes sings the lark,
And little rivers drop between
Hills fairer than dark Mitylene.

Yet something calls me with no voice
And wakes sweet echoes in my mind;
In the fair country of my choice
Nor Peace nor Love again I find,

> Nor anything of rest I know
> When south-east winds are blowing low.

War had not diminished his interst in mythology; from this period in Londonderry, we have *A Dream Dance*.

> Maeve held a ball on the dún,
> Cuculain and Eimer were there,
> In the light of an old broken moon
> I was dancing with Deirdre the fair.
>
> How loud was the laughter of Finn
> As he blundered about thro' a reel,
> Tripping up Caoilte the thin,
> Or jostling the dreamy Aleel.
>
> And when the dance ceased for a song,
> How sweet was the singing of Fand,
> We could hear her far, wandering along,
> My hand in that beautiful hand.

The poetry contained in *Songs Of Peace* was written from mid 1914 until December 1916. It was a period which covered Francis Ledwidge's life in the British Army, in particular it covered active service in Gallipoli and Serbia; it covered his period of recovery in hospital in Egypt. The blood, the horror, the suffering, the death of war affected him to the core. But war and its ways did not impinge upon the central sources of his inspiration or the central fountains of his joy. They remained as they had been in the period in which he wrote *Songs Of The Fields*, nature, home, family, friends, mythology. The terrible events of the Easter Rising and its aftermath must be added to his creative material. *Songs Of Peace* are the clearest evidence of his increasing stature as a writer and a poet, of his subtler concepts, of his purer and simpler language, principally based upon the same inspirations as *Songs Of The Fields*. It may be that the heightened achievement of the last section of *Songs Of Peace*, *In Barracks*, was at least partly a result of the renewed contact, friendship, guidance and inspiration of Lord Dunsany who was in Londonderry for at least some of the period of Ledwidge's service there from June to December 1916.

Ledwidge's service in Ebrington Barracks lasted from June 1916 to December

1916. It was a bonus and luxury of those six months that his old friendship with Lord Dunsany was renewed and revitalised. Ledwidge worked at his house in Londonderry when off-duty. Lord Dunsany advised and assisted in the preparation of his second volume of poetry.

However, these happy days came to an end in December 1916 when he was assigned to the Western Front. He had a few days leave in Slane; he returned to Londonderry. He travelled to England via Dublin; then to Folkestone; then to France on 26 December 1916. He did not spend his last Christmas at home. His family never saw him again.

Francis Ledwidge had a very real capacity for friendship. WB Yeats had not written in 1916 his lovely lines 'Think, where man's glory most begins and ends. Say my glory was I had such friends.' From *The Municipal Gallery Revisited*, if he had, Francis Ledwidge would have certainly have agreed that his friends were very much a part of his own glory. He had very real friends in Slane, particularly Matty

The River Boyne near Slane

PAUL WALLS

McGoona. Bob Christie, with whom he stayed in Belfast on his return to Londonderry, was a close and genuine friend. His relationship with Lord Dunsany was essentially one of friendship. He gathered friends in the different experiences of his life.

An important friend who came into his life towards its end was the distinguished Anglo-Irish writer, Katherine Tynan.

Katherine Tynan first met Francis Ledwidge in 1912 at a private view of AE's pictures in Dublin. He had been taken by Lord Dunsany. In *The Years Of The Shadow* she wrote of Francis Ledwidge:

> He had a high-coloured, eager, winning face. Perhaps it was the excitement made the high colour. I remember that he was wrapped in a big frieze coat, as though some one had carried him off unawares to what used to be something of a fashionable function, and he, protesting that he was not dressed for the like, had wrapped himself up in the big coat. I can see the eager, gentle face, under the dark soft hair, with the desire to please obvious in it. He was very humble and deferential to an older writer. There was nothing self-conscious about him. He was entirely simple and sincere.

She reviewed *Songs Of The Field*, about which she said that she found in it an essential beauty with magical phrases. In respect of *Songs Of Peace* she commented on how little the war had affected his writing experiences. He had she said in *The Years Of The Shadow* 'been at pretty well all the Fronts of war. He had seen the dreadful things which all soldiers must see in these days. The Chariot of War had driven over him and left him untouched. He was still the boy who sat by the roadside in Meath and loved the fields and the thorn-hedges and the long roads fringed with cow parsley, and the blackbird's note, and the colour of blue with which all his poems are coloured, and his mother, and all simple and quiet loves.'

She reviewed *Songs Of Peace* in *The Years Of The Shadow*. She wrote to Francis Ledwidge. He replied by letter dated 6 January 1917.

> If I survive the war, I have great hopes of writing something that will live. If not, I trust to be remembered in my own land for one or two things which its long sorrow inspired. My books have had a greater reception in England, Ireland, and America than I had ever dreamt of, but I never feel that my name should be mentioned in the same breath with my contemporaries. You ask me what I am doing. I am a unit in the Great War, doing and suffering, admiring great endeavour and condemning great dishonour. I may be dead before this reaches you, but I will have done my part. Death is as interesting to me as life. I have seen so much of it from Suvla to Strumnitza and now in France. I am

always homesick. I hear the roads calling, and the hills, and the rivers wondering where I am. It is terrible to be always homesick. I don't like to send you a poem in pencil. If I can borrow a fountain pen I will transcribe one for you. If I go home again I should certainly like to come and see you. I know Claremorris, Ballinrobe, and all the little towns of Mayo.

The foreboding, if not the expectation of death, was upon him in January 1917. He wrote again to Katherine Tynan, in the course of which he said, 'I was with the first British troops who landed at Salonika. We spent all last winter fighting the Bulgars in the hills of Varda and Uskub ... I daresay you know the horrors of the retreat. I love Serbia. It is a delightful country even seen, as I have seen it, under the worst conditions of weather etc. I spent a year in the East going first to the Dardanelles. I was in Egypt, Cyprus, Mitylene, and had a pleasant fortnight in Naples;' with this letter he included two poems:

IN FRANCE

The silence of maternal hills
Is round me in my evening dreams;
And round me music-making bills
And mingling waves of pastoral streams.

Whatever way I turn I find
The path is old unto me still.
The hills of home are in my mind,
And there I wander as I will.

HAD I A GOLDEN POUND

[After the Irish]

Had I a golden pound to spend,
    My love should mend and sew no more.
And I would buy her a little quern,
    Easy to turn on the kitchen floor.

And for her windows curtains white,
    With birds in flight and flowers in bloom,
To face with pride the road to town,
    And mellow down her sunlit room.

And with the silver change we'd prove
The truth of Love to life's own end,
With hearts the years could but embolden,
Had I a golden pound to spend.

These two poems were included in Lord Dunsany's and Alice Curtayne's Complete Poems. He wrote again to Katherine Tynan. The letter throws a fascinating light on his methods of writing:

When I read the proofs of *Songs Of Peace* there were several poems I hardly recognised as my own, for I scribble them off in odd moments, and, if I do not give them to some one, they become part of the dust of the earth and little things stuck on the ends of hedges when the wind has done with them. My MSS are scattered about two hemispheres, some lost for ever, others wandering in the corners of newspapers, like so many little Abrahams, changing their names as if they had given over an old faith and were set on new endeavours. I lament them in sober moments, and forget them again when some new tune breaks out in my mind.

I wish you would come to Louth. There are charming places about Dundalk and Drogheda, and the people are so beautiful. When I am in Louth I always imagine voices are calling me from one distance to another, and at every turn I half expect to see Cuchullin stride over the hills to meet some new champion of Maeve. You could only be happy in Louth or Meath …

What a pity the birds must suffer as we do! I had a special way of feeding them when I was at home in winter. I used to put potatoes on the garden wall for the crows and under a covering of sacks spread bread and meal for the smaller birds. It was taboo to open the kitchen door, for that would disturb them … I may be in Ireland for May Day yet.

He wrote again by letter dated 31 May:

Your letter came yesterday evening like melody from the woods of home, as welcome as rain to the shrivelled lips of June. It was like laughter heard over a low hill. I would have written to thank you for the sweets, only that lately we were unsettled, wandering to and fro between the firing-line and resting billets immediately behind. This letter is antedated by two hours, but before midnight we may be wandering in single and slow file, with the reserve line two or three hundred yards behind the fire trench. We are under an hour's notice. Entering and leaving the line is most exciting, as we are usually but about thirty yards from the enemy, and you can scarcely understand how bright the nights are made by his rockets. These are in continual ascent and descent from dusk to dawn, making a beautiful crescent from Switzerland to the sea. There are white lights, green, and red, and whiter, bursting into red and changing again, and blue bursting into purple drops and reds fading into green. It is all like the end of a beautiful world. It is only horrible when you remember that every colour is a signal to waiting reinforcements or artillery, and God help us, if we are caught in the open, for then up go a thousand reds, and hundreds of rifles and machine-guns are emptied against us, and all amongst us shells of every calibre are thrown, shouting destruction amd death. We can do nothing but fling ourselves into the first shell-hole and wonder as we wait where we will be hit. But why all this?

Katherine Tynan's own son was on active service. Hence the correspondence with Francis Ledwidge had a sharp edge to it for her:

I am writing odd things in a little book whenever I can. Just now I engaged in a poem about the *Lanawn Shee*, who, you remember, is really the Irish Muse. One who sees her is doomed to sing. She is very close to you. I am writing it in the traditional style of the 'Silk of the Kine'.

This poem was finished and called *The Lanawn Shee*. Lord Dunsany refers to it as Ledwidge's last poem. This letter continues 'If I do not tire of it you will read it all some day (D.V.). I enclose a little thing written on Ascension Thursday. It is time I remembered you would be weary of this letter and will close with regret.'

ASCENSION THURSDAY, 1917

Lord, Thou hast left Thy footprints in the rocks,
    That we may know the way to follow Thee,
But there are wide lands opened out between
    Thy Olivet and my Gethsemane.

And oftentimes I make the night afraid,
    Crying for lost hands when the dark is deep,
And strive to reach the sheltering of Thy love
    Where Thou art herd among Thy folded sheep.

Thou wilt not ever thus, O Lord, allow
    My feet to wander when the sun is set,
But through the darkness, let me still behold
    The stony bye-ways up to Olivet.

This poem reminds us, if we needed reminding, that Francis Ledwidge was alive to the call of God in his life.

He wrote to Katherine Tynan on 19 June 1917, some six weeks before his death on 31 July. 'This is my birthday [In fact his birthday was 19 August. [Many people in Ireland are vague on the exact date of their birthday]. I am spending it in a little red town in an orchard. There is a lovely valley just below me, and a river that goes gobbling down the fields, like turkeys coming home in Ireland. It is an idle little vagrant that does no work for miles and miles except to turn one mill-wheel for a dusty old man who has five sons fighting for France. I was down here earlier in the spring, when all the valley wore its confirmation dress, and was glad to return again in the sober moments of June. Although I have a conventional residence I sleep out in the orchard, and every morning a cuckoo comes to a tree quite close, and calls out his name with a clear voice above the rest of the morning's song, like a tender stop heard above the lower keys in a beautiful organ…

You are in Meath now, I suppose. If you go to Tara, go to Rath-na Ri and look around you from the hills of Drum-condrath in the north to the plains of Enfield in the south, where Allan Bog begins, and remember me to every hill and wood and ruin, for my heart is there. If it is a clear day you will see Slane Hill blue and distant. Say I will come back again surely, and maybe you will hear pipes in the grass or a fairy horn and the hounds of Finn – I have heard them often from Tara.

Be sure to remember me to Lord Fingall if he is at home. I am greatly afraid Lord Edward will never reach me … My next book is due in October. Did you ever know I wrote a play? It is a one-act thing called *A Crock Of Gold*, and is about a man who went to dig for gold which another man dreamt about. I showed it to many in London and Dublin, and they liked it … I will show you the play when I come to see you. About the mine – it made a greater explosion in the newspapers than on Hill 60, but was beautiful all the same. It is growing dusk now: it is 'the owls' light', and I must draw to a close.'

He sent three poems with this letter:

THE FIND

I took a reed and blew a tune
And sweet it was and very clear
To be about a little thing
That only few hold dear.

Three times the cuckoo named himself,
    But nothing heard him on the hill,
Where I was piping like an elf,
    The air was very still.

'Twas all about a little thing,
    I made a mystery of sound,
I found it in a fairy ring
    Upon a fairy mound.

STANLEY

On Stanley Hill the bees are loud
    And loud a river wild,
And there, as wayward as a cloud,
    I was a little child.

I knew not how mistrustful heart
    Could lure with hidden wile,
And wound us in a fateful part
    With dark and sudden guile.

And yet for all I've known and seen
    Of Youth and Truth reviled,
On Stanley Hill the grass is green
    And I am still a little child.

THE OLD GODS

I thought the old gods still in Greece
    Making the little fates of man,
So in a secret place of Peace
    I prayed as but a poet can:

And all my prayer went crying faint
    Around Parnassus' cloudy height,
And found no ear for my complaint,
    And back unanswered came at night.

Ah, foolish that I was to heed
The voice of folly, or presume
To find the old gods in my need,
So far from AE's little room.

His last letter to Katherine Tynan is dated 20 July:

We have just returned from the line after an unusually long time. It was very exciting this time, as we had to contend with gas, lachrymatory shells and other devices new and horrible. It will be worse soon. The camp we are in at present might be in Tir-n'an-Og, it is pitched amid such splendours. There is barley and rye just entering harvest days of gold, and meadow-sweet rippling, and where a little inn named 'In den Neerloop' holds its gable up to the swallows, blue-bells and goldilocks swing their splendid censers. There is a wood hard by where hips glisten like little sparks, and just at the edge of it mealey leaves sway like green fire. I will hunt for a secret place in that wood to read Lord Edward. I anticipate beautiful moments.

I daresay you have left Meath and are back again in the brown wides of Connaught. I would give £100 for two days in Ireland with nothing to do but ramble on from one delight to another. I am entitled to leave now, but I'm afraid there are many before my name in the list … Special leaves are granted, and I have to finish a book for the autumn. But, more particularly, I want to see again my wonderful mother, and to walk by the Boyne to Crewbawn and up through the brown and grey rocks to Crocknaharna. You have no idea of how I suffer with this longing for the swish of the reeds at Slane and the voices I used to hear coming over the low hills at Currabwee. Say a prayer that I may get this leave, and give as a condition my punctual return and sojourn till the war is over. It is midnight now and the glowworms are out. It is quiet in camp, but the far night is loud with our own guns bombarding the positions we must soon fight for.

I hope your boy in Macedonia is doing well and that your other boy is still in Ireland.

This last letter shows the whole man, fully related to nature, home, family, friends and ever concerned about other people. Katherine Tynan's last lines on Ledwidge constitute an epitaph.

One is quite sure that the blameless soul of Francis Ledwidge, before it sped on its way to its ultimate Source and Goal, flew over the fields of Meath and hovered a while near those scenes and friends for whom he had so tender and faithful an attachment.

Another prominent man of letters to meet and concern himself about Francis Ledwidge and his writing was Padraic Colum. Padraic Colum, born in 1891, was a poet, playwright, novelist and essayist of distinction. '*The Road Round Ireland*' by him is charming. In it he wrote about Francis Ledwidge.

The Road Round Ireland
PADRAIC COLUM

Francis Ledwidge's is the poetry of the plain – specially of the demesne land that is the County Meath. The land is beautiful under the light that gives its fields the greenness of jade, but it has scant variety of interest: fields, hedgerows and streams; larks, blackbirds and pigeons, with a castle or an ancient ruin amongst ivy-enwreathed trees, are what the eye of a poet would mostly note there. There are villages and people, of course, but the poet I have just been re-reading might not approach the people unless they grouped themselves as people in an idyll.

He has been compared to Robert Burns, because his poetry came out of country life as seen through the eyes of a young man of the soil. But Francis Ledwidge saw country people and saw the country not at all in the way that Burns saw them. Indeed, his genius was at the other side of Burns' – it was idyllic where Burns' was dramatic; Francis Ledwidge responded not to the tumult but to the charm of life; it was his triumph that he made us know the creatures of his world as things freshly seen, surprisingly discovered … I have said that his genius was at the other side of Burns.' It was idyllic and akin to the genius of Theocritus. Indeed Francis Ledwidge was the Sicilian singer of our day, and it is probable that he would have made the discovery that Theocritus was his master.

I kept for a long time a letter that I had from him. It was a letter written in small back-sloping handwriting the winter before the great war and was headed 'Janeville, County Meath'. I had a notion that 'Janeville' was a cottage, rose-covered, and just off a country road. But I never saw Ledwidge's home. I had told him that I had never been at the Boyne in Meath, and had never seen the Brugh of Angus. His letter was to tell me that he would meet me at a place near his home and be my guide to the Brugh. I never made the journey with him. Then I saw him – it was for the last time – at Christmas. I met him in a street in Dublin with a writer whose death, like Ledwidge's, is an irreparable loss – the writer of 'The Weaver's Grave'. We went to the back of a coffee house to have a talk. Francis Ledwidge had been out of Ireland for a while – he had been in Manchester, I think – and he was going back that evening to his home in Meath. I well recall his big frieze overcoat and how – although he had not thought of entering the army at the time – he looked a young lance corporal. He was a big-boned, ruddy-faced, handsome youth. He was boyish and eager that evening but with something of a drift in his mind. He had no notion of what he wanted to do with himself. The 'Saturday' and 'The English Review' were paying him four or five guineas for poems. He was pleased that he could show us he was getting such sums. All very well, but what was he going to do for a living? He had worked in a shop in Ireland and he had been doing something in England. These things were now over for him. Even the profession he was working to acquire – engineering – seemed too prosaic. I felt that he had a boyish notion that he might become a Byron and live magnificently on the sales of the books he was about to publish.

Silly stories were current about his origin and his employments. There was a suggestion that he was hardly literate. The publishers of his *Songs Of The Fields* informed the world that he had been a scavenger on the roads. Nothing of the sort. He struck me as the sort of a boy who might have belonged to a good Irish farmer family. His education was probably better than the education of an American youth who has been through the ordinary college. I know he had been only in National school in a country place. But the National school with all its drawbacks is – or was – capable of giving a boy a good literary education.

Later in *The Road Round Ireland* he details the friendship between Lord Dunsany and Francis Ledwidge.

Lord Dunsany was Francis Ledwidge's great neighbour, and Lord Dunsany had made himself talked about on account of his enthusiasm for imaginative things. It was to Lord Dunsany that Francis Ledwidge took his first song-offerings. The elder poet helped him with his verse, eulogised him in Dublin, and influenced the important London reviews towards publishing his poems. This intervention put the youth of twenty with the poets of the day. For all this Francis Ledwidge had a personal loyalty to Lord Dunsany – the loyalty that the simple-hearted young Irishman always gives to the leader who captures his imagination. His entering the army was, I think, an expression of personal loyalty.

We have looked in detail at the circumstances which prompted Francis Ledwidge to enter the Army. The view that his entering the Army was an expression of personal loyalty to Lord Dunsany is seriously erroneous.

It is clear that Padraic Colum liked Francis Ledwidge and admired his poetry. The friendship did not develop in correspondence over the years as the friendship with Katherine Tynan developed. This was no doubt because Katherine Tynan had a particular sensitivity towards and interest in young men on active service. Her own son was in the Army. There was no specific point of contact between Padraic Colum in Ireland and Francis Ledwidge at war. If Ledwidge had survived the war Padraic Colum would have been a sympathetic contact for him in the Dublin literary scene. He lived until 1972.

ELEVEN

LAST POST

F RANCIS LEDWIDGE SAILED FOR FRANCE from Folkestone on 26 December 1916. He never returned. He had time to write on 26 December *Spring Love*:

> I saw her coming through the flowery grass,
> Round her swift ankles butterfly and bee
> Blent loud and silent wings; I saw her pass
> Where foam-bows shivered on the sunny sea.
>
> Then came the swallow crowding up the dawn,
> And cuckoo-echoes filled the dewy South.
> I left my love upon the hill, alone,
> My last kiss burning on her lovely mouth.

As he sailed to war the imagery of his poetry was still the imagery of County Meath.

He was serving with the Royal Inniskilling Fusiliers. He was stationed at Pickvizing, near Amiens. The weather was arctic. The conditions were dreadful as detailed from different spheres by Wilfred Owen and many others.

It is clear from Francis Ledwidge's correspondence with Kathleen Tynan that he had come fully to terms with death in battle. In the course of a letter written to her on the 6 January 1917 he said 'If I can survive the war I have great hopes of writing something that will live. If not, I trust to be remembered in my own land for one or two things which its long sorrow inspired ... I may be dead before this reaches you,

but I shall have done my part. Death is as interesting to me as life. I have so much
of it from Suvla to Serbia and now in France.'

Within a short time in France he had written *Soliloquy*.

When I was young I had a care
Lest I should cheat me of my share
Of that which makes it sweet to strive
For life, and dying still survive,
A name in sunshine written higher
Than lark or poet dare aspire.

But I grew weary doing well;
Besides, 'twas sweeter in that hell,
Down with the loud banditti people
Who robbed the orchards, climbed the steeple
For jackdaw's eggs and made the cock
Crow ere 'twas daylight on the clock.
I was so very bad the neighbours
Spoke of me at their daily labours.
And now I'm drinking wine in France
The helpless child of circumstance.
To-morrow will be loud with war.
How will I be accounted for?

It is too late now to retrieve
A fallen dream, too late to grieve
A name unmade, but not too late
To thank the gods for what is great;
A keen-edged sword, a soldier's heart,
Is greater than a poet's art.
And greater than a poet's fame
A little grave that has no name,
Whence honour turns away in shame.

It is clear that the meanings of war had got through to the deepest areas of his
heart.

How did death on every side affect his writing? The answer is that death on every
side drove him back to the sources of his joy and the sustaining strength of home,
family, friends, the Boyne and County Meath.

His reliance in the last months of his life on the Western Front on the strengths of home, family, friends, the Boyne and County Meath were greatly increased by the fact that quite apart from the horrors of war, he was positively homesick for home. In the same letter to Katherine Tynan he wrote: 'I am always homesick. I hear the roads calling, and the hills, and the rivers wondering where I am. It is terrible to be always homesick.'

By 29 December 1916 he had written *Ceol Sidhe (Fairy Music)*:

> When May is here, and every morn
> Is dappled with pied bells,
> And dewdrops glance along the thorn
> And wings flash in the dells,
> I take my pipe and play a tune
> Of dreams, a whispered melody,
> For feet that dance beneath the moon
> In fairy jollity.
>
> And when the pastoral hills are grey
> And the dim stars are spread,
> A scamper fills the grass like play
> Of feet where fairies tread.
> And many a little whispering thing
> Is calling to the Shee.
> The dewy bells of evening ring,
> And all is melody.

On 6 January 1916 he wrote *The Rushes*:

> The rushes nod by the river
> As the winds on the loud waves go,
> And the things they nod of are many,
> For it's many the secret they know.
>
> And I think they are wise as the fairies
> Who lived ere the hills were high,
> They nod so grave by the river
> To everyone passing by.

If they would tell me their secrets
I would go by a hidden way,
To the rath when the moon retiring
Dips dim horns into the gray.

And a fairy-girl out of Leinster
In a long dance I should meet,
My heart to her heart beating,
My feet in rhyme with her feet.

The language of this poem is a return to County Meath. The concept of things of nature, in this case rushes, as living beings, as wise as the fairies, is a return to one of the central themes of his poetry when he was living in County Meath.

On 7 January 1917 he wrote *The Dead Kings*. Again the imagery is of the places of his infancy and youth but the hint of war and death is never far away (see p.36).

Shortly after arrival in Picquingy the Royal Inniskilling Fusiliers were moved closer to the front line.

On 26 January they marched to the front line. Francis Ledwidge was in the trenches. The horrific conditions were described by Phillip Gibbs, 'Bodies, and bits of bodies, and clots of blood, and green, metallic-looking slime, made by explosive gases, were floating on the surface of that water below the crater banks. Our men lived there, crouched below the sandbags and burrowed in the sides of the craters. Lice crawled over them in legions. Human flesh, rotting and stinking, mere pulp, was pasted into the mudbanks. If they dug to get deeper cover, their shovels went into the softness of dead bodies who had been their comrades. Scraps of flesh, booted legs, blackened hands, eyeless heads, came flying over them when the enemy trenches-mortared their position or blew up a new mine shaft.'

He wrote two poems in February 1917 while in the front line trenches. On 6 February *Fairies*.

Maiden-poet, come with me
To the heaped up cairn of Maeve,
And there we'll dance a fairy dance
Upon a fairy's grave.

In and out among the trees,
Filling all the night with sound,
The morning, strung upon her star,
Shall chase us round and round.

> What are we but fairies too,
> Living but in dreams alone,
> Or, at the most, but children still,
> Innocent and overgrown?

On 11 February *In A Café*:

> Kiss the maid and pass her round,
> Lips like hers were made for many.
> Our loves are far from us to-night,
> But these red lips are sweet as any.
>
> Let no empty glass be seen
> Aloof from our good table's sparkle,
> At the acme of our cheer
> Here are francs to keep the circle.
>
> They are far who miss us most –
> Sip and kiss – how well we love them,
> Battling through the world to keep
> Their hearts at peace, their God above them.

Towards the end of February the Royal Inniskilling Fusiliers were transferred to La Novelle, where they stayed until the end of March when they were moved towards Arras, about which Lord Dunsany wrote in detail.

On 8 March he wrote *Spring*:

> Once more the lark with song and speed
> Cleaves through the dawn, his hurried bars
> Fall, like the flute of Ganymede
> Twirling and whistling from the stars.
>
> The primrose and the daffodil
> Surprise the valleys, and wild thyme
> Is sweet on every little hill,
> When lambs come down at folding time.

In every wild place now is heard
The magpie's noisy house, and through
The mingled tunes of many a bird
The ruffled wood-dove's gentle coo.

Sweet by the river's noisy brink
The water-lily bursts her crown,
The kingfisher comes down to drink
Like rainbow jewels falling down.

And when the blue and grey entwine
The daisy shuts her golden eye,
And peace wraps all those hills of mine
Safe in my dearest memory.

On 11 March he wrote *Pan:*

He knows the safe ways and unsafe
And he will lead the lambs to fold,
Gathering them with his merry pipe,
The gentle and the overbold.

He counts them over one by one,
And leads them back by cliff and steep,
To grassy hills where dawn is wide,
And they may run and skip and leap.

And just because he loves the lambs
He settles them for rest at noon,
And plays them on his oaten pipe
The very wonder of a tune.

In these thirteen poems written by Francis Ledwidge between arrival in France on 26 December 1916 and departure for Arras in late March 1917 there is hardly a mention of war and no description of the terrible conditions which inspired Wilfred Owen to write his great poems. Apart from the line of awaking to a bomb blast in Picardy in *The Dead Kings* and the description of a keen-edged sword in *Soliloquy* these thirteen poems could all have been written in County Meath. They were certainly inspired by the people and places, and faeries of County Meath.

The Royal Inniskilling Fusiliers were positioned near Arras. Arras was to be a launching base for the next British offensive; a role which invited heavy German artillery upon it.

There was an extensive system of tunnels beneath Arras described by Phillip Gibbs and quoted by Alice Curtayne: 'I went through the tunnels when long columns of soldiers in single file moved slowly forward to another day's battle in the fields beyond, and when another column came back, wounded and bloody after their morning's fight. The wounded and the unwounded passed each other in these dimly lighted corridors. Their steel hats clinked together. Their bodies touched. Wafts of stale air laden with a sickly stench came out of the vaults. Faint whiffs of poison-gas filtered through the soil above and made men vomit. For the most time the men were silent as they passed each other, but now and then a wounded man would say 'Oh, Christ!.' In the vaults dug into the sides of the passages were groups of tunnellers and other men half screened by blanket curtains. Their rifles were propped against the quarried rocks. They sat on ammunition boxes and played cards in the light of candles stuck in bottles, which made their shadows flicker fantastically on the walls. They took no interest in the procession beyond their blankets – the walking wounded and the troops going up. Some of them slept on the stone floors with their heads covered by their overcoats and made pillows of their gas-masks.'

Francis Ledwidge was in these tunnels until his platoon was ordered out on 13 April and into trenches near Monchy-le-Preux. Terrible fighting took place in mid-April between the British and German armies in conditions of wind, rain and snow. The mud claimed the lives of many wounded. Conditions were so dreadful that eight French divisions mutinied which threw an additional burden on the British forces.

In May the weather improved but the fighting raged. Francis Ledwidge wrote to Katherine Tynan on 31 May: 'Entering and leaving the line is most exciting, as we are usually but about thirty yards from the enemy, and you can scarcely understand how bright the nights are made by his rockets. These are in continual ascent and descent from dusk to dawn, making a beautiful crescent from Switzerland to the sea. There are white lights, green, and red, and whiter, bursting into red and changing again, and blue bursting into purple drops and reds fading into green. It is all like the end of a beautiful world. It is only horrible when you remember that every colour is a signal to waiting reinforcements of artillery and God help us if we are caught in the open, for then up go a thousand reds, and hundreds of rifles and machine-guns are emptied against us, and all amongst us shells of every calibre are thrown, shouting destruction and death. We can do nothing but fling ourselves into the first shell-hole and wonder as we wait where we will be hit.'

It is not surprising that in April and May he wrote very little. In April he wrote *With Flowers*:

These have more language than my song,
Take them and let them speak for me.
I whispered them a secret thing
Down the green lanes of Allary.

You shall remember quiet ways
Watching them fade, and quiet eyes,
And two hearts given up to love,
A foolish and an overwise.

He was also working by May 1917 on one of his longest poems *The Lanawn Shee*, completed very shortly before his death.

On 6 June he wrote a long letter to Professor Lewis Chase of the University of Wisconsin in answer to an enquiry asking for information about himself and for his poems to use in the course of his university work on contemporary poets. Ledwidge's answer is the nearest we have to an autobiography. The letter is highly instructive of Ledwidge's attitude to contemporary politics; and to the sources of his own literary inspiration; and to his own method of writing poetry; and to his ambitions for the future and to his realisation that he might have no future in this world:

Your letter of May 15 reached me this afternoon. I have to thank you for introducing my books into your library and for the interest which you take in my poems and will endeavour to supply you with what details you require of myself and my work for the composition of your proposed lecture. You will, of course, understand that I am writing this under the most inept circumstances between my watches, for I am in the firing line and may be busy at any moment in the horrible work of war. I am on active service since the Spring of 1915, having served in the Dardanelles and the first British expeditionary force to Serbia and after a brief interval at home came to France in December 1916.

I am sorry that party politics should ever divide our two tents but am not without hope that a new Ireland will arise from her ashes in the ruins of Dublin, like the Phoenix, with one purpose, one aim, and one ambition. I tell you this in order that you may know what it is to me to be called a British soldier while my own country has no place amongst the nations but the place of Cinderella.

I set myself certain studies and these I pursued at night when I should have been resting from a laborious day. I read books on logic and astronomy and could point out the planets and discuss the nebulae of the Milky Way. I read and studied the poets of England from the age of Chaucer to Swinburne, turning especially to the Elizabethans and the ballads that came before the great renaissance. I thirsted for travel and adventure and longed to see the Italy of Shelley and the Greece of Byron. But the poems of Keats and his sad life appealed to me most. I began to pick faults with Longfellow and Tennyson, and the poems of the former which had erstwhile pleased me seemed too full of colour, too full of metaphor and often too disconnected, like a picture which an artist began at one window and finished at another. Tennyson was too conventional for my taste and nearly always spoiled his work with a prologue, or an epilogue, full of loud bombast or conceit. Shelley was innocent of such sins and poor Keats never heard of them. For a long time I did little but criticise and rearrange my books, separating as it were the sheep from the goats. I put Longfellow and Tennyson at the back of the shelf and gave Keats, Swinburne, Shelley and the anthologies the foremost place in the light. I burned many copybooks which contained fugitive pieces of my own because I thought it were better for them to die young and be happy than live to be reviled.

My taste, I think, became extremely acute and I was more inclined to blow warm and cold over such works as Yeats than sit to admire as I do now. I have never met Yeats but hope to one day for I have much to say to him. I don't think he has quite ever reached the hearts of the people and if any of his works live it will be his early poems on *Maeve* and *Cuchullain*. If you remember his earlier works you will agree with me in saying that the revisions which he made in them in later years have robbed them of much enchantment. I agree that many of his far-fetched metaphors required elucidation, but, in attempting this, he has not always been successful. Take for instance two lines which appeared in the first version of the *Wanderings of Ossian.*

> 'Empty of purple hours as a beggar's cloak in the rain: As a grass seed crushed by a pebble, or a wolf sucked under a weir.'

I always pointed out these similes as the most ludicrous of Yeats. They do not illustrate his meaning, and were probably written in a rainstorm in a moment certainly happy for rhyme, not for reason. In the revised edition it reads: *'As a haycock out on the flood, etc'* which is better because it gives you a picture of things adrift, of loneliness and the beauty of a cataclysm. This is a single exception in his work of where his second thoughts were better than his inspiration. I am afraid Masefield is getting this bad habit also. When his *Dauber* appeared first in *The English Review* I was struck by a wonderful line in the kitchen scene of which Dauber spoke. His sister was dusting and 'A wagging corner of the duster flicked', but when it appeared in book form this line was replaced by another which had no thought. What a pity it is that these men won't remember that they do the Gods' work and not their own. I never revise. It is too dangerous. I can't dictate to the Gods.

Georgian Poetry (with my three excluded) contains, I think, the best poems of the century. What could be sweeter than the songs at the gates of Damascus, or Stephens' *Goat-paths*? It is not always Stephens plucks all flowers but I have not found a weed on the crooked paths that wind every way up the hill.

Of myself: I am a fast writer and very prolific. I have long silences, often for weeks, then the mood comes over me and I must write and write no matter where I be or what the circumstances are. I do my best work in the spring. I have had many disappointments in life and many sorrows but in my saddest moment song came to me and I sang. I get more pleasure from a good line than from a big cheque. Tho' I love music I cannot write within earshot of any instrument. I cannot carry a watch on account of the tick, real or imaginary, and might as well try to sleep under the bell of Bruges as in a room where a clock stands. I write a lot late at night in my room, though mostly my poems are written out of doors.

I have been to Naples, Egypt, Greece, Serbia, Spain and France, but in no country have I found a people as wonderful or as strange as my own. I have written many short stories and one play: *The Wife of Llew* was written in a meadow full of flowers and singing birds. *The Lost Ones* was written in a sad mood when I remembered all whom I knew and who were lost and away for ever. I wanted someone to console me by assuring me that beyond the dark they would meet me again.

My favourite amongst my own are always changing. Of my published works, I perhaps like *Thomas MacDonagh* best. Better work than you have yet seen from me is being selected for my next book, but my best is not yet written. I mean to do something really great if I am spared, but out here one may at any moment be hurled beyond life.

Everything about this letter is fascinating. It is balanced; it is confident; it is curiously dismissive of Yeats. In 1917, when this letter was written, Yeats was the acknowledged leader in the world of Irish letters; by the time of his death in 1939 he was the uncrowned king of poetry in the English speaking world. It is indicative of Ledwidge's extensive knowledge of modern poetry and of the great romantic poets on his thinking.

It is not surprising that *Thomas MacDonagh* was perhaps Ledwidge's favourite poem of his own writing. It is a wonderful poem and reminds us of the importance of the Easter Rising and its terrible aftermath for Francis Ledwidge.

The letter is a wonderful insight into Ledwidge's methods of work. It emphasises for us his great love for his own people of Ireland.

The letter is tragically confident for his own future with his ever conscious awareness of the precarious quality of his life.

The letter gives the clue as to why he was writing of County Meath, his Boyne home and friends with the battle raging around him. They were his sustaining strength.

He sent *With Flowers* and *Pan* with this letter. By June 1917 he was out of the line and back in reserve. On 1 July he wrote to Edmund Marsh who had published some of his *Georgian Poetry*. 'Just now a big strafe is worrying our dug-outs and putting out our candles, but my soul is by the Boyne cutting new meadows under a thousand wings and listening to the cuckoos at Crocknahara. They say there will be peace soon.

If you visit the Front don't forget to come to the line at night to watch the German rockets. They have white crests which throw a pale flame across no-man's land and white bursting into green and green changing into blue and blue bursting and dropping down in purple torrents. It is like the end of a beautiful world.'

This letter was tragically prophetic in its thoughts of German rockets. But he continued to write poetry about the Boyne and not about German rockets. He wrote *A Fairy Hunt* and *The Sylph* shortly before or after this letter:

A FAIRY HUNT

Who would hear the fairy horn
Calling all the hounds of Finn
Must be in a lark's nest born
When the moon is very thin.

I who have the gift can hear
Hounds and horn and tally ho,
And the tongue of Bran as clear
As Christmas bells across the snow.

And beside my secret place
Hurries by the fairy fox,
With the moonrise on his face,
Up and down the mossy rocks.

Then the music of a horn
And the flash of scarlet men,
Thick as poppies in the corn
All across the dusky glen.

Oh! the mad delight of chase!
Oh! the shouting and the cheer!
Many an owl doth leave his place
In the dusty tree to hear.

THE SYLPH

I saw you and I named a flower
That lights with blue a woodland space,
I named a bird of the red hour
And a hidden fairy place.

And then I saw you not, and knew
Dead leaves were whirling down the mist,
And something lost was crying through
An evening of amethyst.

The Royal Inniskilling Fusiliers were part of the next major British-Franco offensive. They were positioned near Ypres. On 12 July Francis Ledwidge wrote to Lizzie Healey 'You will be surprised to hear from me again after a silence nearly three years long. The reason I write is because I have been dreaming about you and it has made me rather anxious. I sincerely hope that nothing troubles you in body or soul. It must be quite beautiful on the bog now. How happy you are to be living in peace and quietude where birds still sing and the country wears her confirmation dress. Out here the land is broken up by shells and the woods are like skeletons and when you come to a little town it is only to find poor homeless people lamenting over what was once a cheery home. As I write this a big battle is raging on my left hand and if it extends to this part of the line I will be pulling triggers like a man gone mad. Please, dear Lizzie, send me a flower from the bog, plucked specially for me. I may be home again soon. In fact I am only waiting to be called home. God send it soon.'

The third battle of Ypres started on 15 July. A robin inspired his second to last poem. Even in battle the joys and strengths of home were easily and powerfully triggered. He wrote *Home* in the midst of battle. It covered in a few lines every part of the day and many of the images of County Meath:

> A burst of sudden wings at dawn,
> Faint voices in a dreamy noon,
> Evenings of mist and murmurings,
> And nights with rainbows of the moon.
>
> And through these things a wood-way dim,
> And waters dim, and slow sheep seen
> On uphill paths that wind away
> Through summer sounds and harvest green.
>
> This is a song a robin sang
> This morning on a broken tree,
> It was about the little fields
> That call across the world to me.

On 20 July he wrote to Katherine Tynan. On 22 July he wrote *To One Who Comes Now And Then*, a reflection on his greatest friend Matty McGoona (see p.24).

The weather at the end of July was dreadful. Rain, mist and mud were the conditions in which the battle was being fought out; mustard gas was added to the bombardment of shells, three thousand men suffered from it in the last three weeks of July.

On 30 July Francis Ledwidge attended Confession. On 31 July he was at Mass and received Holy Communion.

An attack on the German lines was launched on 30 July. It was far from conclusive. One hundred and thirty-five thousand men were lost in one day. One hundred yards were gained.

Francis Ledwidge was in the reserve on 30 July. He was not among the one hundred and thirty-five thousand killed by machine-gun fire. He was engaged with many others in road making. Road making, the construction of wooden tracks, was an essential ingredient of the advance. It was a highly dangerous occupation. It was carried on in immediate proximity to the firing line and well within range of German artillery. German shells started to land behind Ledwidge's position. He and other Royal Inniskilling Fusiliers continued the task of track construction. While drinking a cup of tea beside the track Francis Ledwidge and six other soldiers were blown to bits by a German shell. He had been writing *The Lanawn Shee* for some weeks before his death. The last two verses are a dream for Ellie Vaughey, his first and greatest love. They probably constitute his most fitting epitaph:

Powdered and perfumed the full bee
Winged heavily across the clover,
And where the hills were dim with dew,
Purple and blue the west leaned over.

A willow spray dipped in the stream,
Moving a gleam of silver ringing,
And by a finny creek a maid
Filled all the shade with softest singing.

Listening, my heart and soul at strife,
On the edge of life I seemed to hover,
For I knew my love had come at last,
That my joy was past and my gladness over.

I tiptoed gently up and stooped
Above her looped and shining tresses,
And asked her of her kin and name,
And why she came from fairy places.

She told me of a sunny coast
Beyond the most adventurous sailor,
Where she had spent a thousand years
Out of the fears that now assail her.

And there, she told me, honey drops
Out of the tops of ash and willow,
And in the mellow Sleep
Doth sweetly keep her poppy pillow.

Not Autumn with her brown line marks
The time of larks, the length of roses,
But song-time there is over never
Nor flower-time ever, ever closes.

And wildly through uncurling ferns
Fast water turns down valleys singing,
Filling with scented winds the dales,
Setting the bells of sleep a-ringing.

And when the thin moon lowly sinks,
Through cloudy chinks a silver glory
Lingers upon the left of night
Till dawn delights the meadows hoary.

And by the lakes the skies are white,
(oh, the delight!) when swans are coming,
Among the flowers sweet joy-bells peal,
And quick bees wheel in drowsy humming.

The squirrel leaves her dusty house
And in the boughs makes fearless gambol,
And falling down in fire-drops, red,
The fruit is shed from every bramble.

Then, gathered all about the trees
Glad galaxies of youth are dancing,
Treading the perfume of the flowers,
Filling the hours with mazy glancing.

And when the dance is done, the trees
Are left to Peace and the brown woodpecker,
And on the western slopes of sky
The day's blue eye begins to flicker.

But at the sighing of the leaves,
When all earth grieves for lights departed
An ancient and a sad desire
Steals in to tire the human-hearted.

No fairy aid can save them now
Nor turn their prow upon the ocean,

The hundred years that missed each heart
Above them start their wheels in motion.

And so our loves are lost, she sighed,
And far and wide we seek new treasure,
For who on Time or Timeless hills
Can live the ills of loveless leisure?

('Fairer than Usna's youngest son,
O, my poor one, what flower-bed holds you?
Or, wrecked upon the shores of home,
What wave of foam with white enfolds you?

'You rode with kings on hills of green,
And lovely queens have served you banquet,
Sweet wine from berries bruised they brought
And shyly sought the lips which drank it.

'But in your dim grave of the sea
There shall not be a friend to love you.
And ever heedless of your loss
The earth ships cross the storms above you.

'And still the chase goes on, and still
The wine shall spill, and vacant places
Be given over to the new
As love untrue keeps changing faces.

'And I must wander with my song
Far from the young till Love returning,
Brings me the beautiful reward
Of some heart stirred by my long yearning,')

Friend, have you heard a bird lament
When sleet is sent for April weather?
As beautiful she told her grief,
As down through leaf and flower I led her.

And, friend, could I remain unstirred
Without a word for such a sorrow?
Say, can the lark forget the cloud
When poppies shroud the seeded furrow?

Like a poor widow whose late grief
Seeks for relief in lonely byeways,
The moon, companionless and dim,
Took her dull rim through starless highways.

I was too weak with dreams to feel
Enchantment steal with guilt upon me,
She slipped, a flower upon the wind,
And laughed to find how she had won me.

From hill to hill, from land to land,
Her lovely hand is beckoning for me,
I follow on through dangerous zones,
Cross dead men's bones and oceans stormy.

Some day I know she'll wait at last
And lock me fast in white embraces,
And down mysterious ways of love
We two shall move to fairy places.

Francis Ledwidge was buried, No 5, in Row B of the second plot in Artillery
Wood cemetery, about three miles north of Ypres in Belgium.

The slaughter of English speaking poets in the First World War was horrendous. Did our allies the French and our enemies the Germans sustain the terrible losses among their poets suffered by the English speaking world? Some famous names are in the history of the nation – such as Rupert Brooke, Julian Grenfell, Wilfred Owen and Siegfried Sassoon. But there were many poets who fell in the war whose writing is not part of remembered literature. An extraordinary feature of the fallen poets was the sheer universality of their origins and occupations. They came from every quarter of Great Britain and Ireland. They represented every class, every profession, every calling.

> The naked earth is warm with Spring,
> And with green grass and bursting trees
> Leans to the sun's gaze glorying,
> And quivers in the sunny breeze.
> And Life is Colour and Warmth and Light,
> And a striving evermore for these;
> And he is dead who will not fight,
> And who dies fighting has increase.
>
> *Into Battle,* Julian Grenfell DSO

The last line of this lovely poem is correct: the poets of England, Ireland, Scotland and Wales had massive increase in the years 1914–1918.

After the war.

Now is the story over.
Over the grief and pain,
And down in the purple clover
The red lips meet again.

But one in the dewy shadows
Waited thro all the noon,
And they told her out of the meadows
Someone was coming soon.

Some lips spoke of to-morrow,
And some of yesterday spoke.
But O! the heart in sorrow
On the rocks of trouble broke!

~~I longed to have sung de~~
I longed for to sing delighted,
And laugh with the newly gay.
But a gloom on my soul alighted
And would not go away.

A hitherto unpublished poem by Francis Ledwidge
from a private collection

INDEX OF TITLES

*unpublished poem